TREVOR APPLESON

LOS LOSS

Photographs Made in Mexico

TABLE OF CONTENTS

LOS LOSS

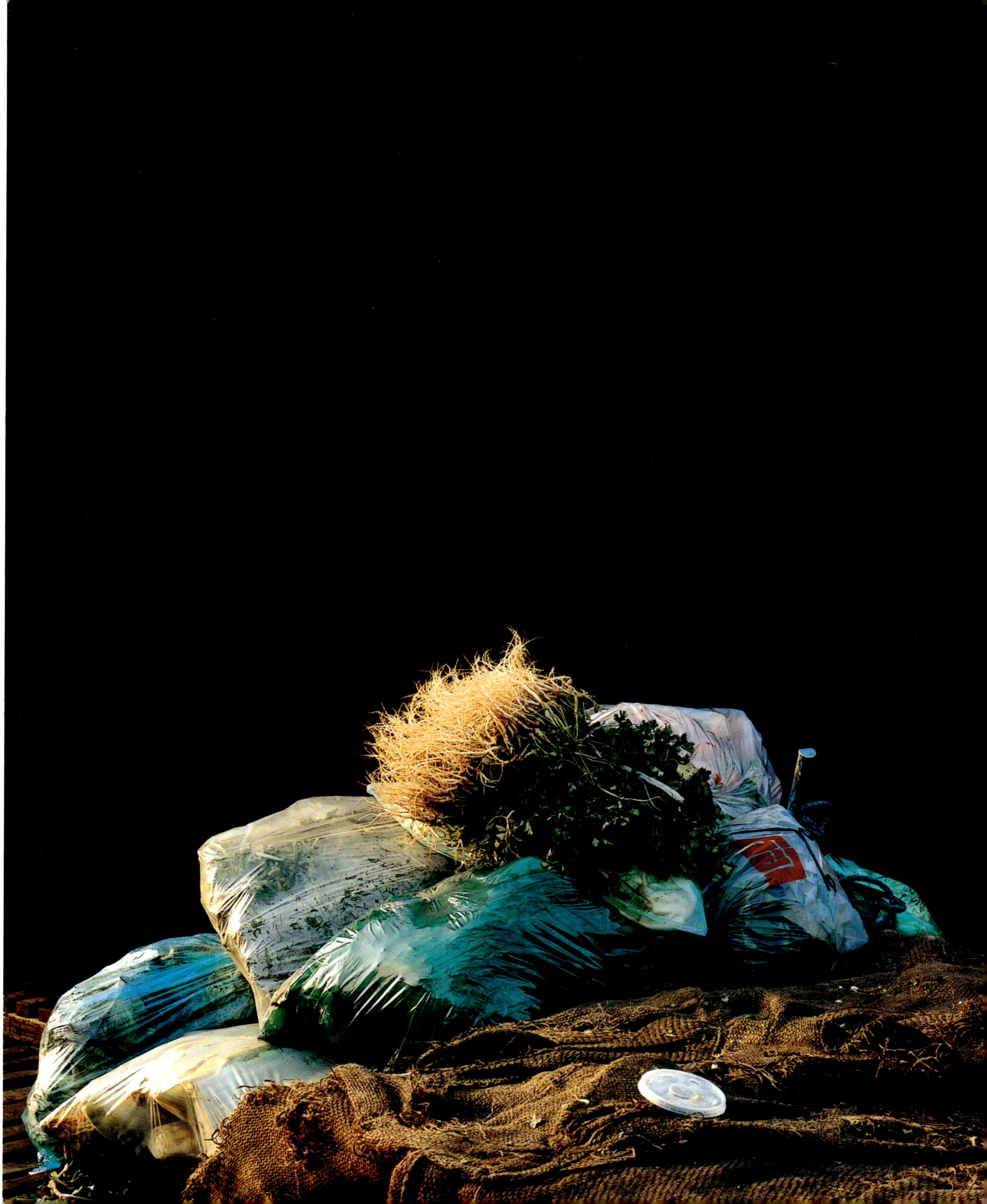

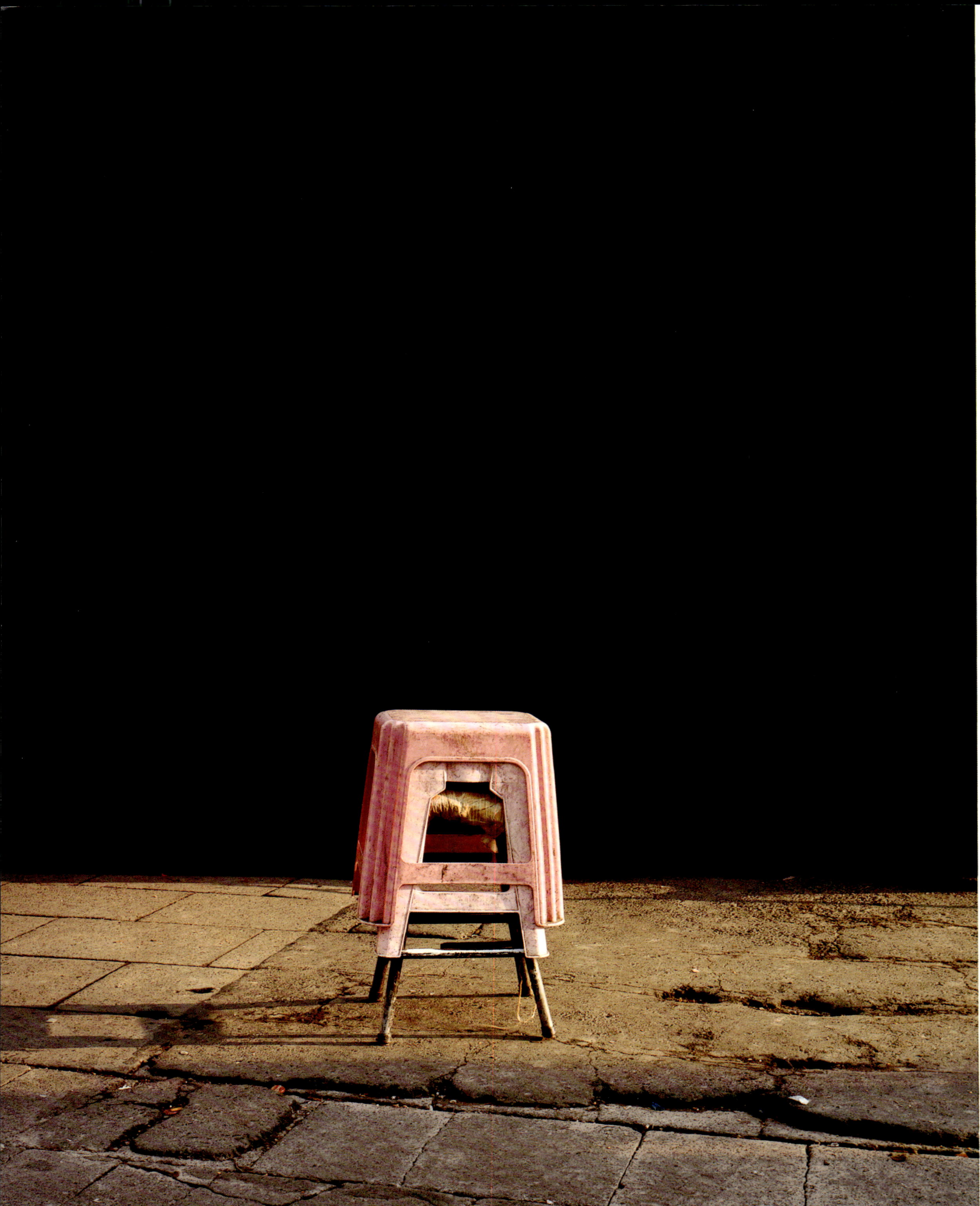

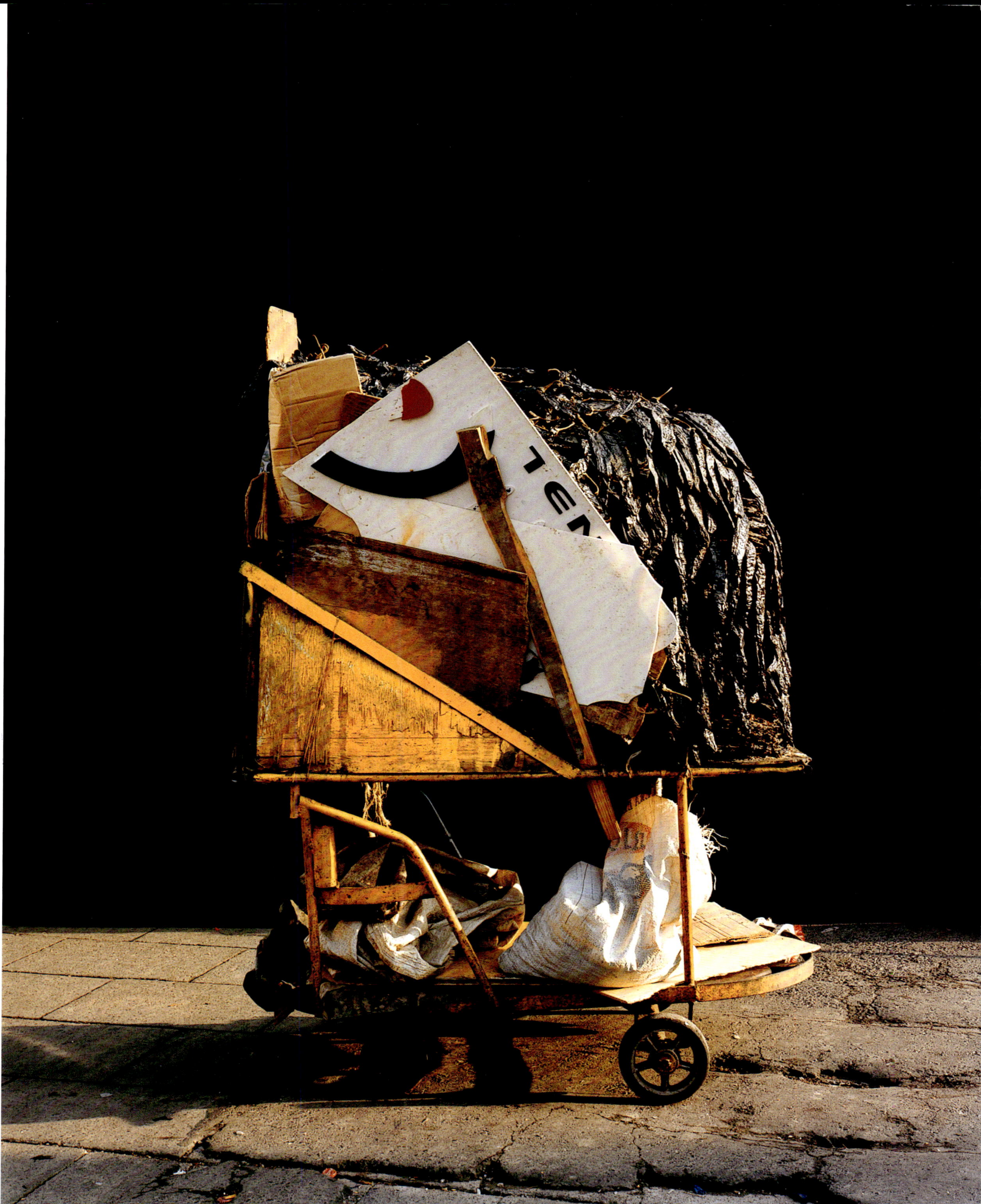

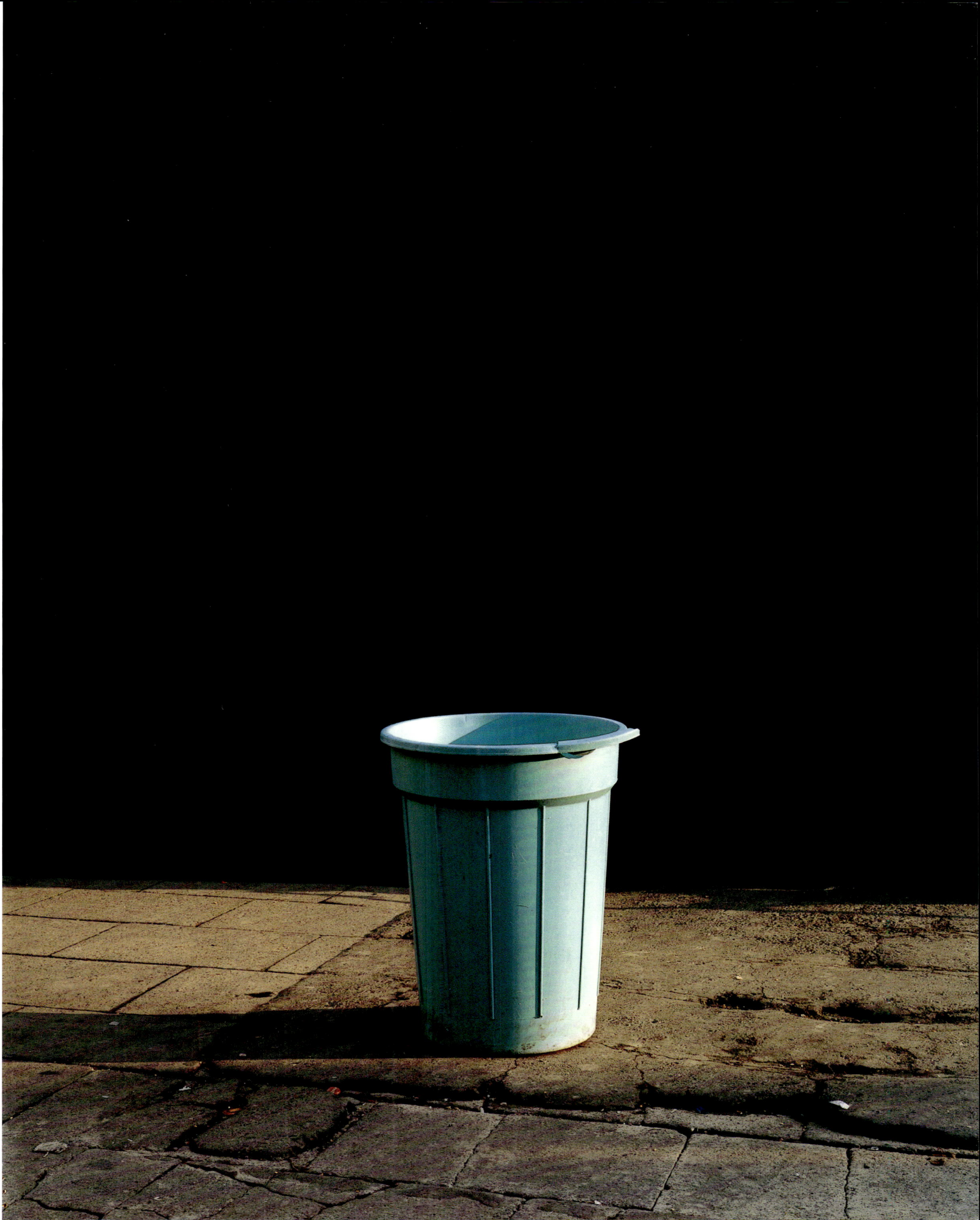

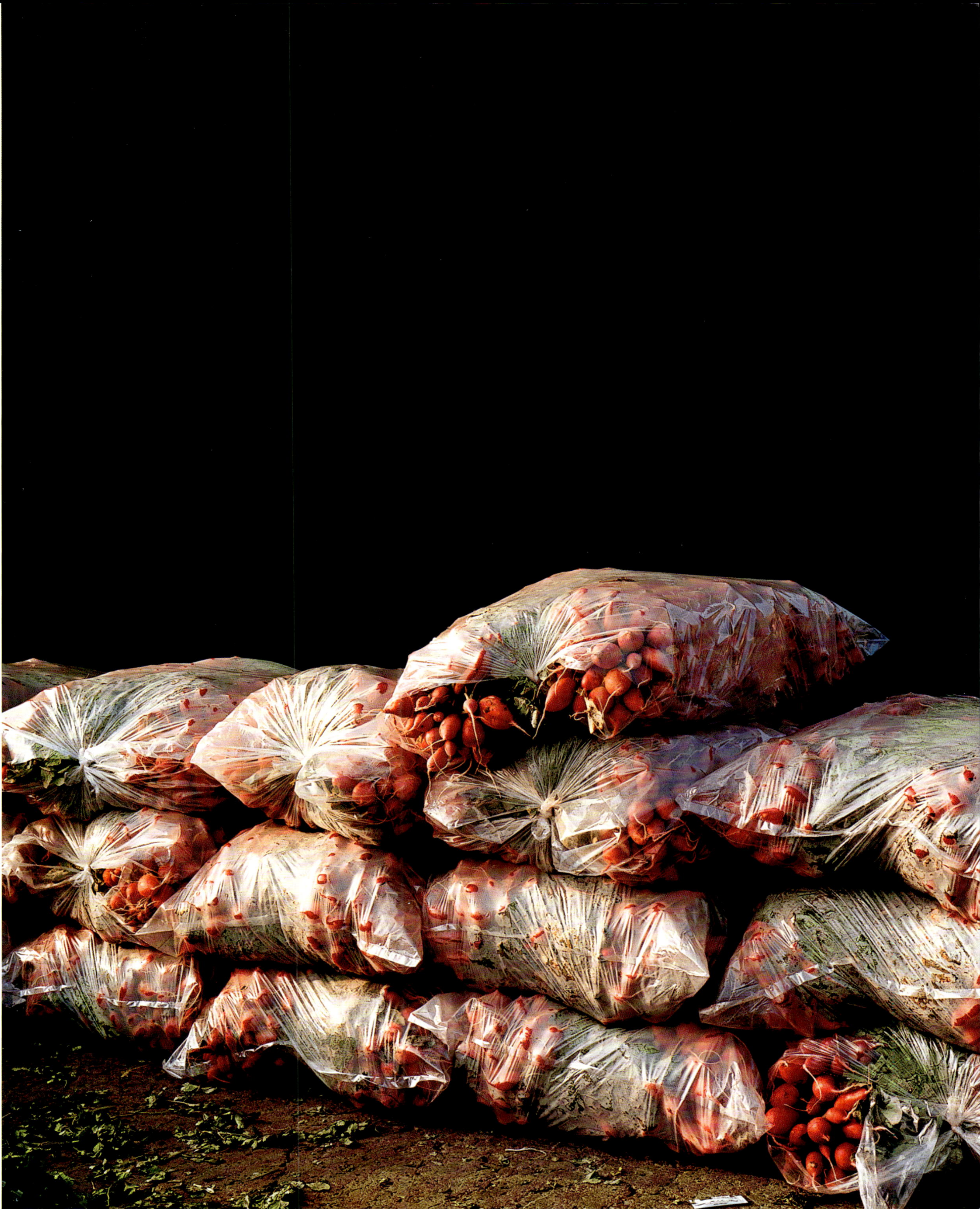

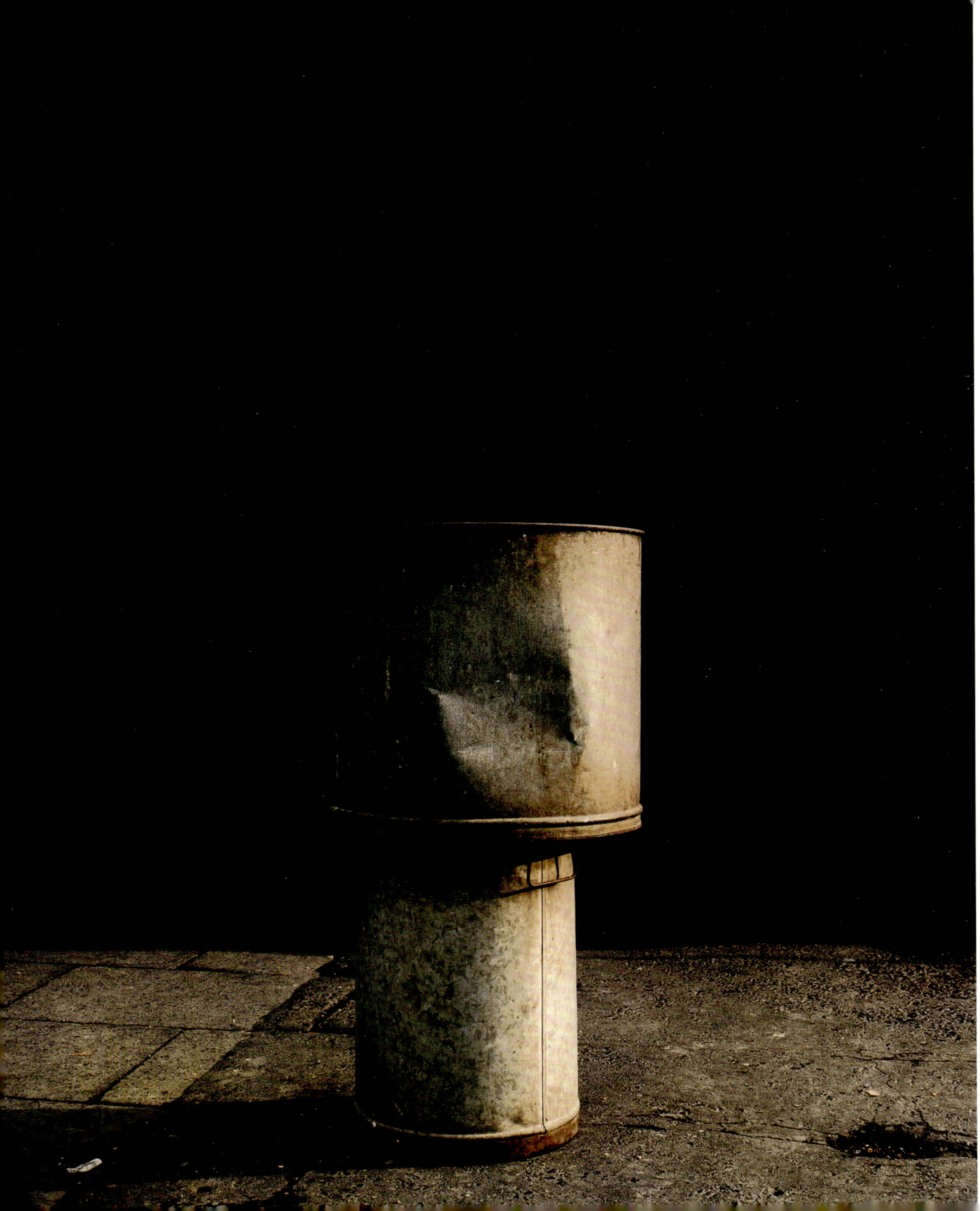

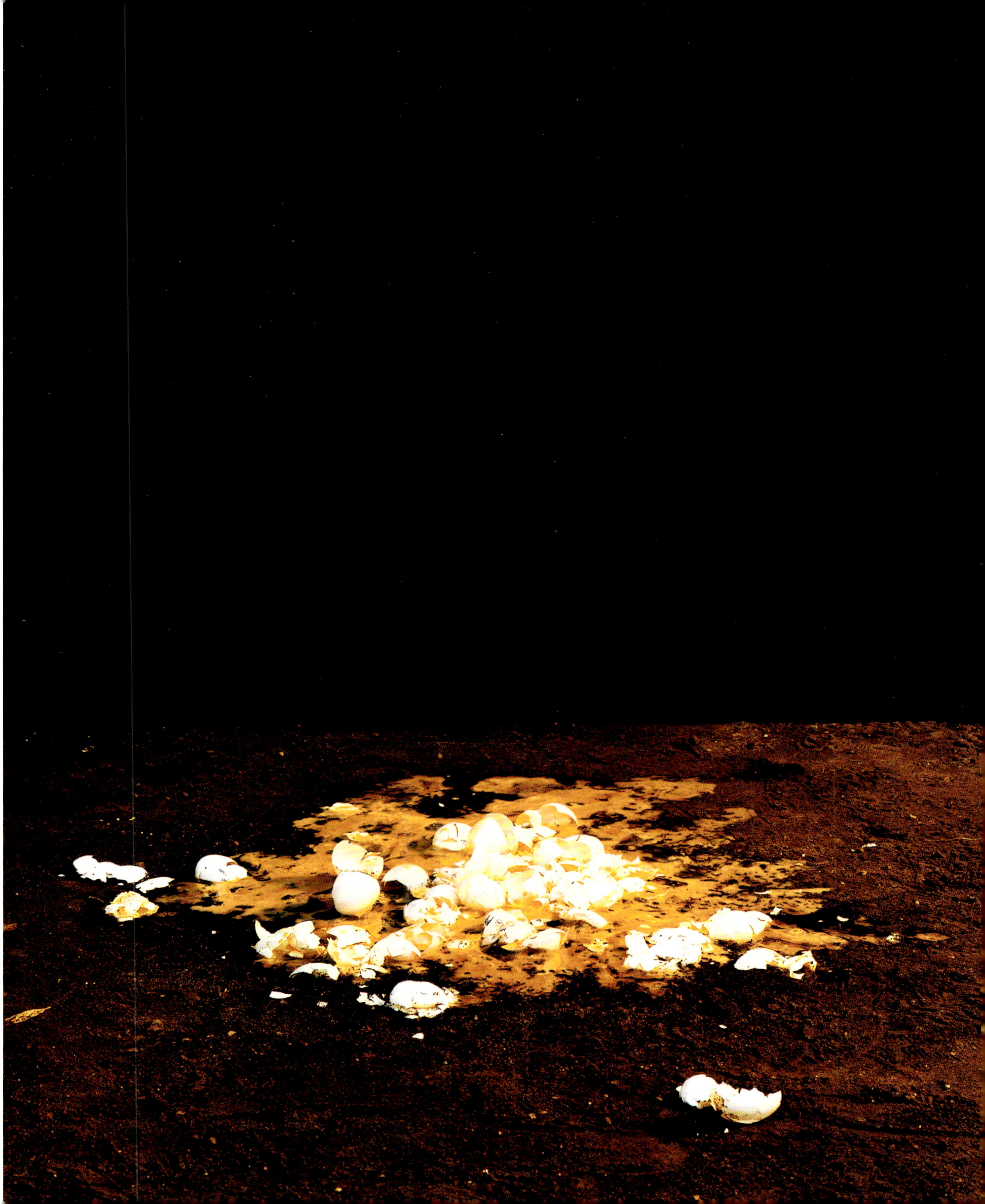

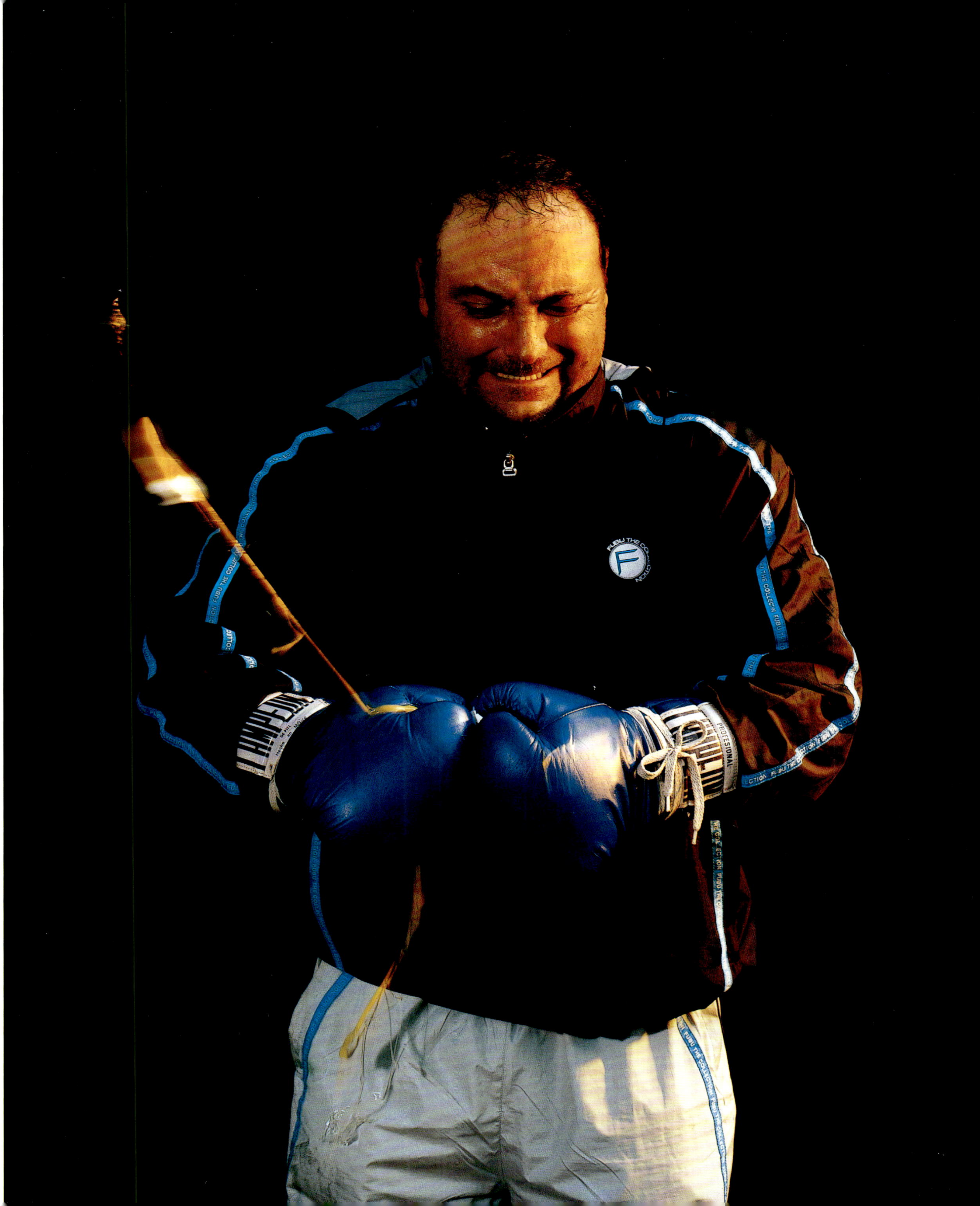
PROFESIONAL

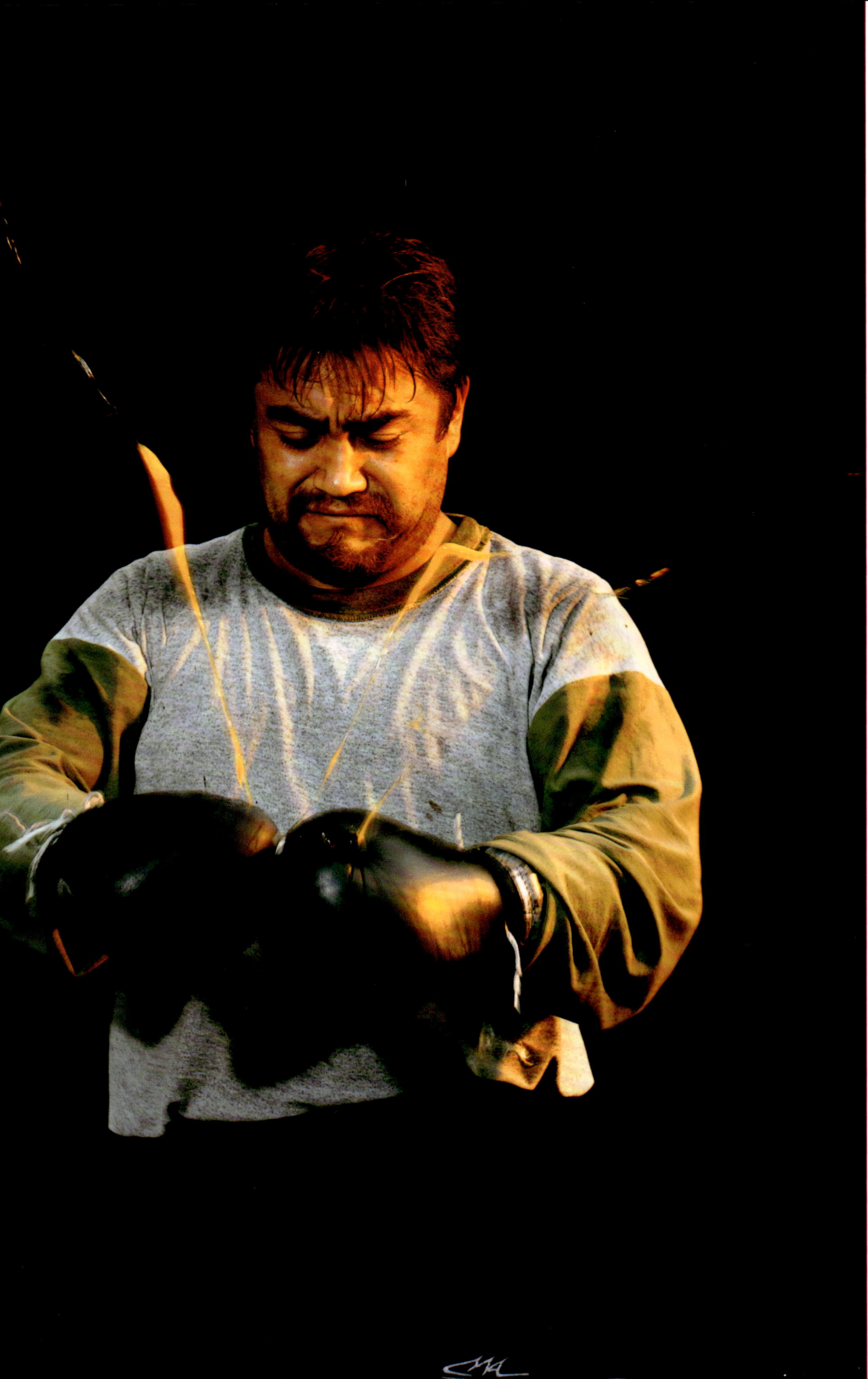

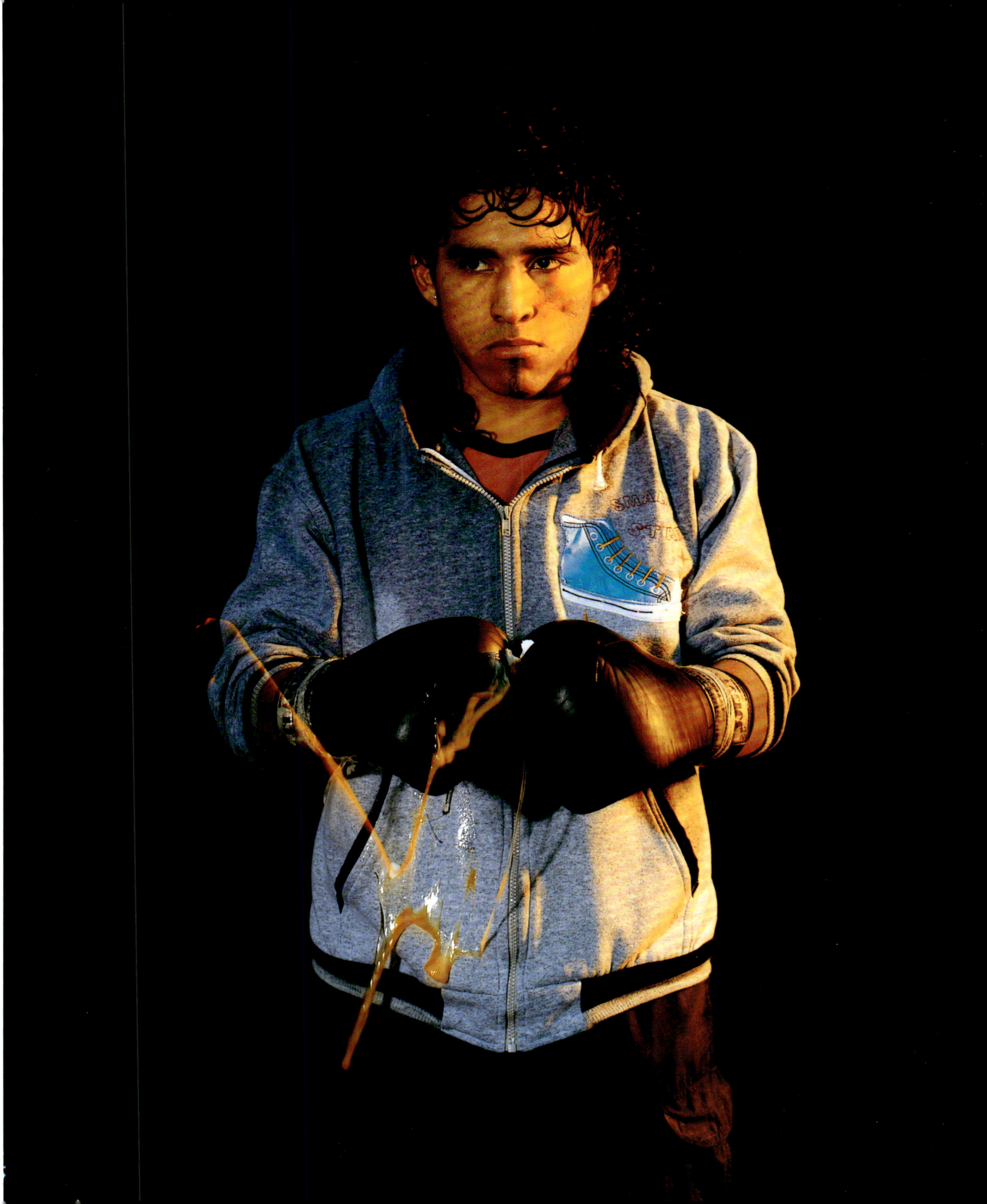

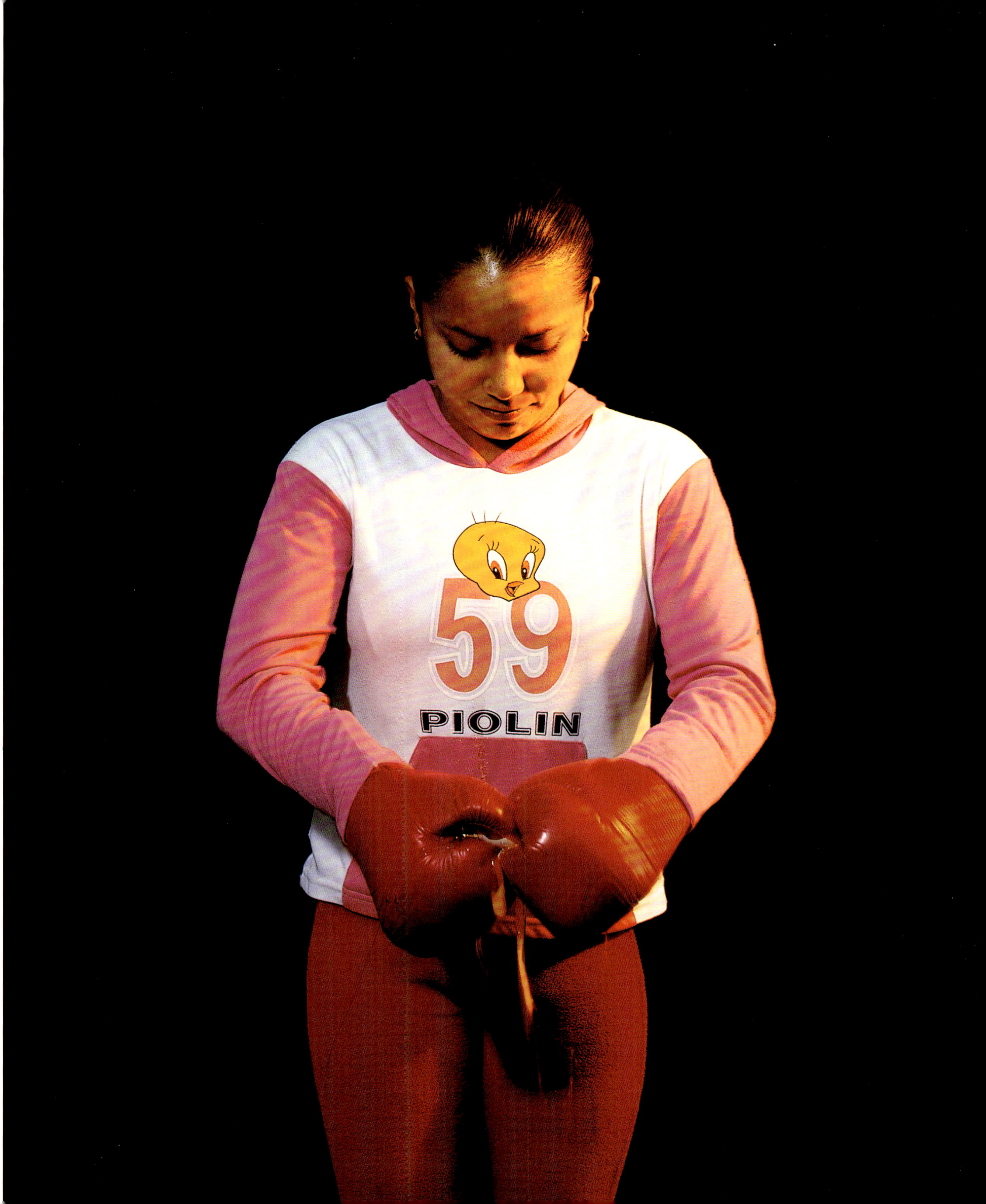
59
PIOLIN

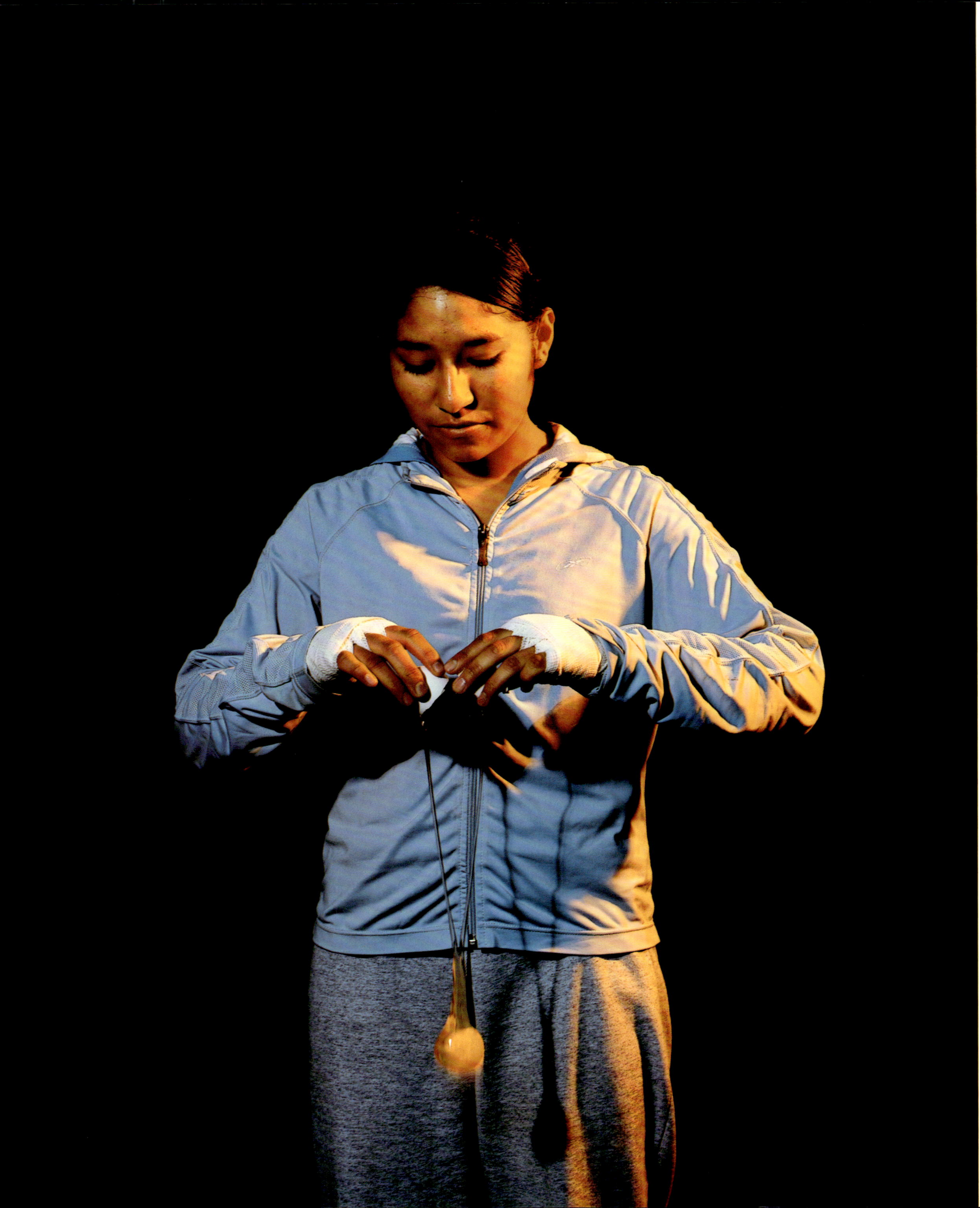

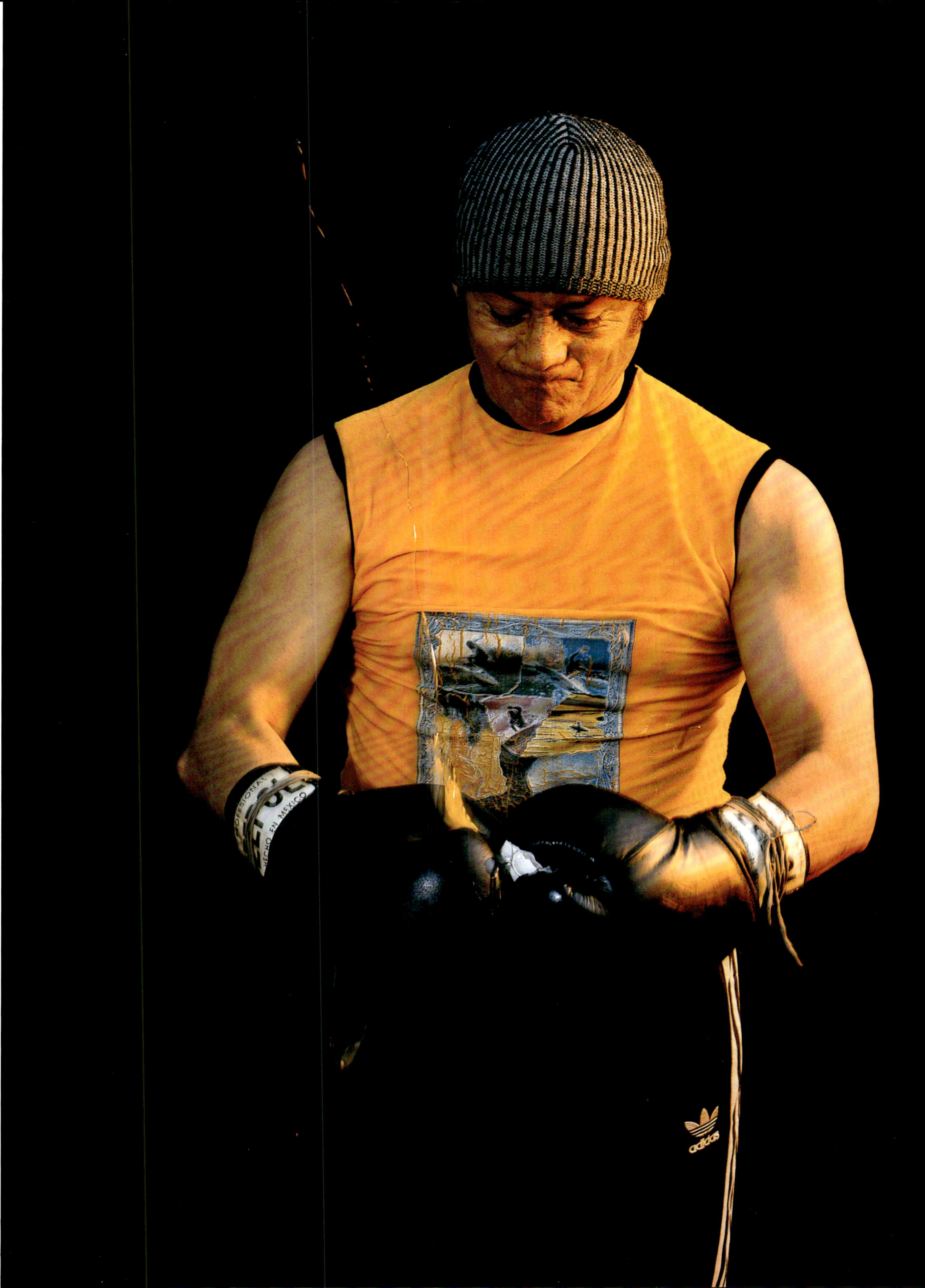
HECHO EN MEXICO
adidas

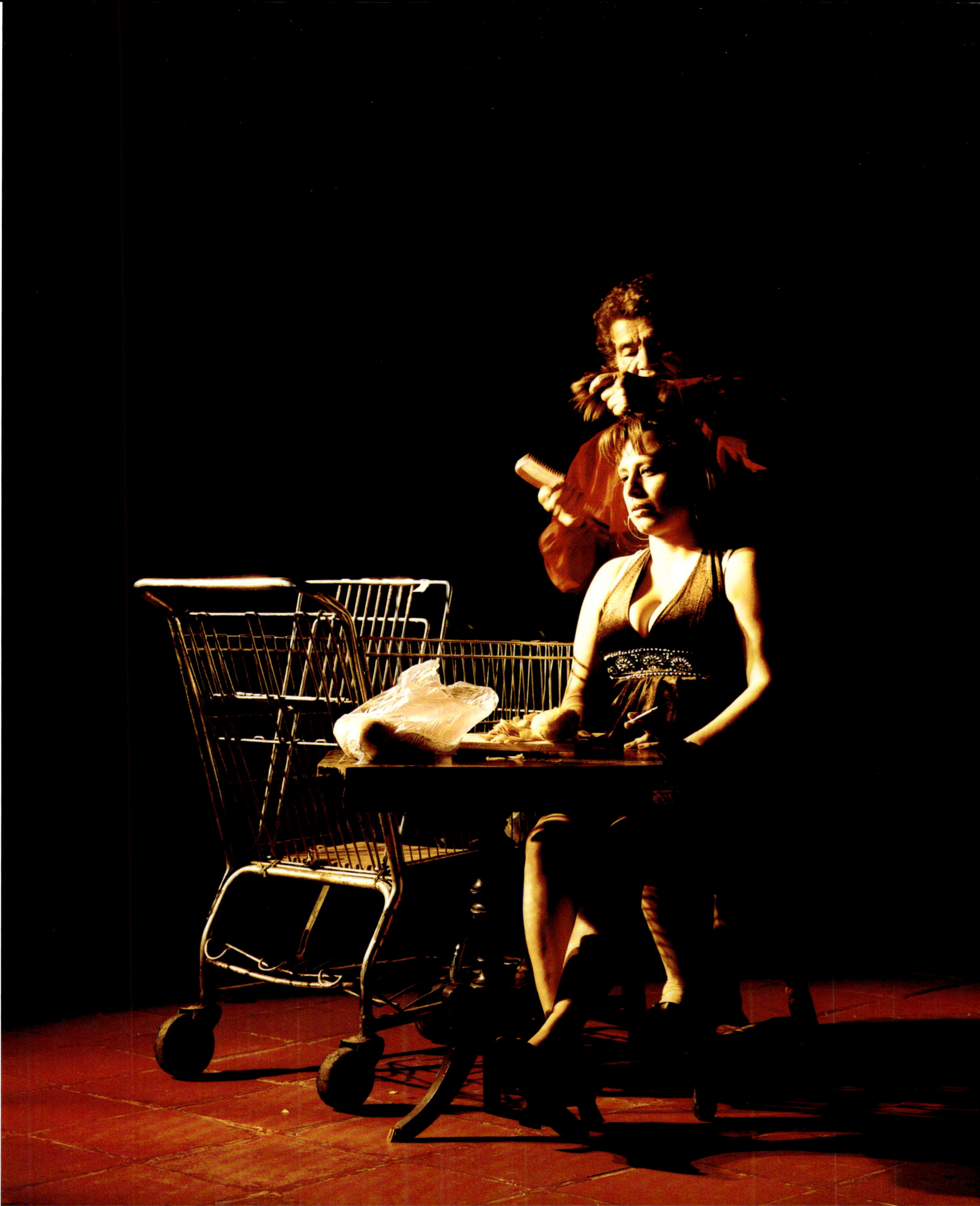

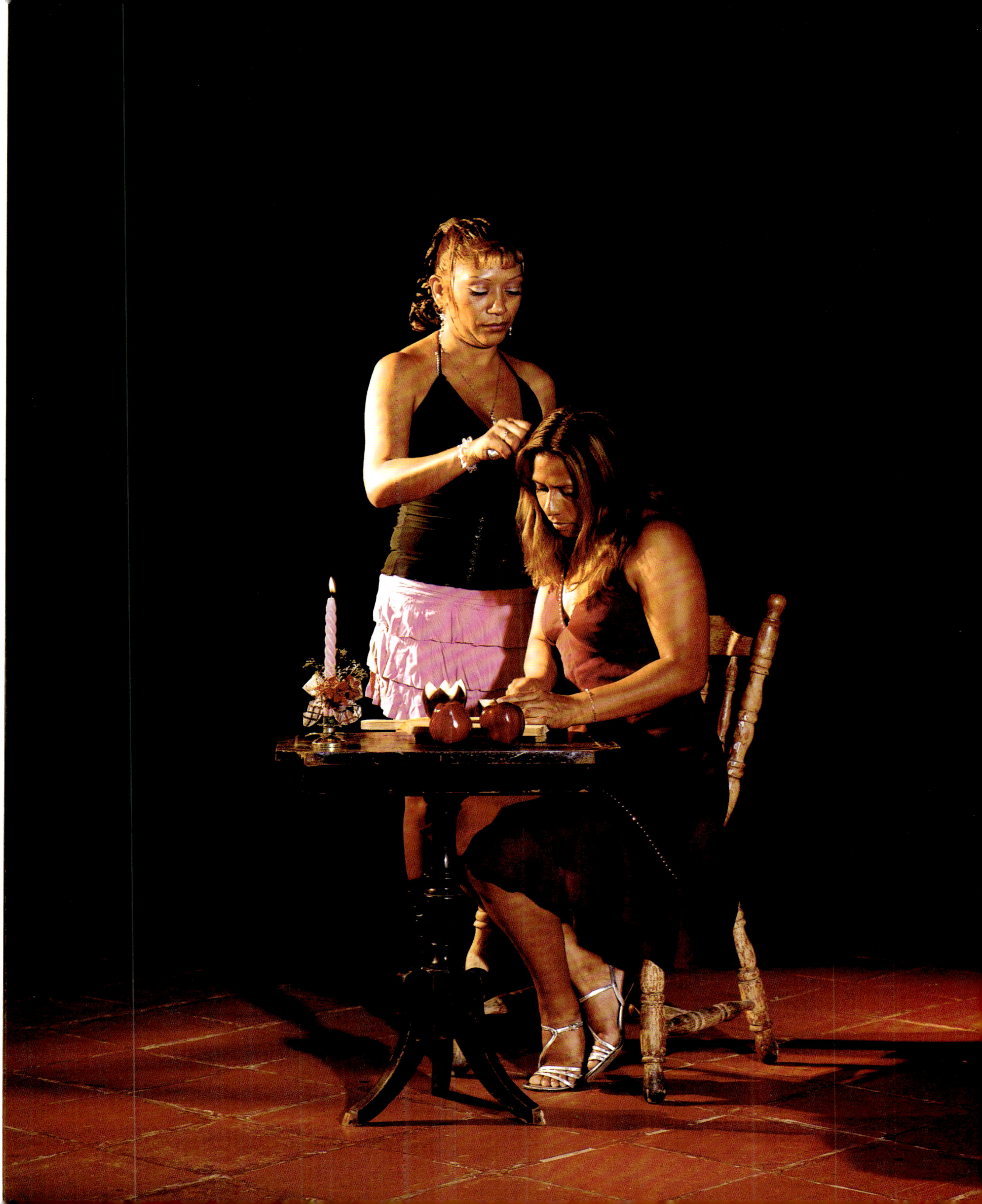

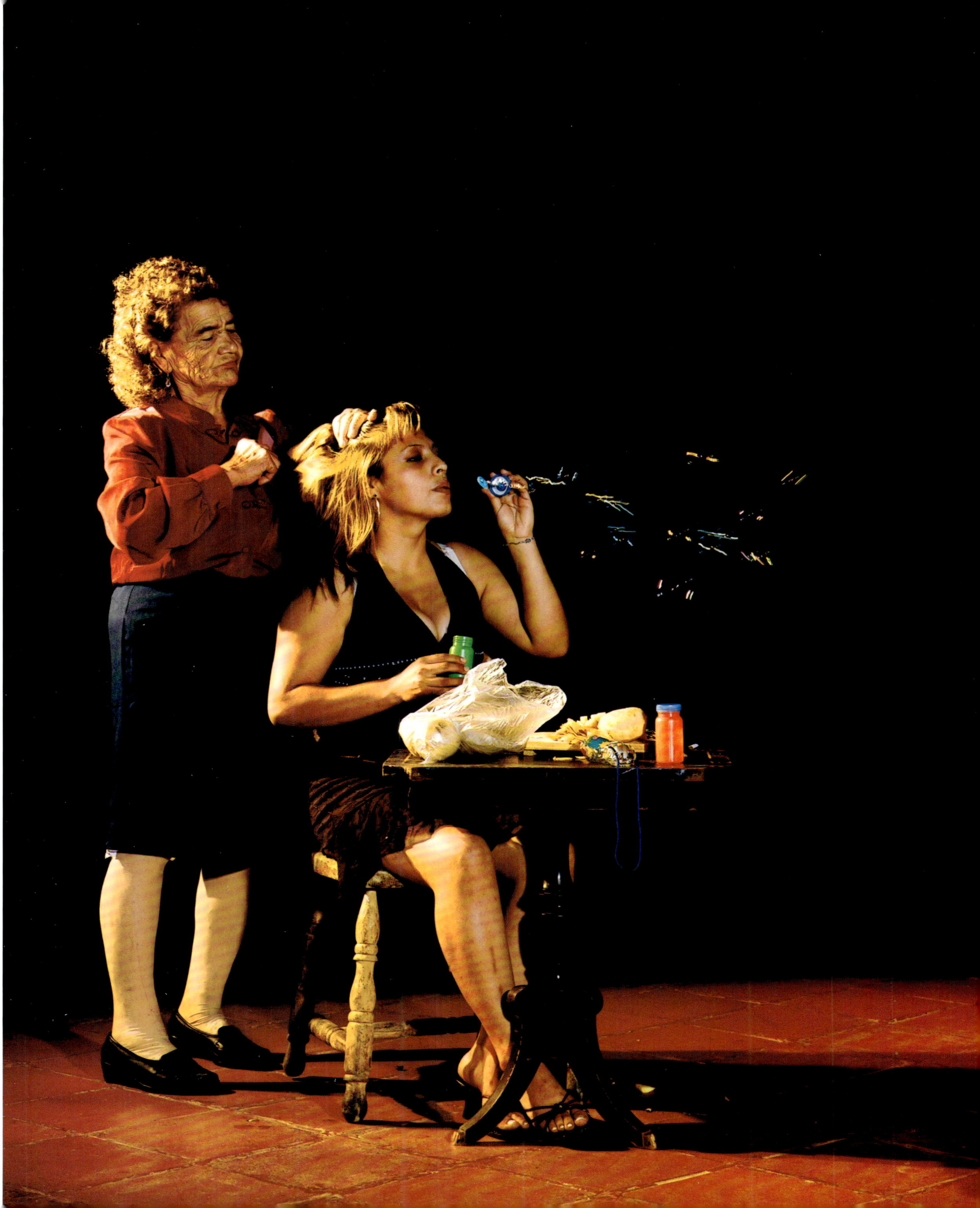

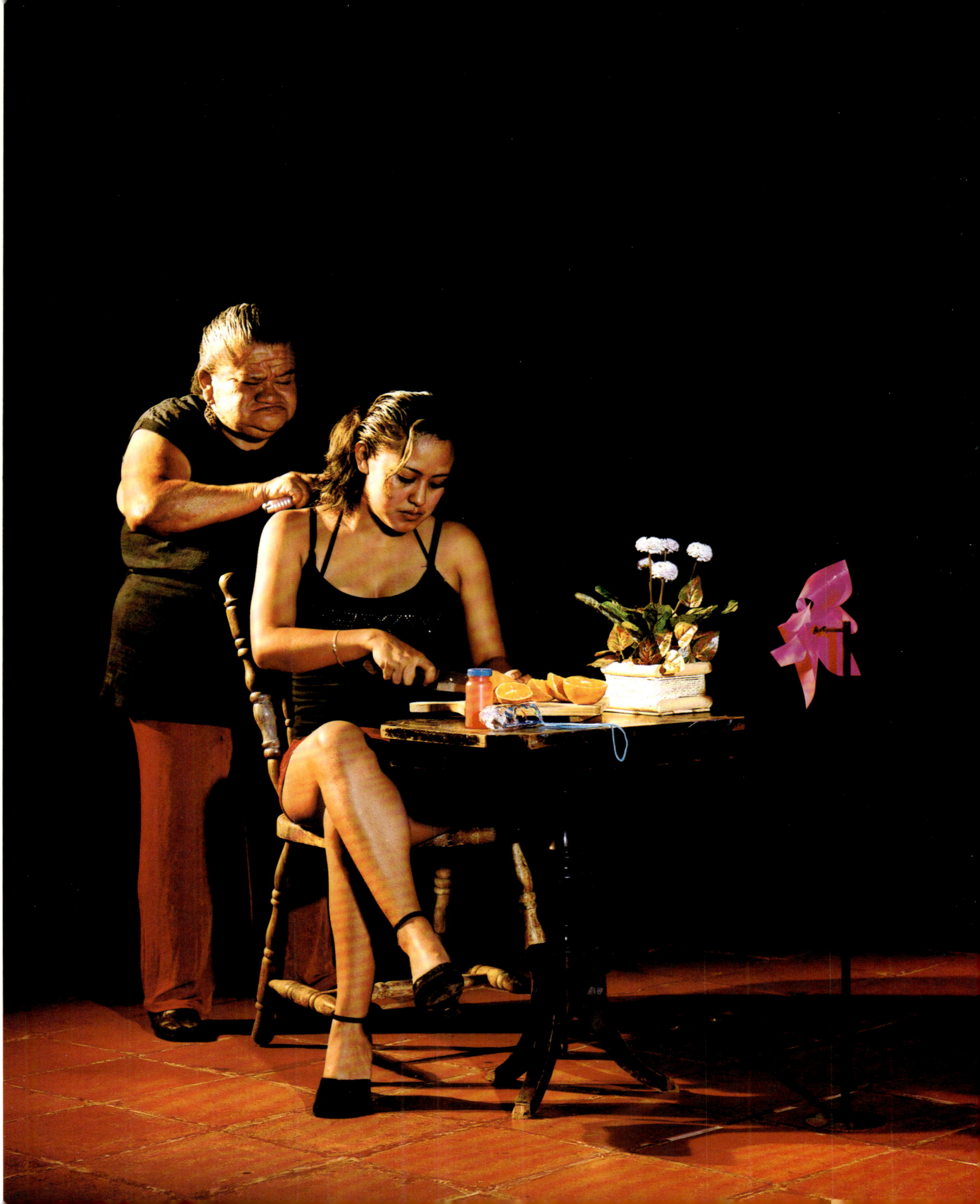

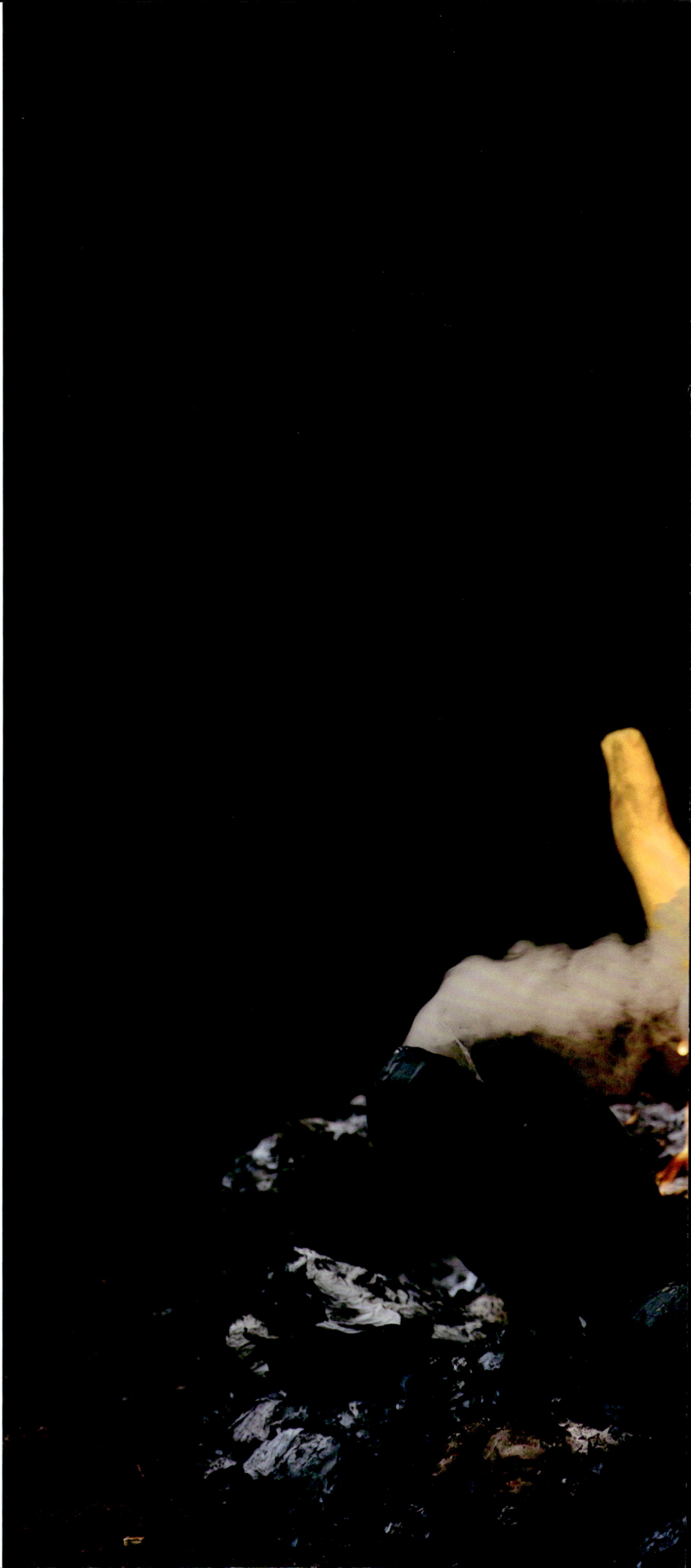

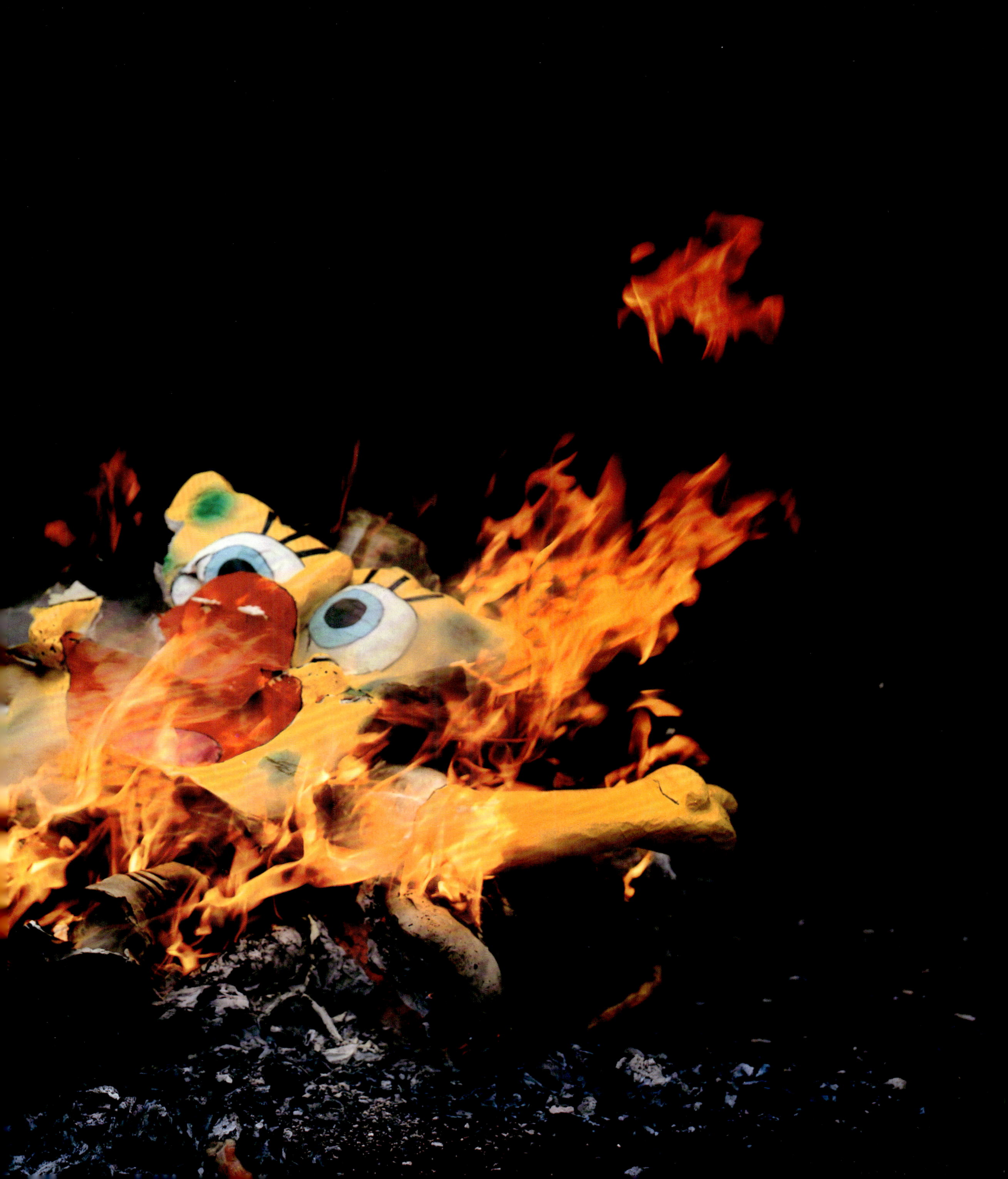

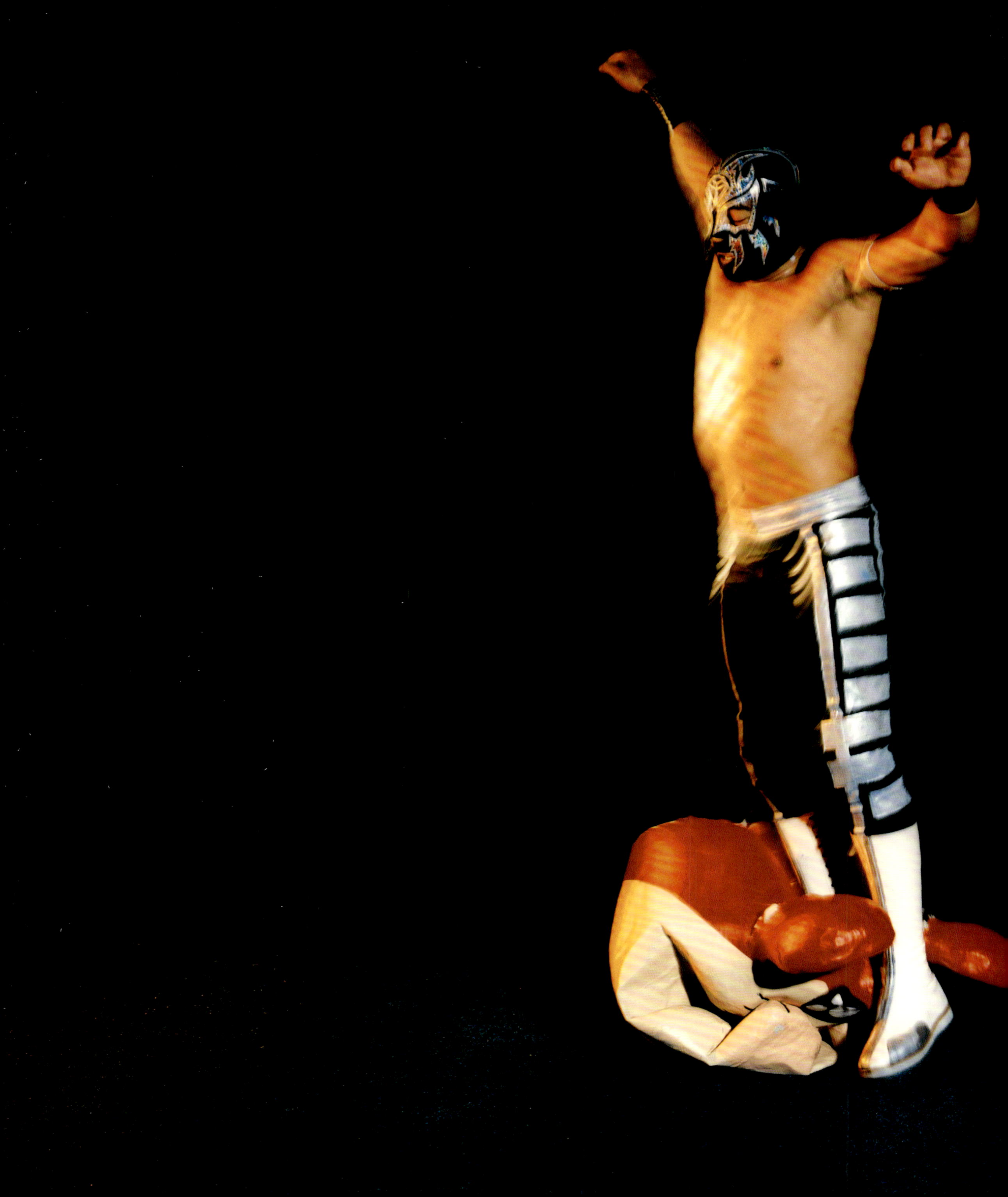

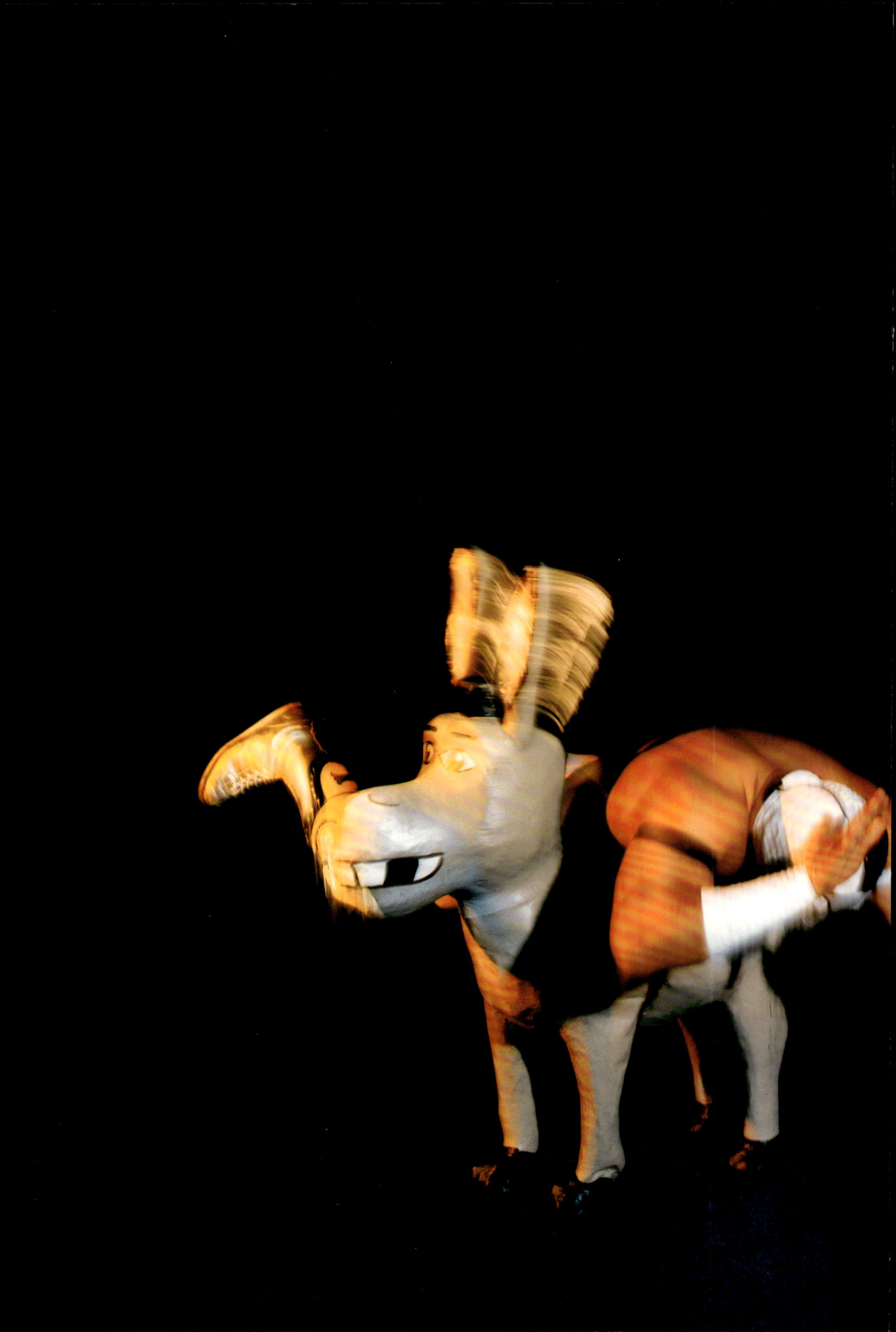

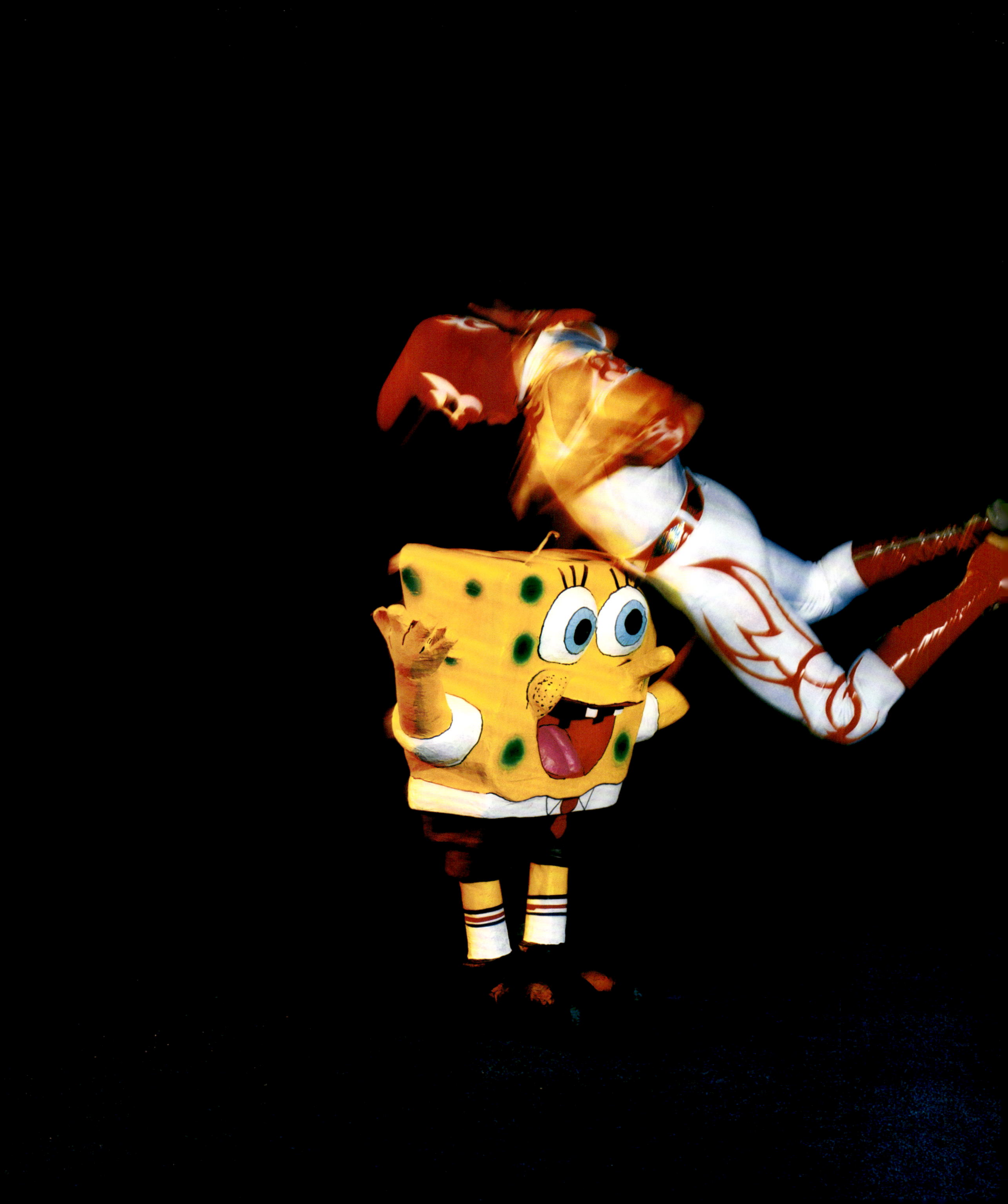

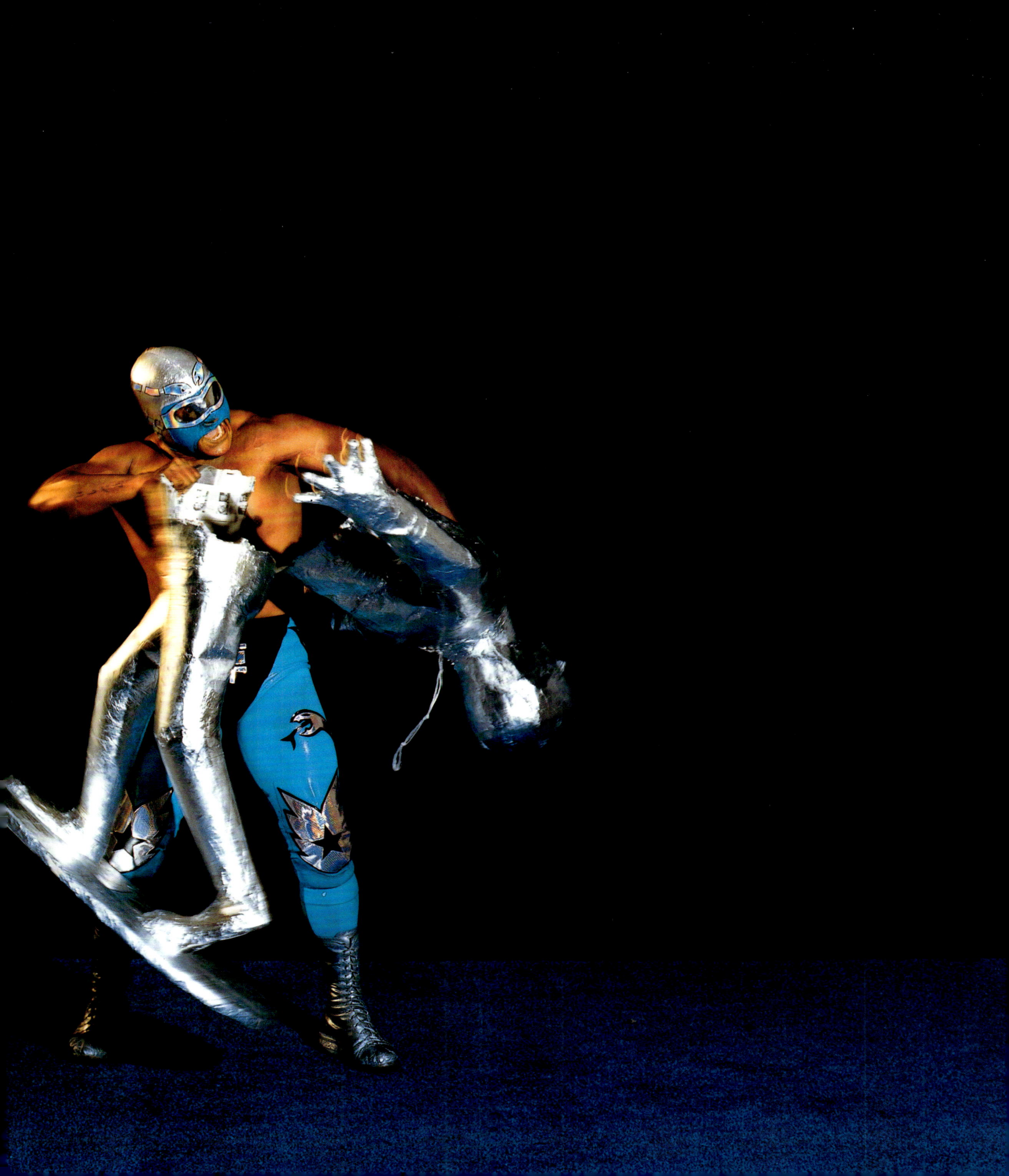

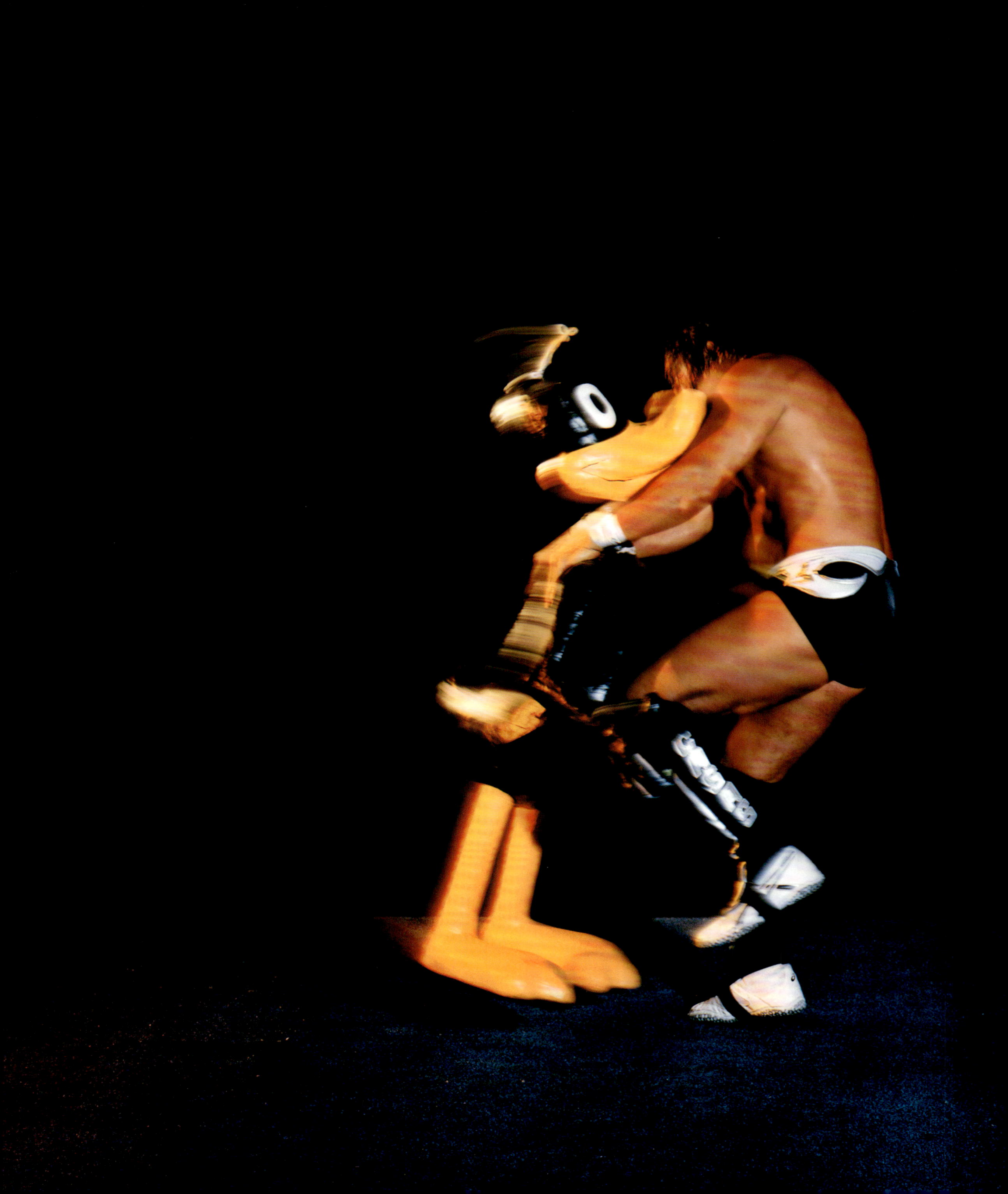

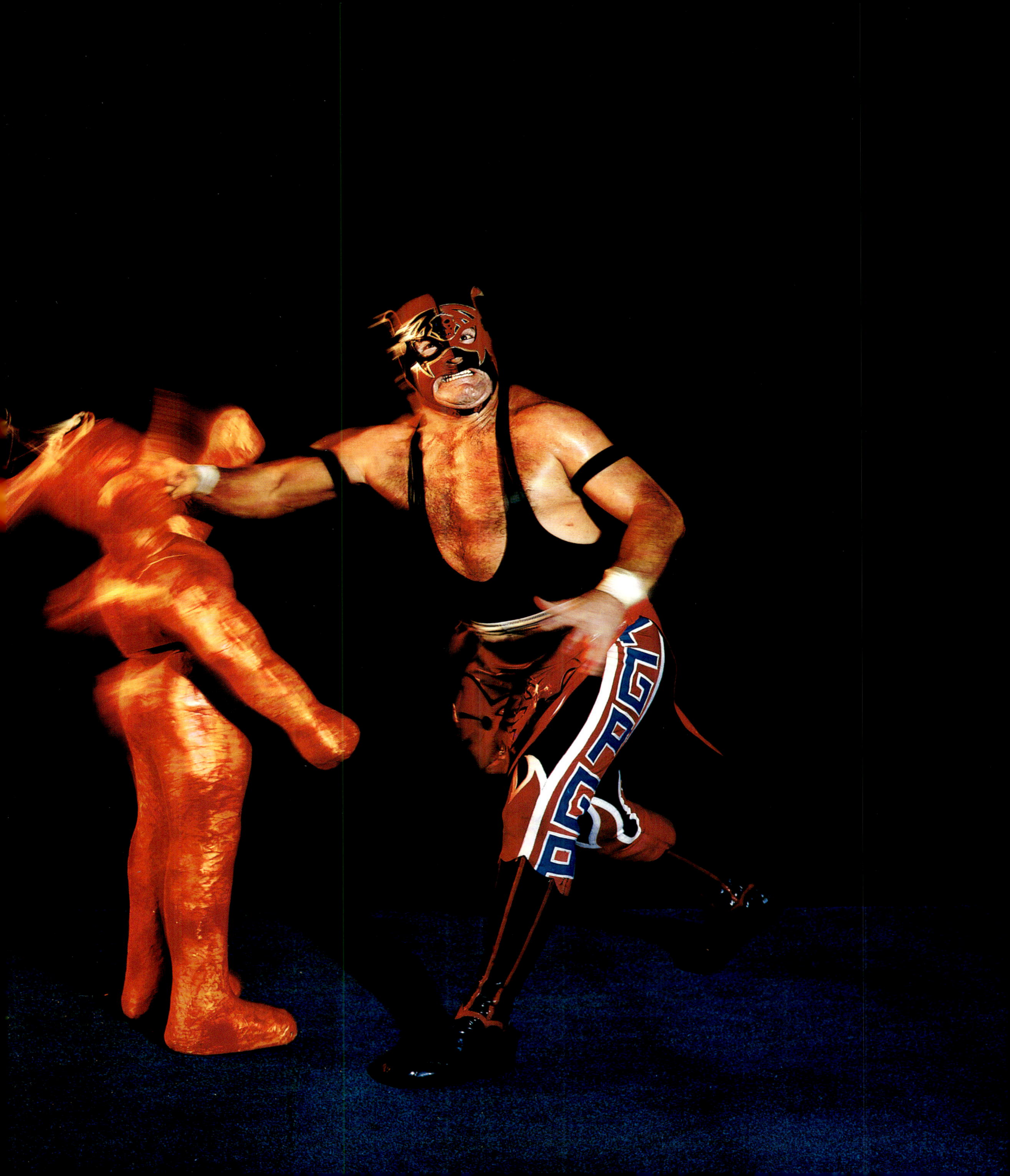

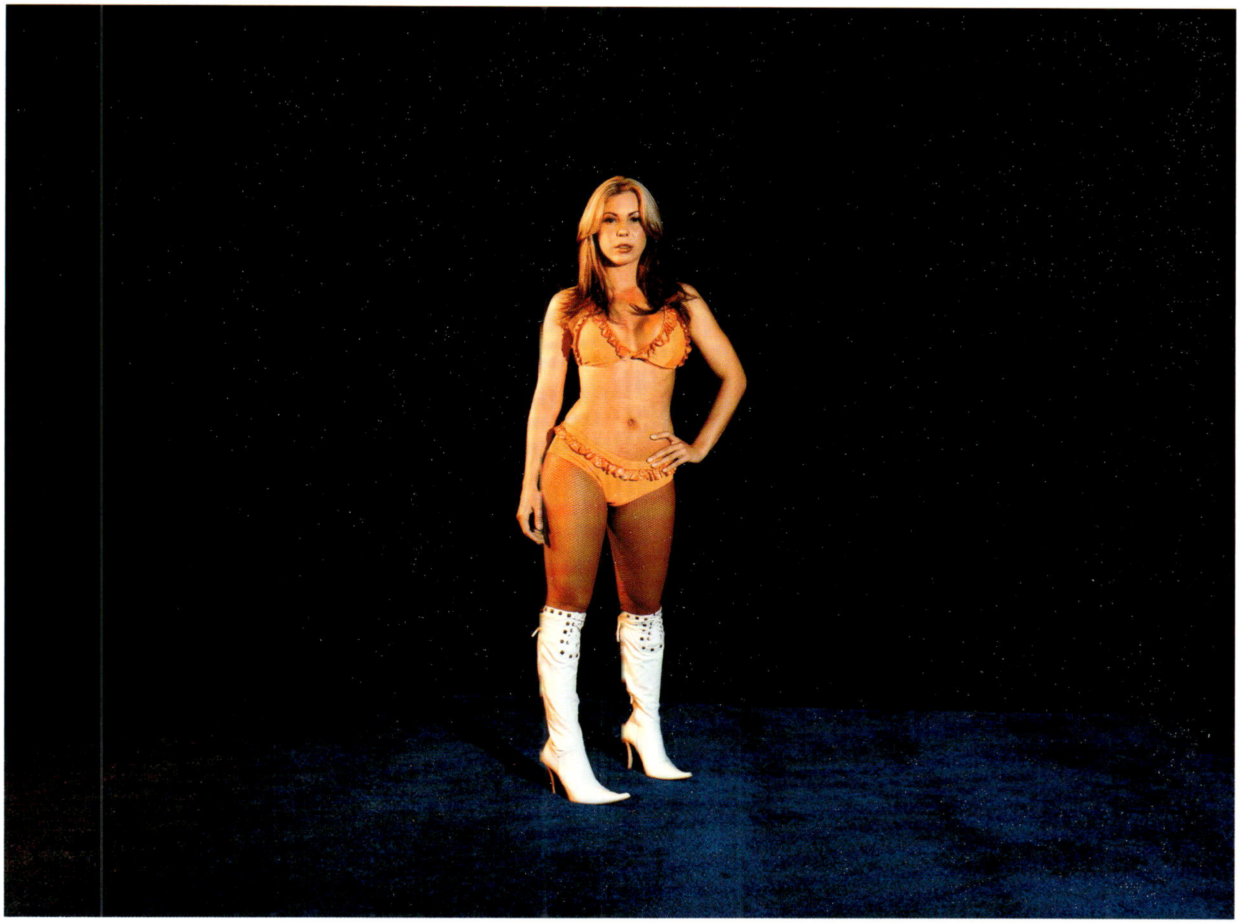

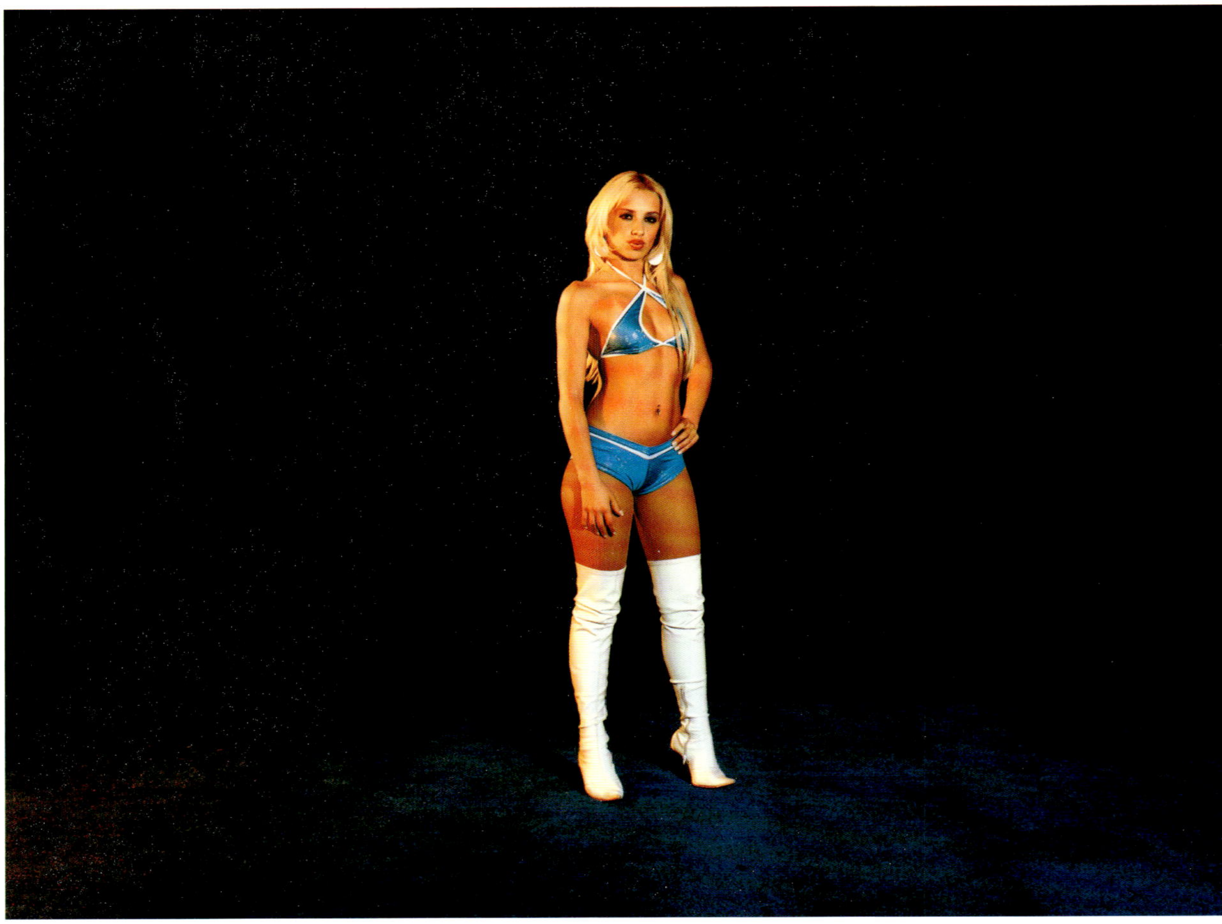

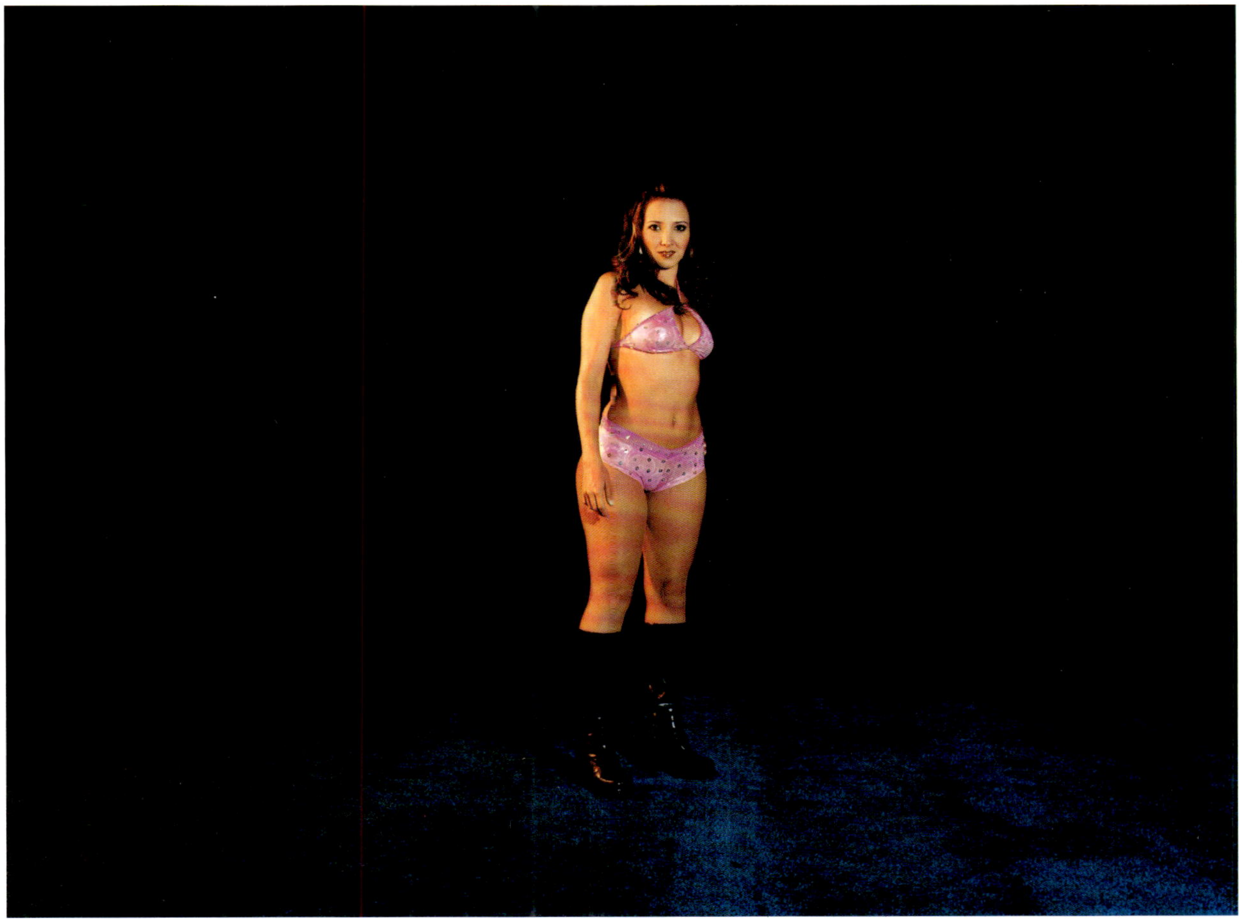

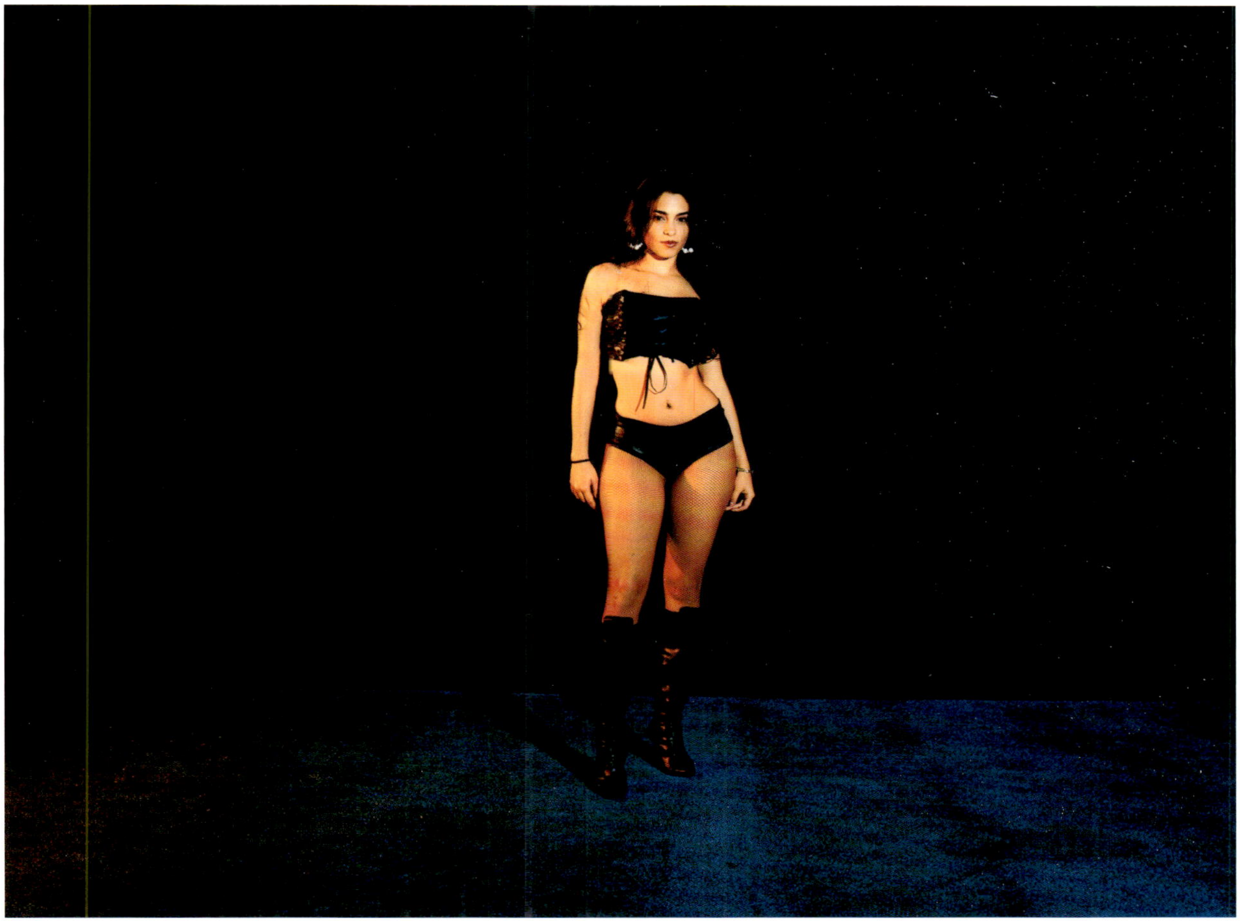

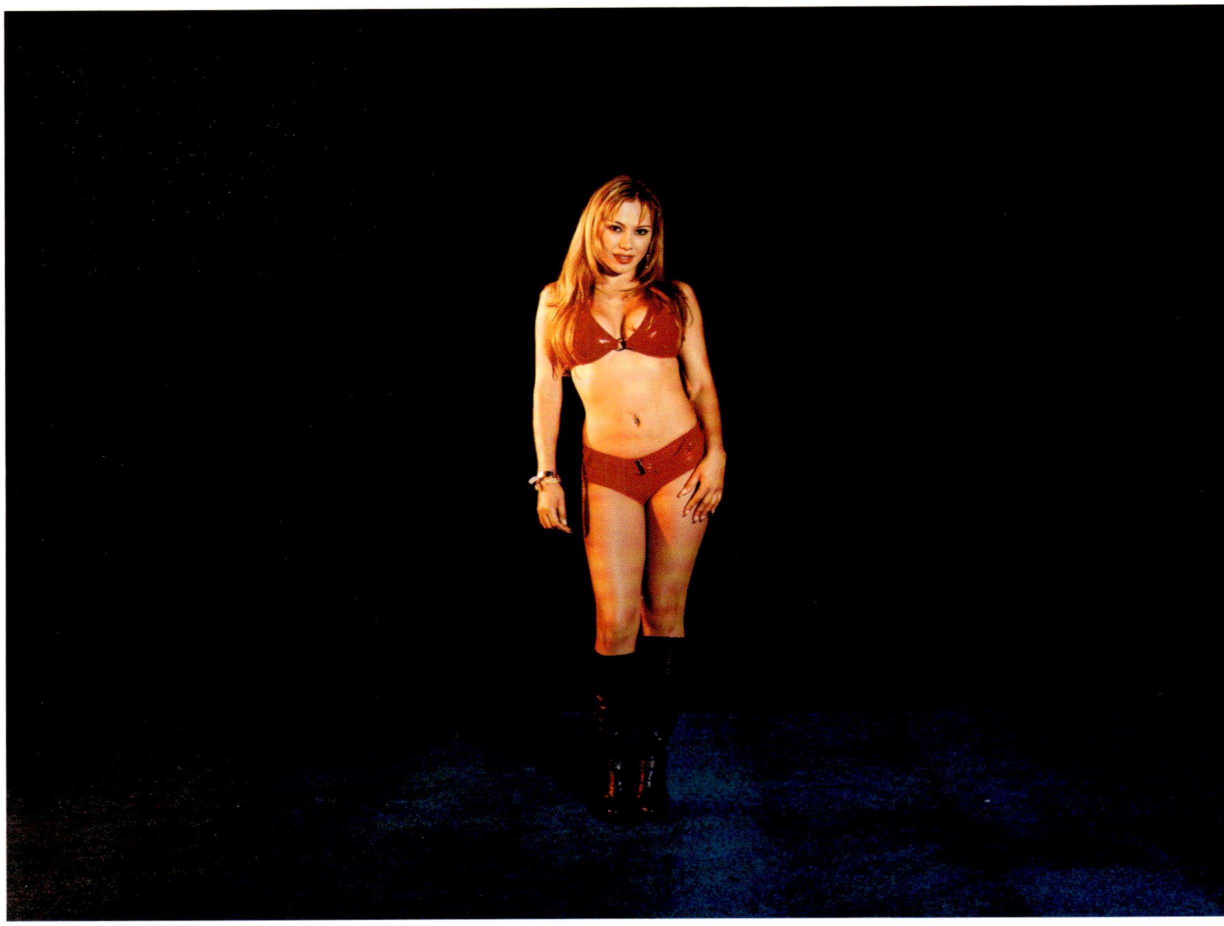

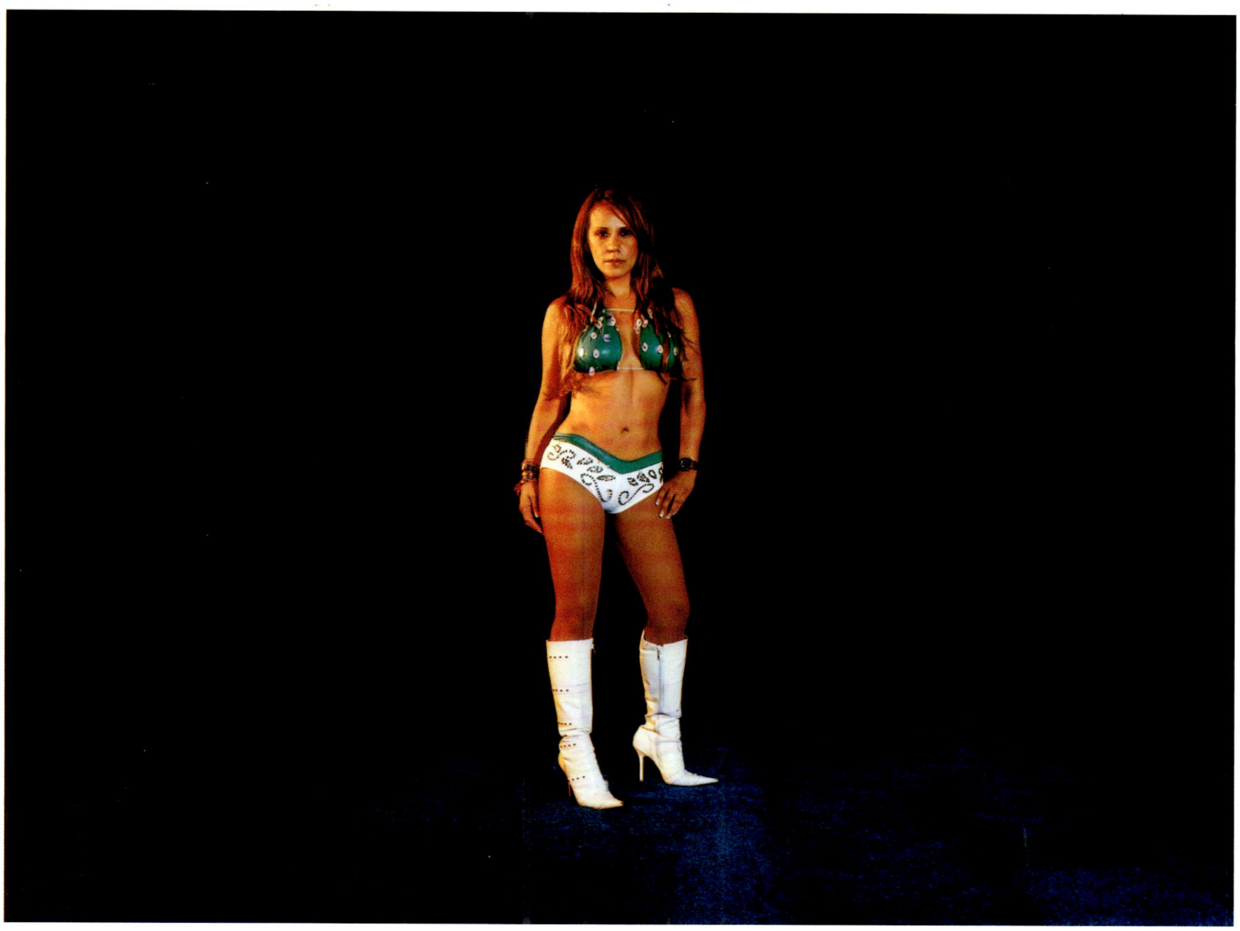

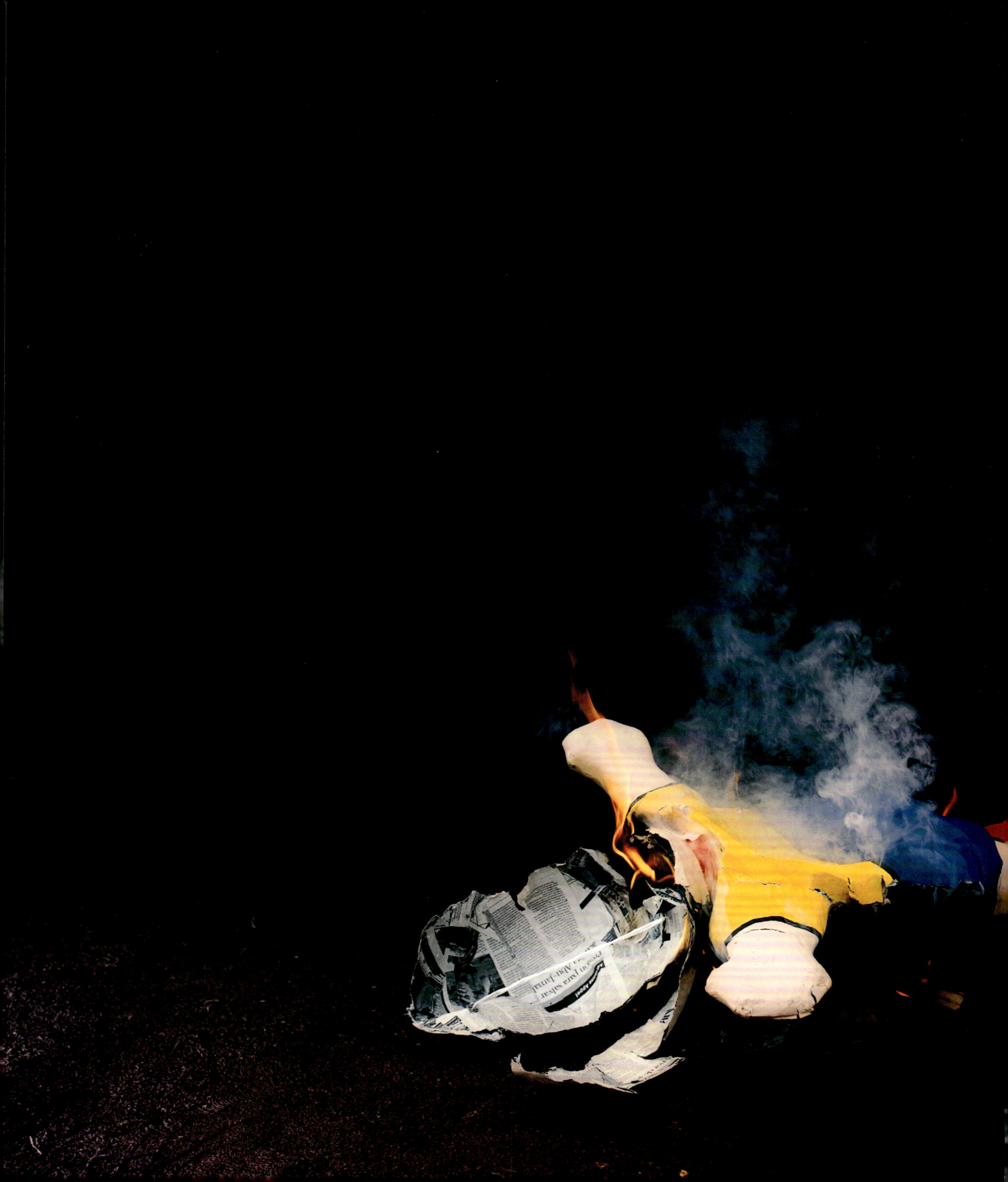

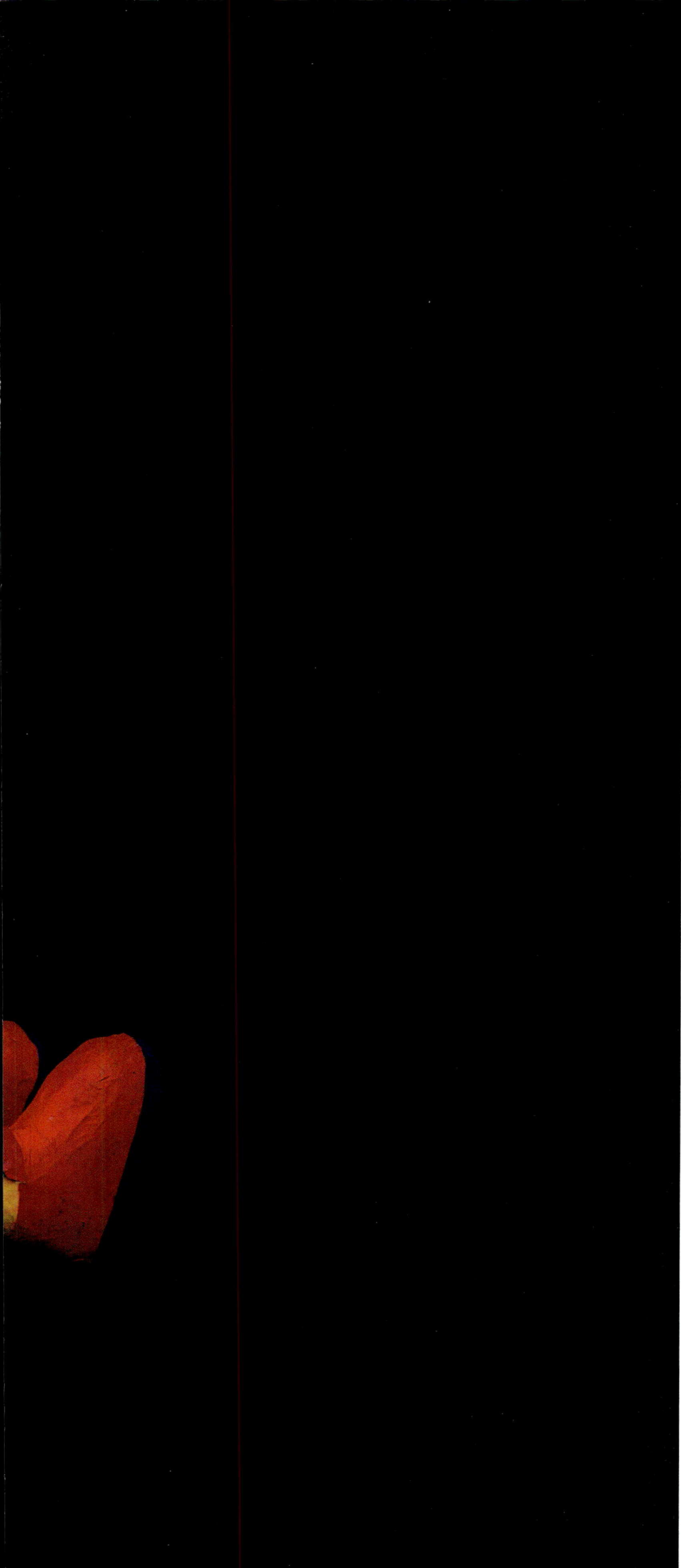

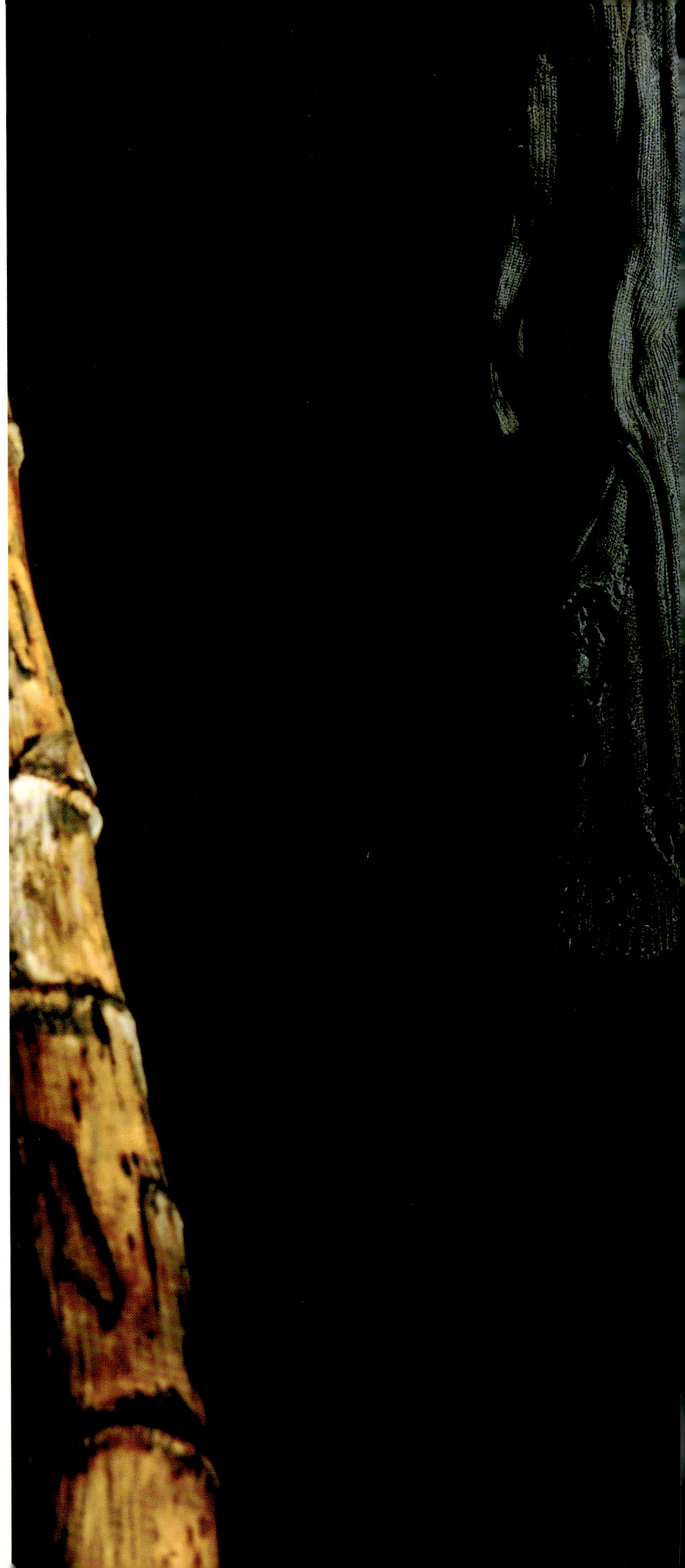

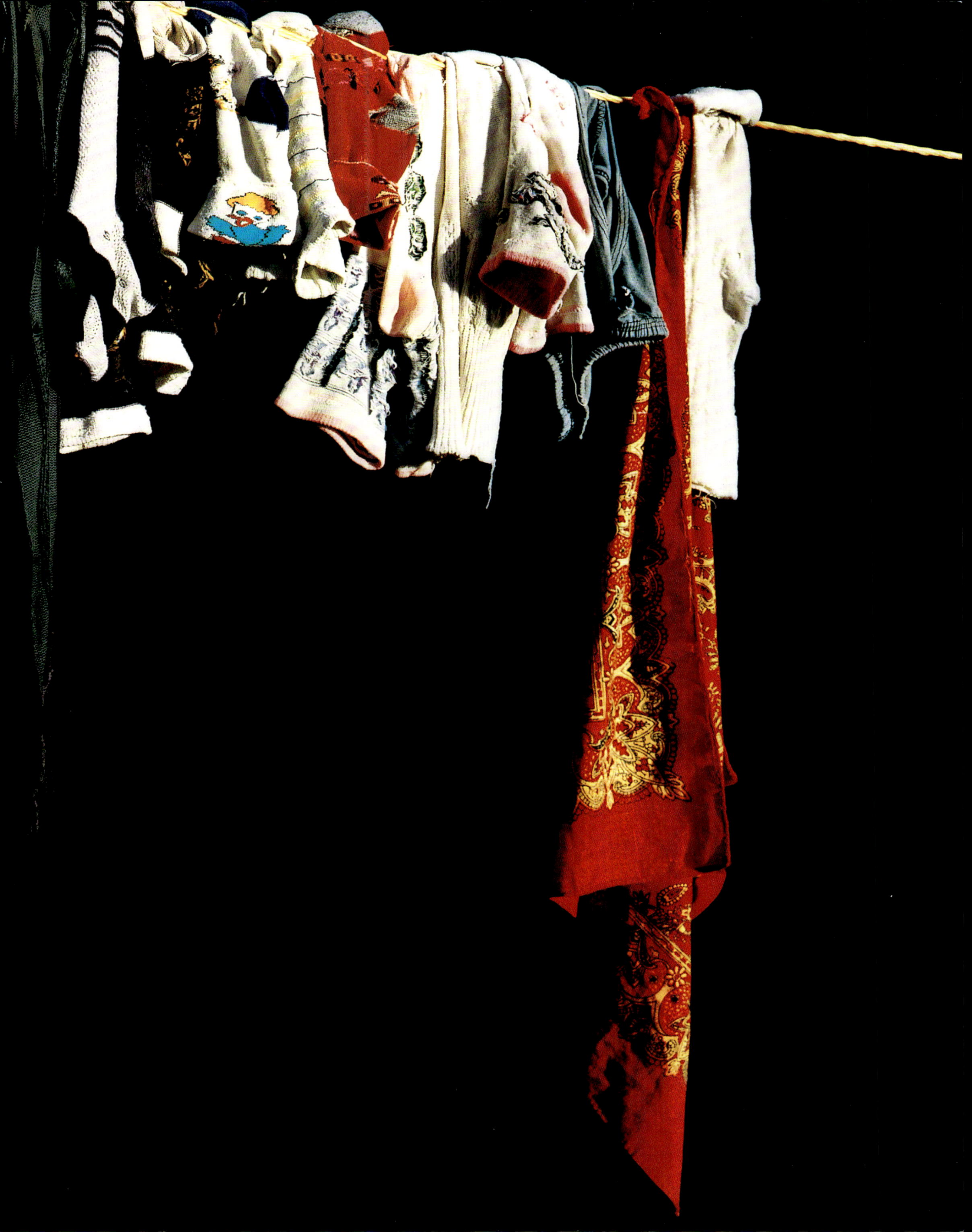

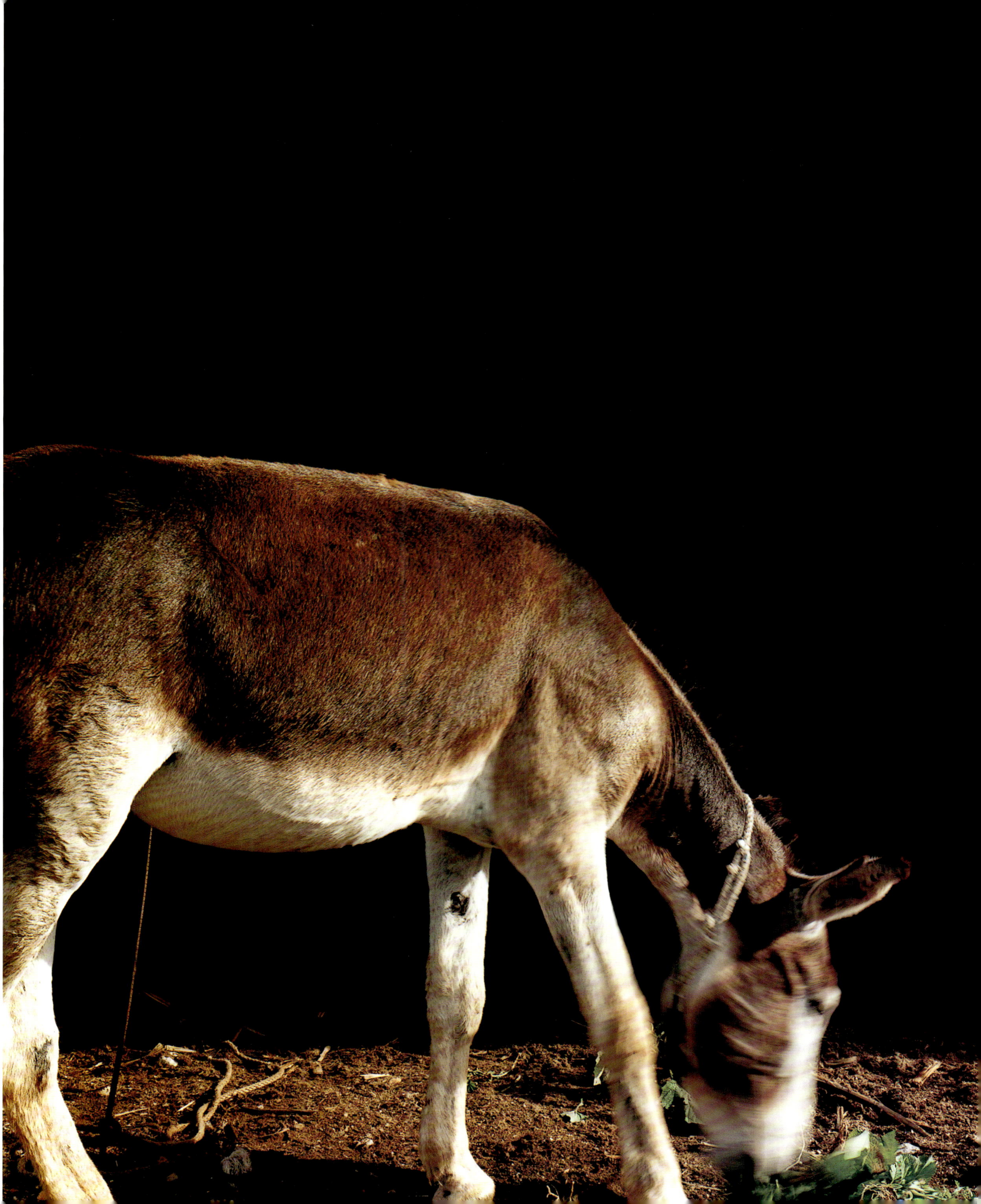

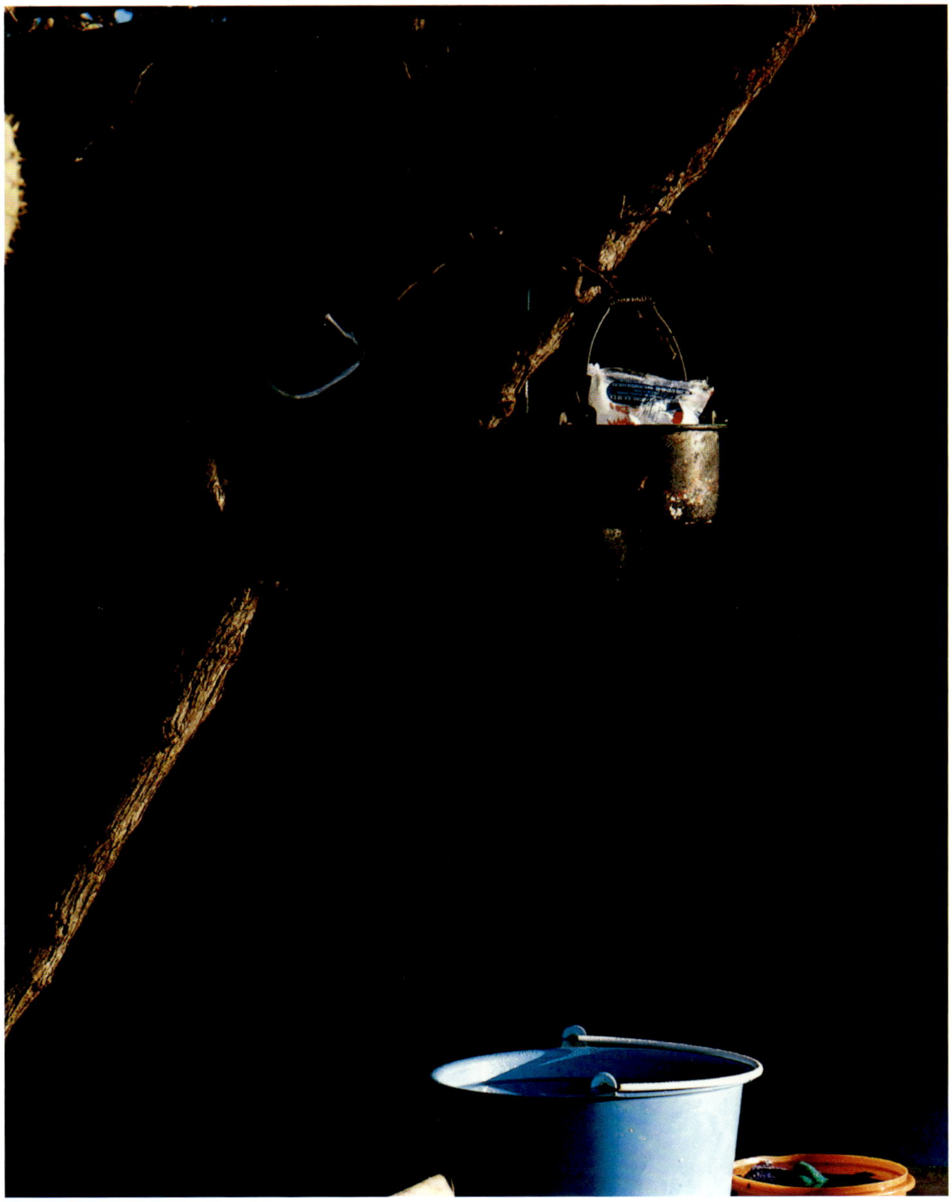

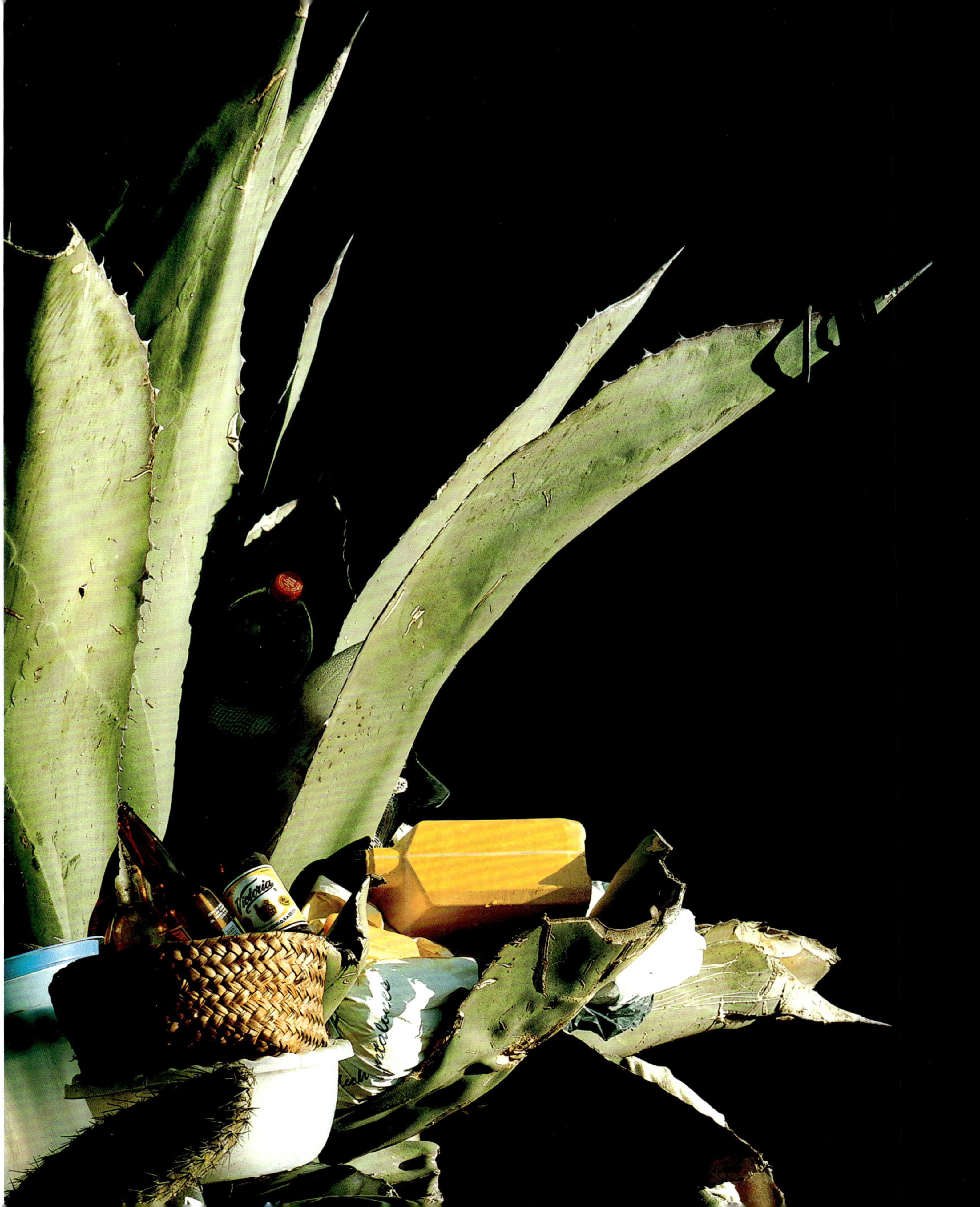
Victoria

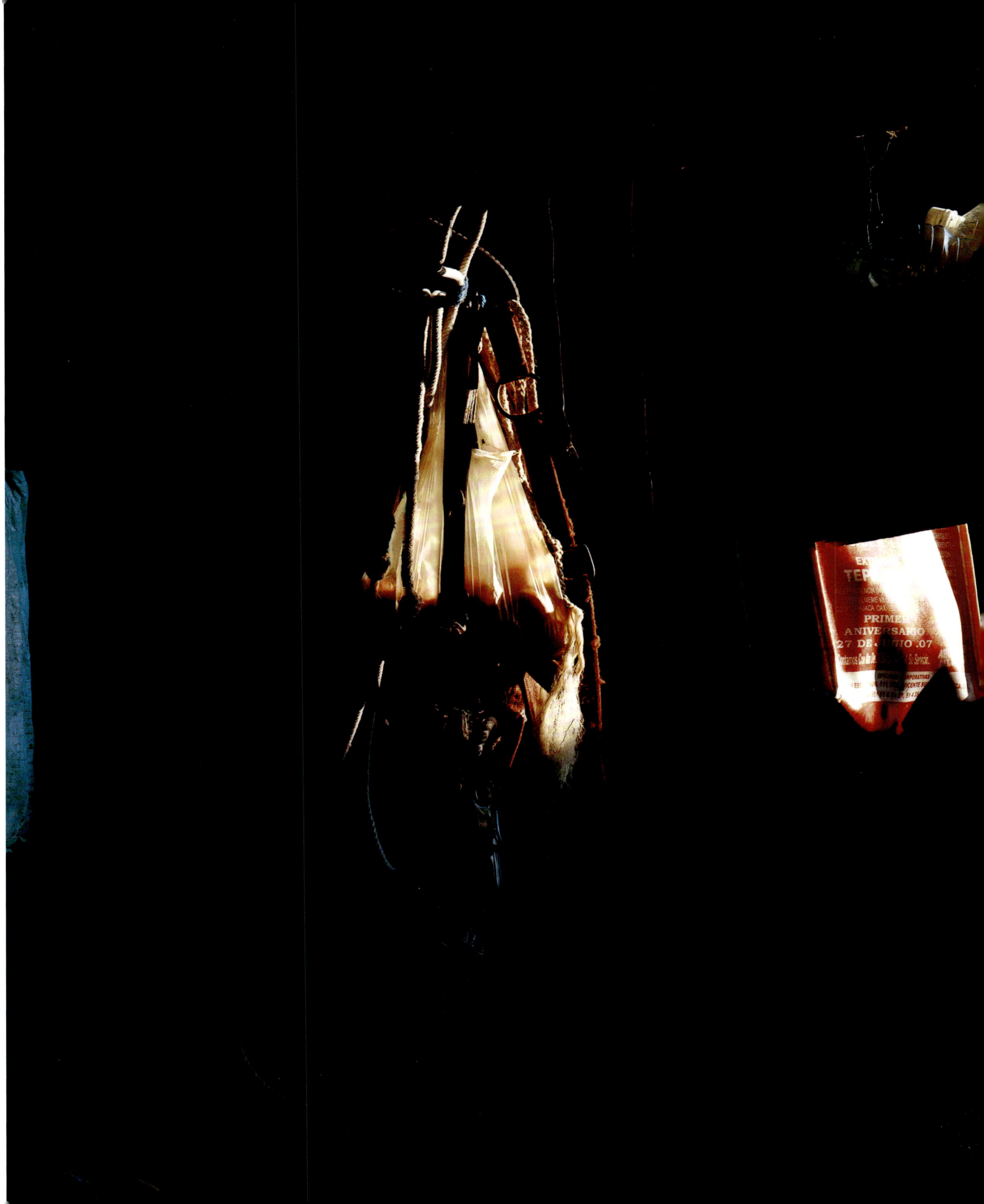
ANIVERSARIO

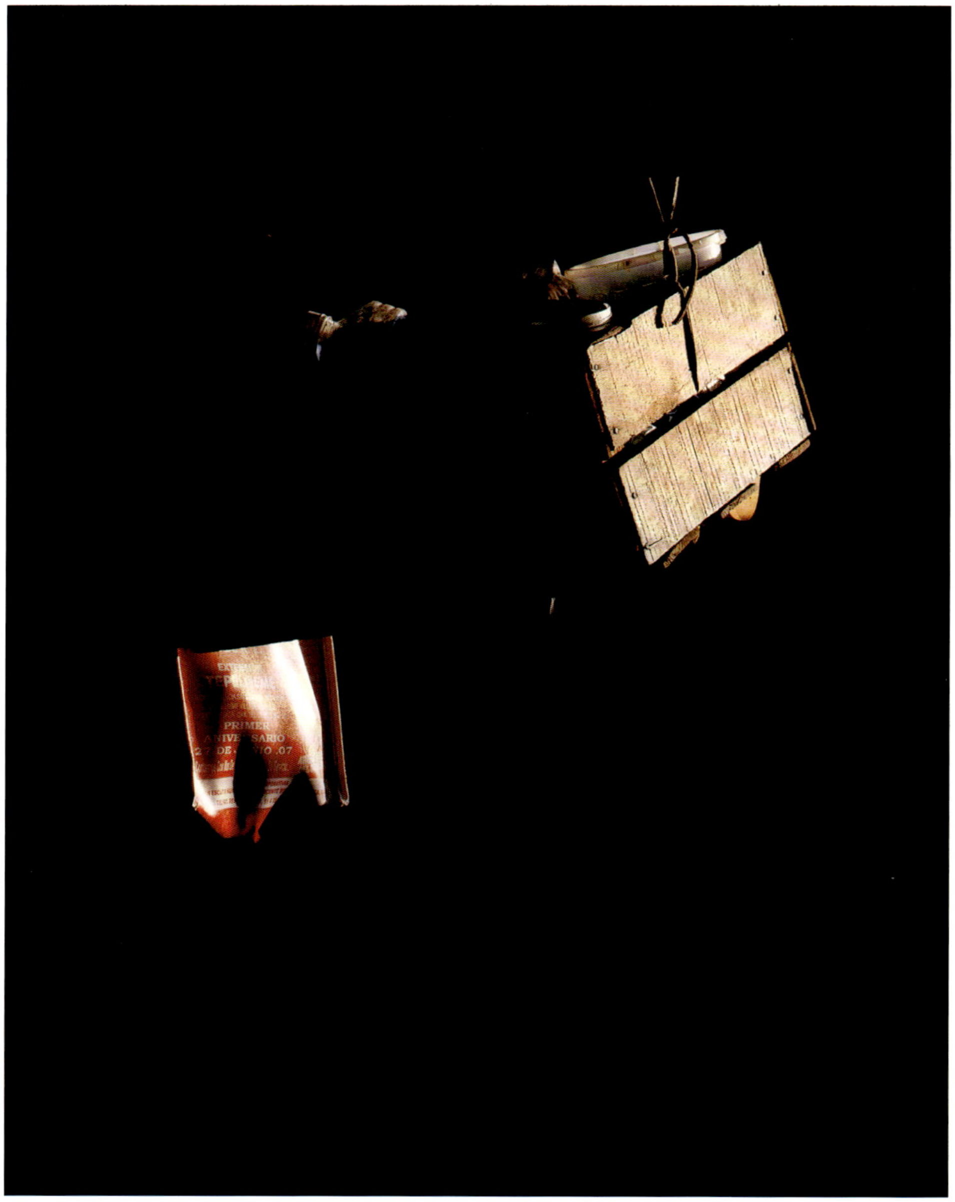
PRIMER

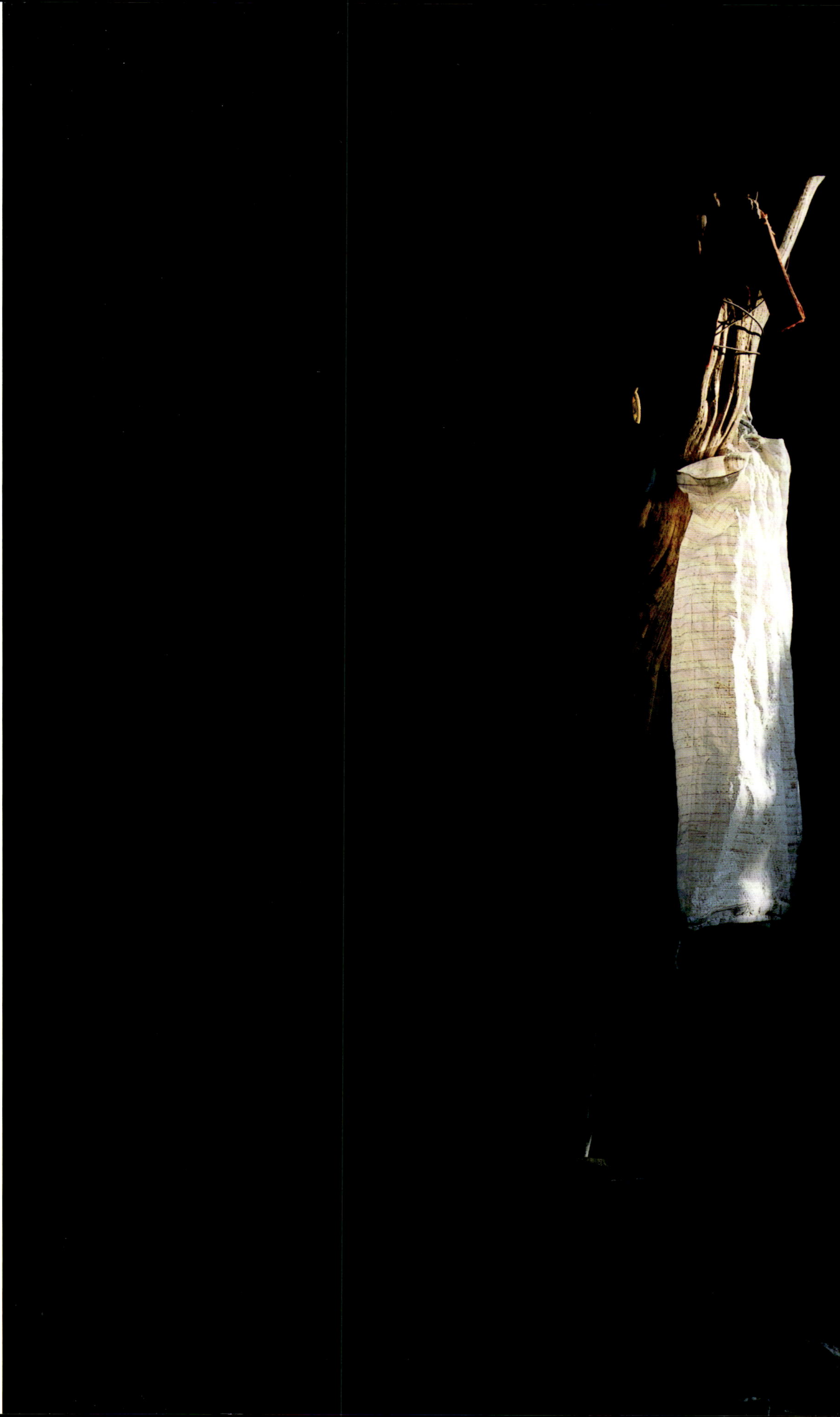

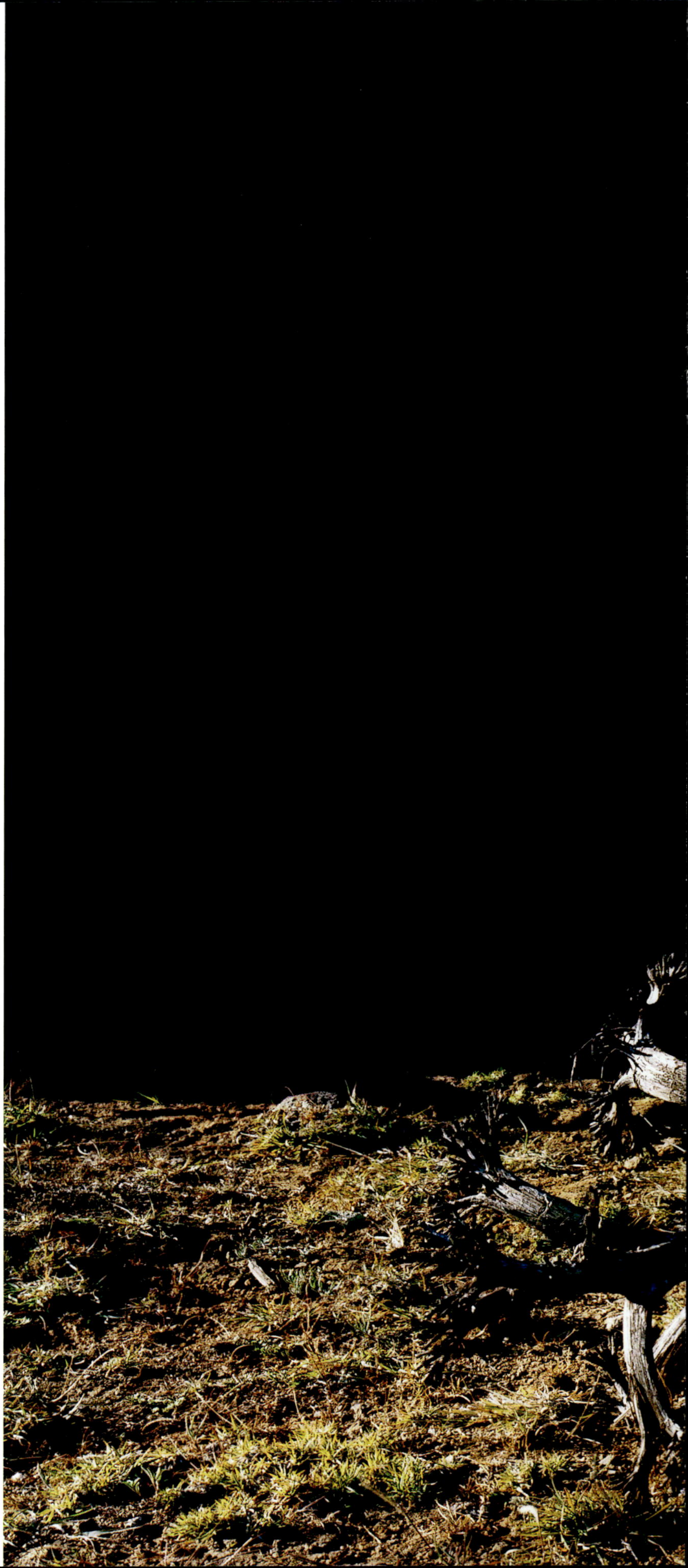

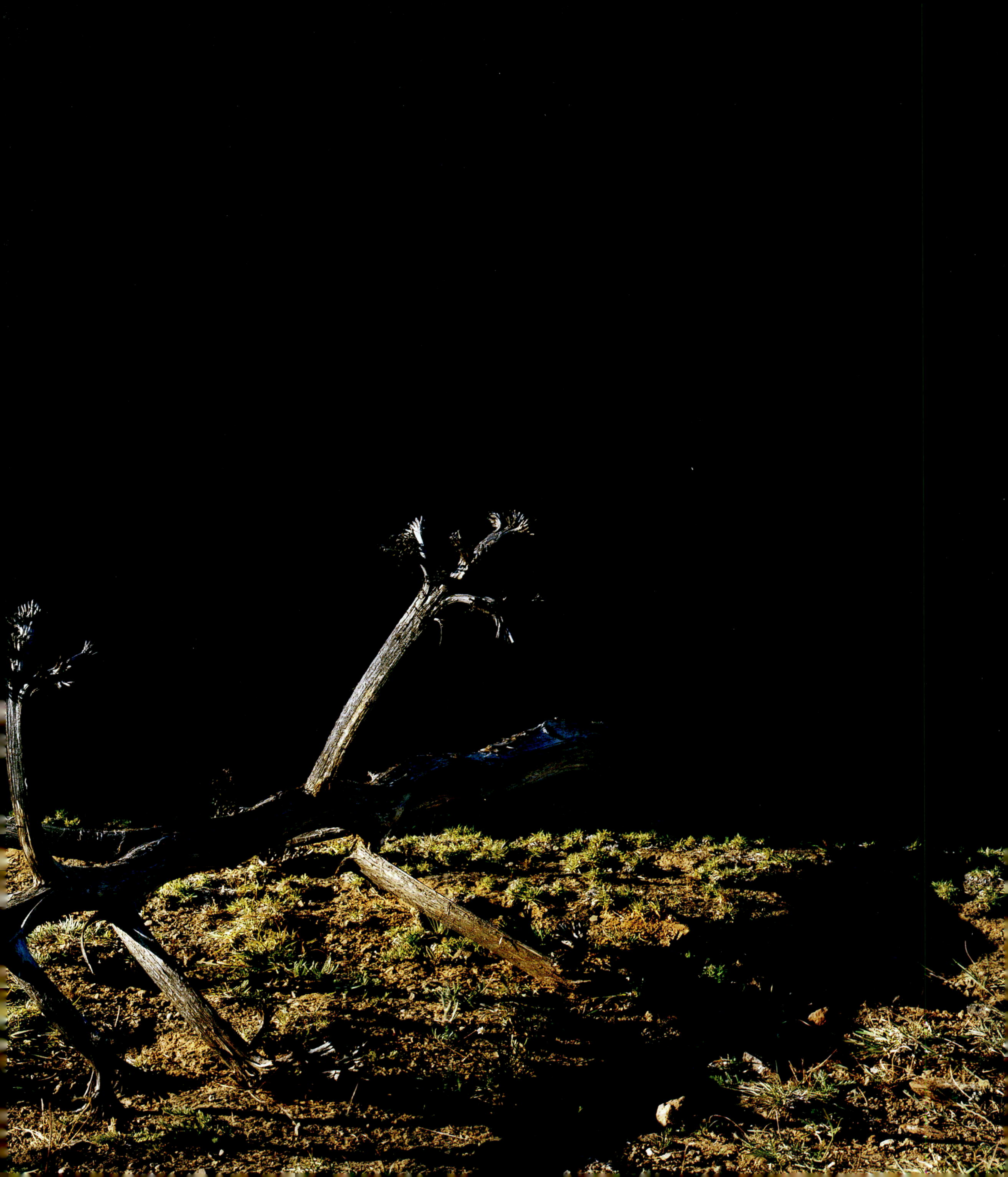

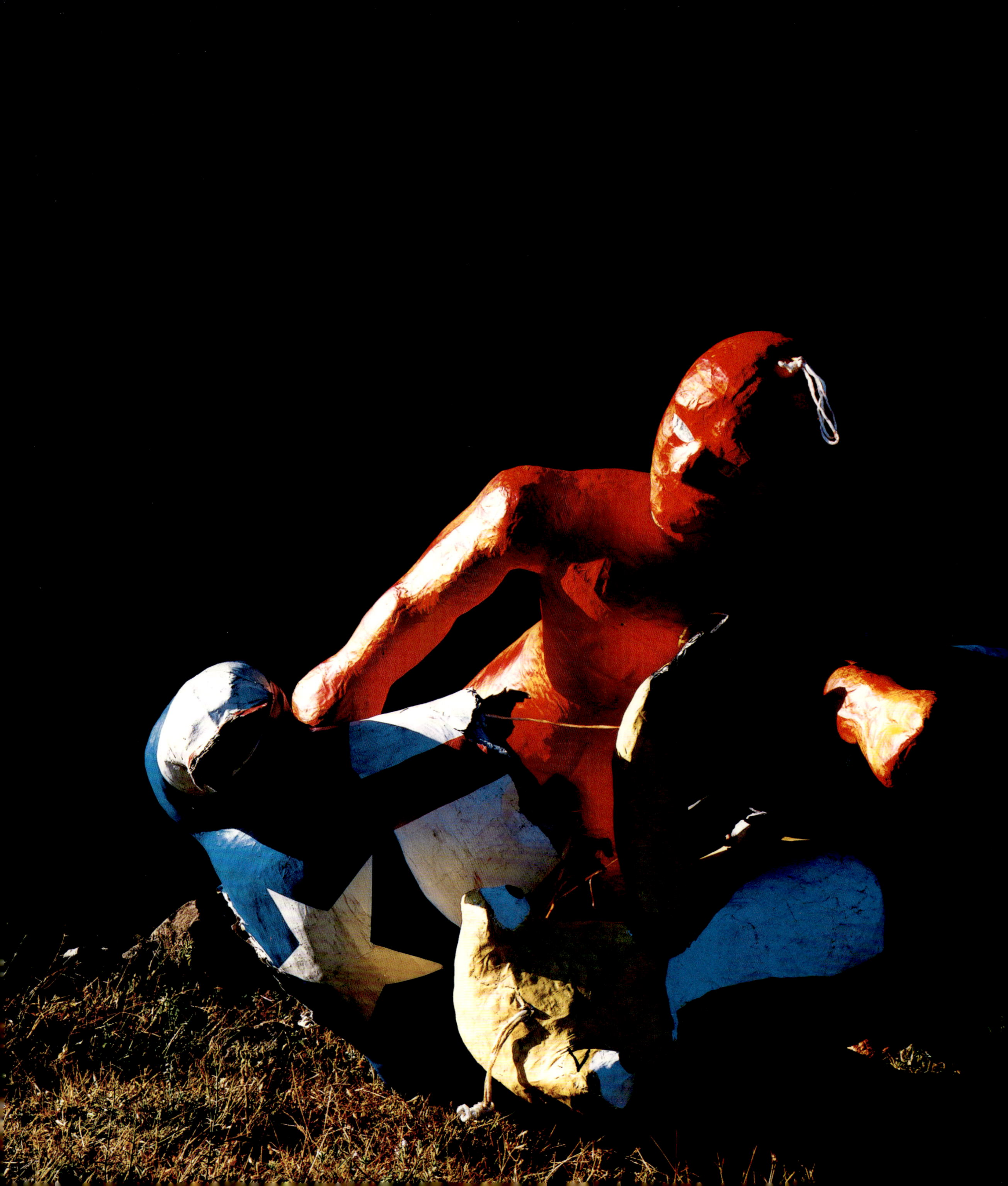

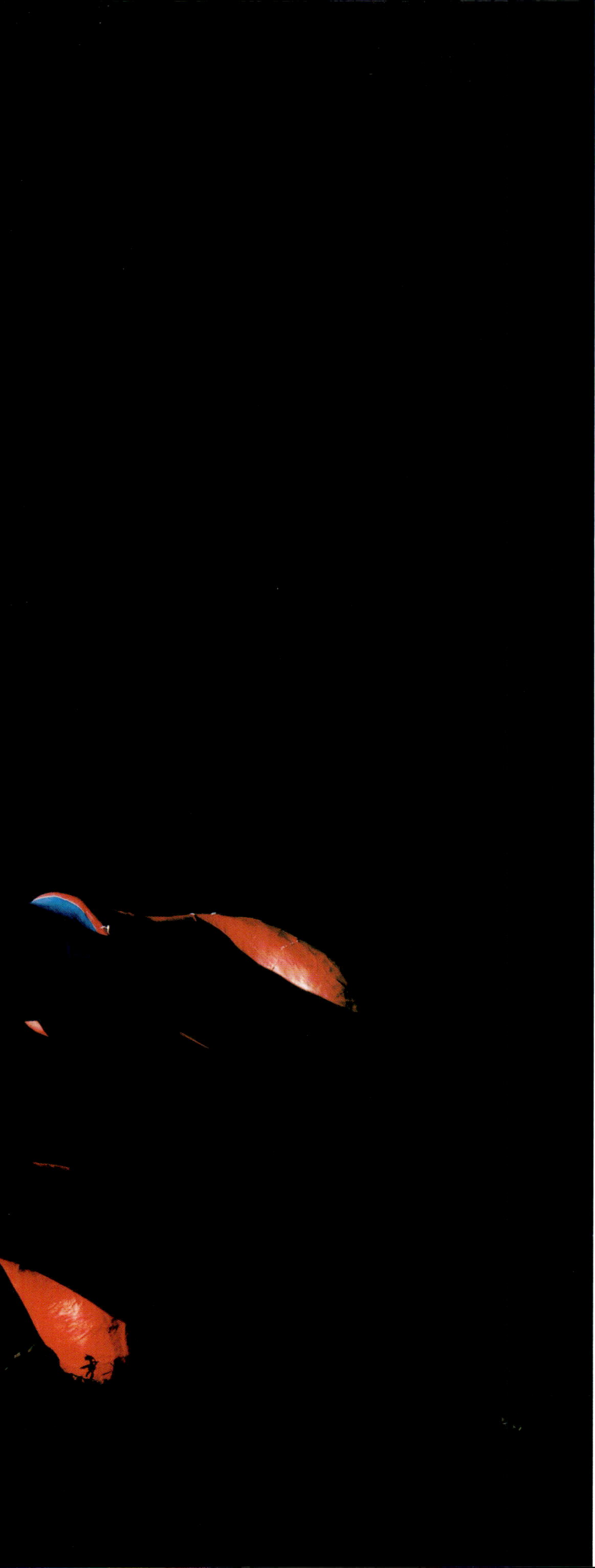

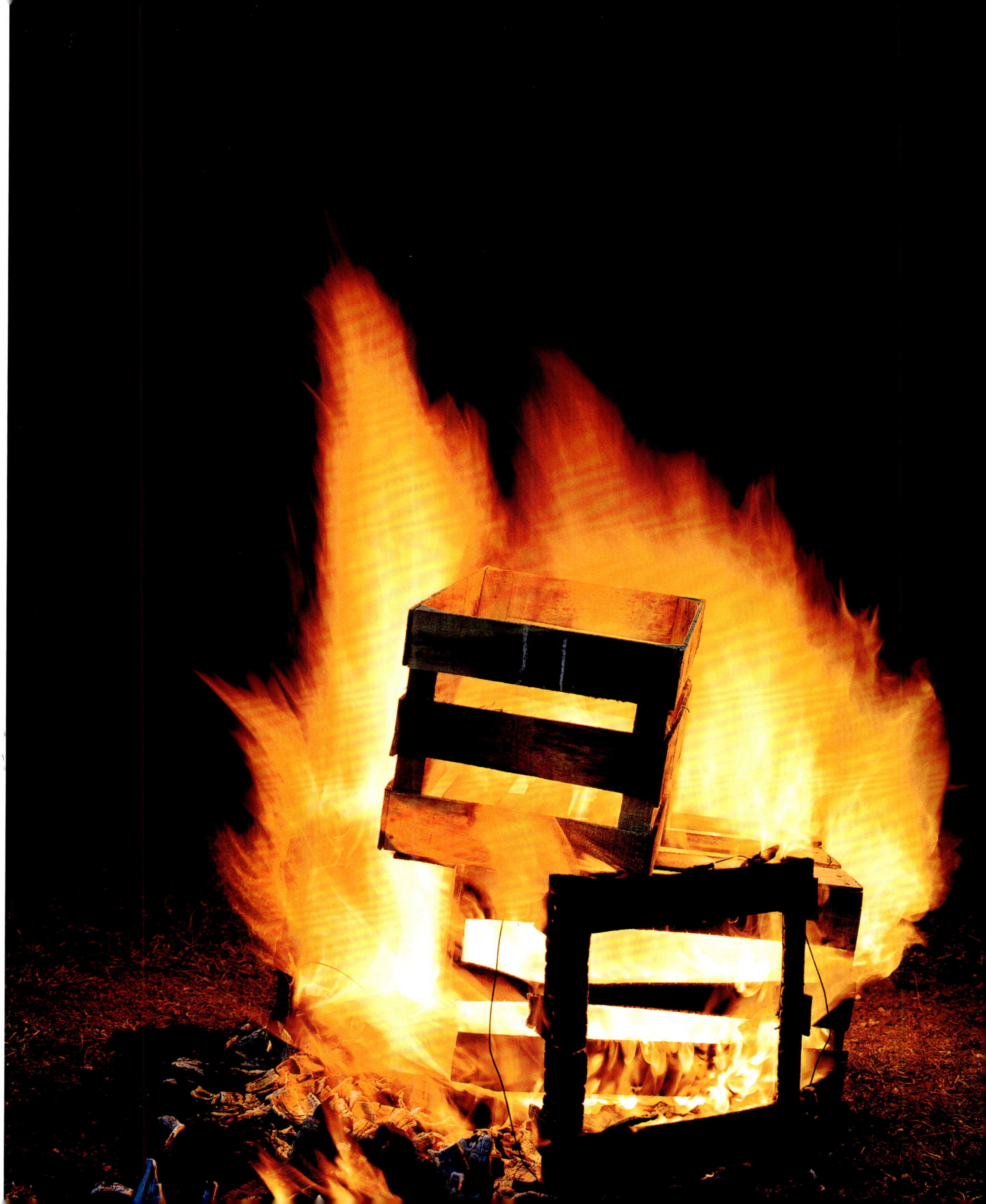

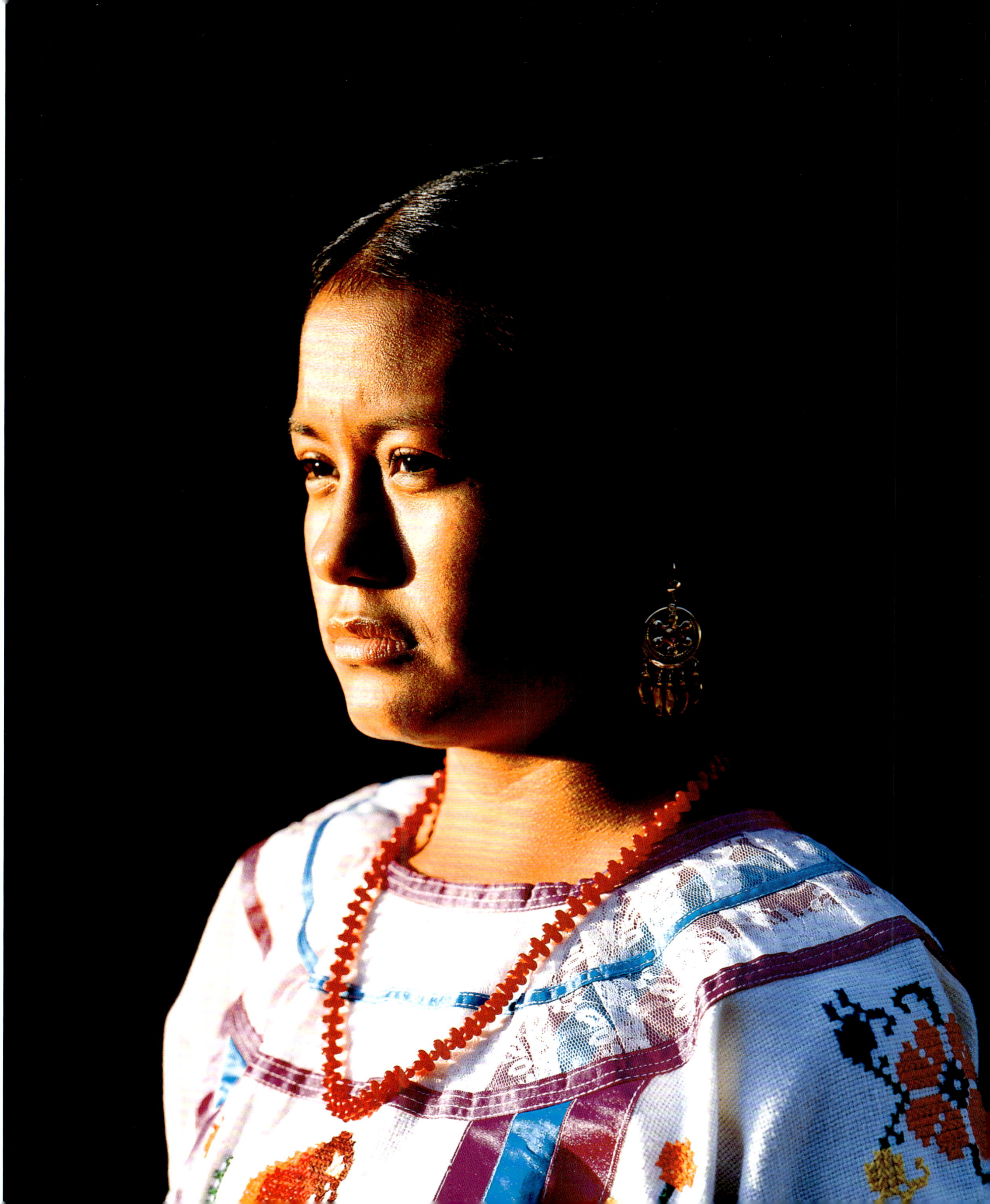

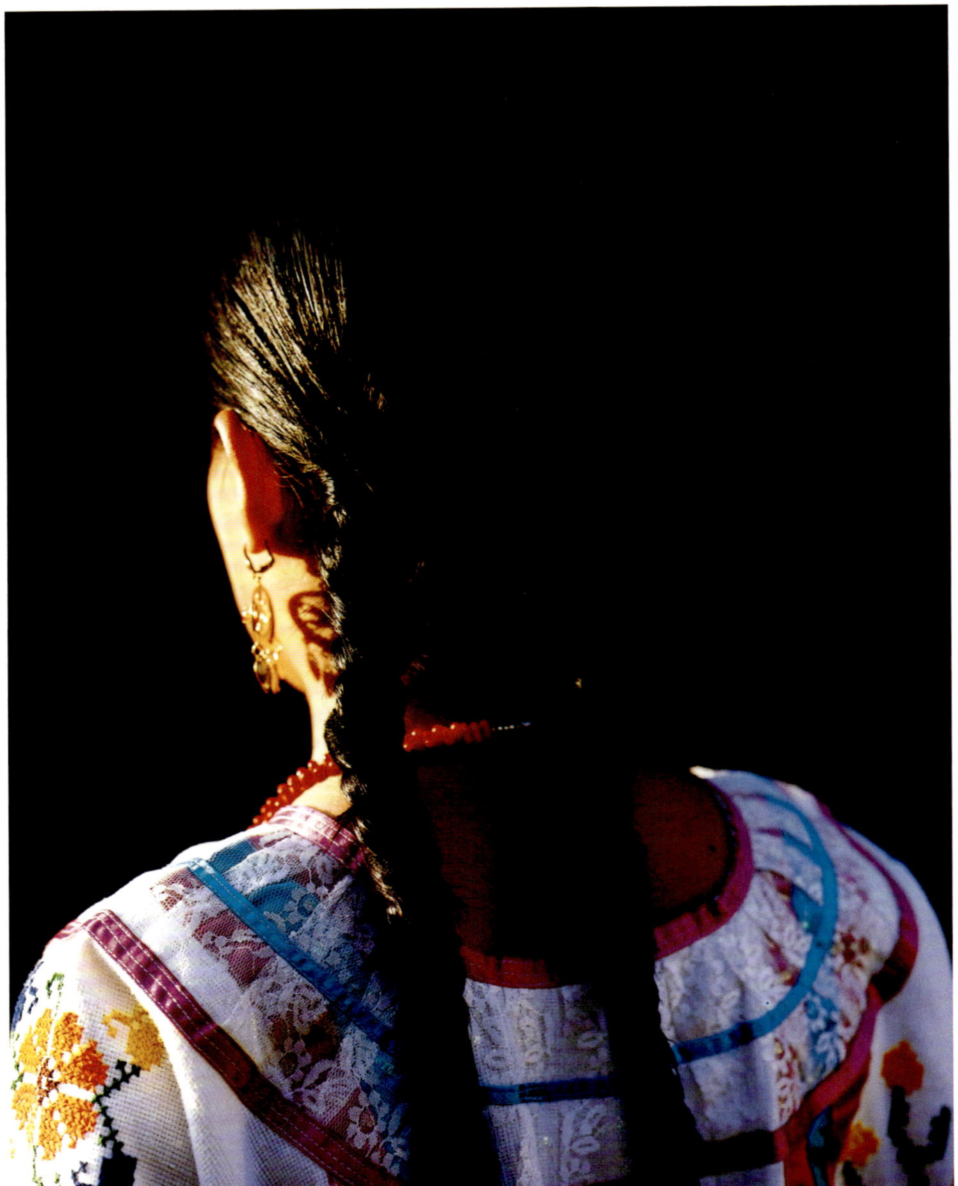

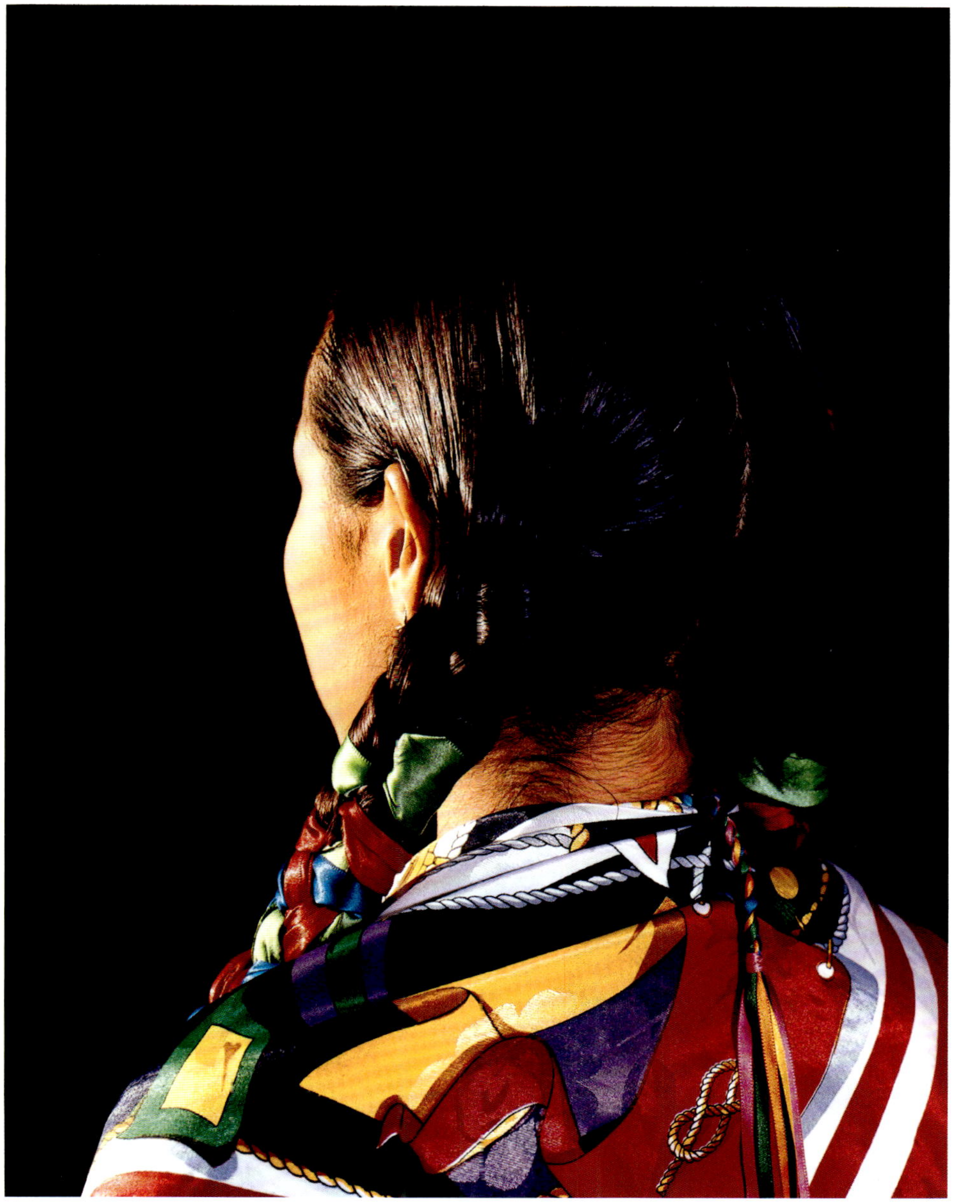

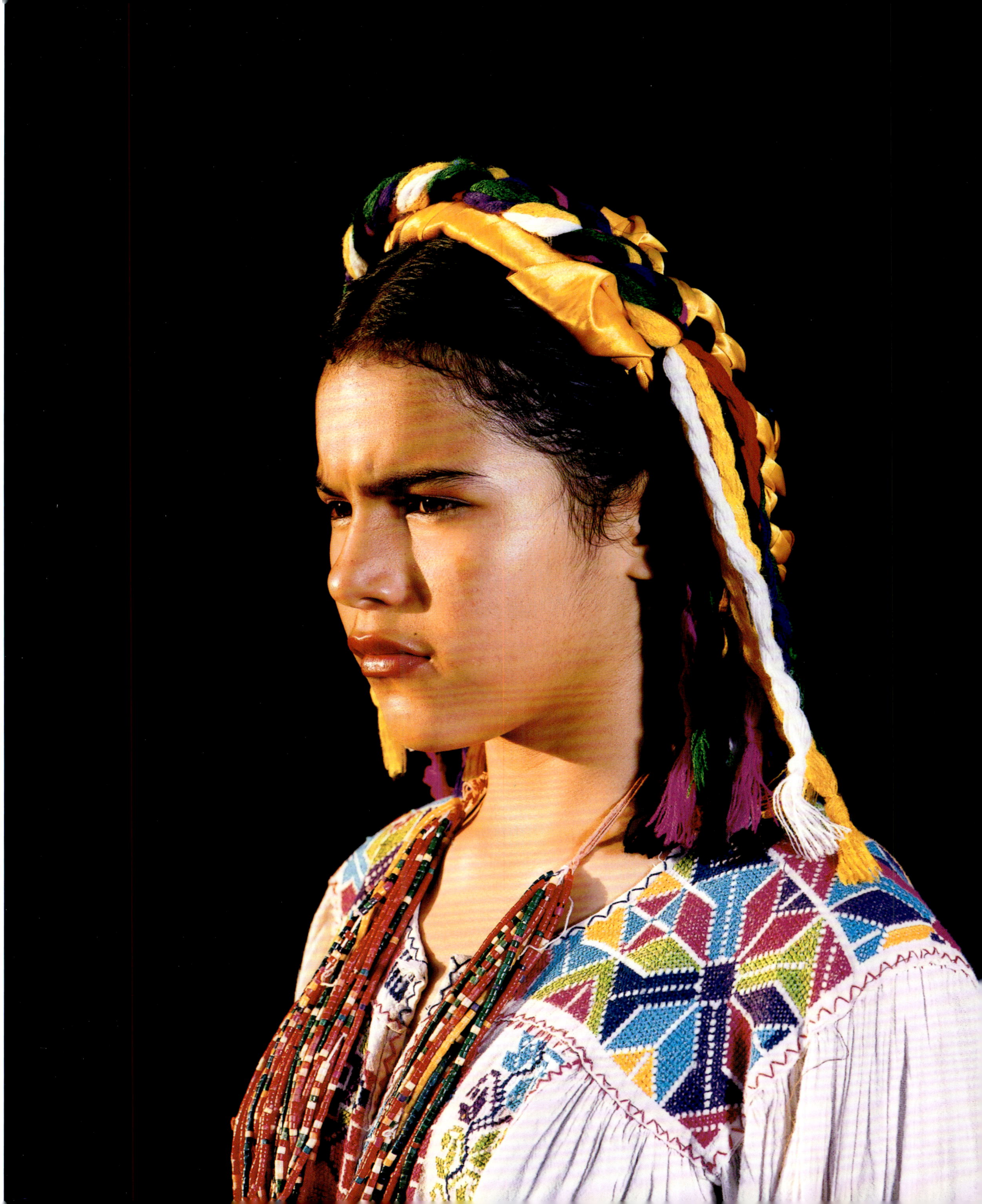

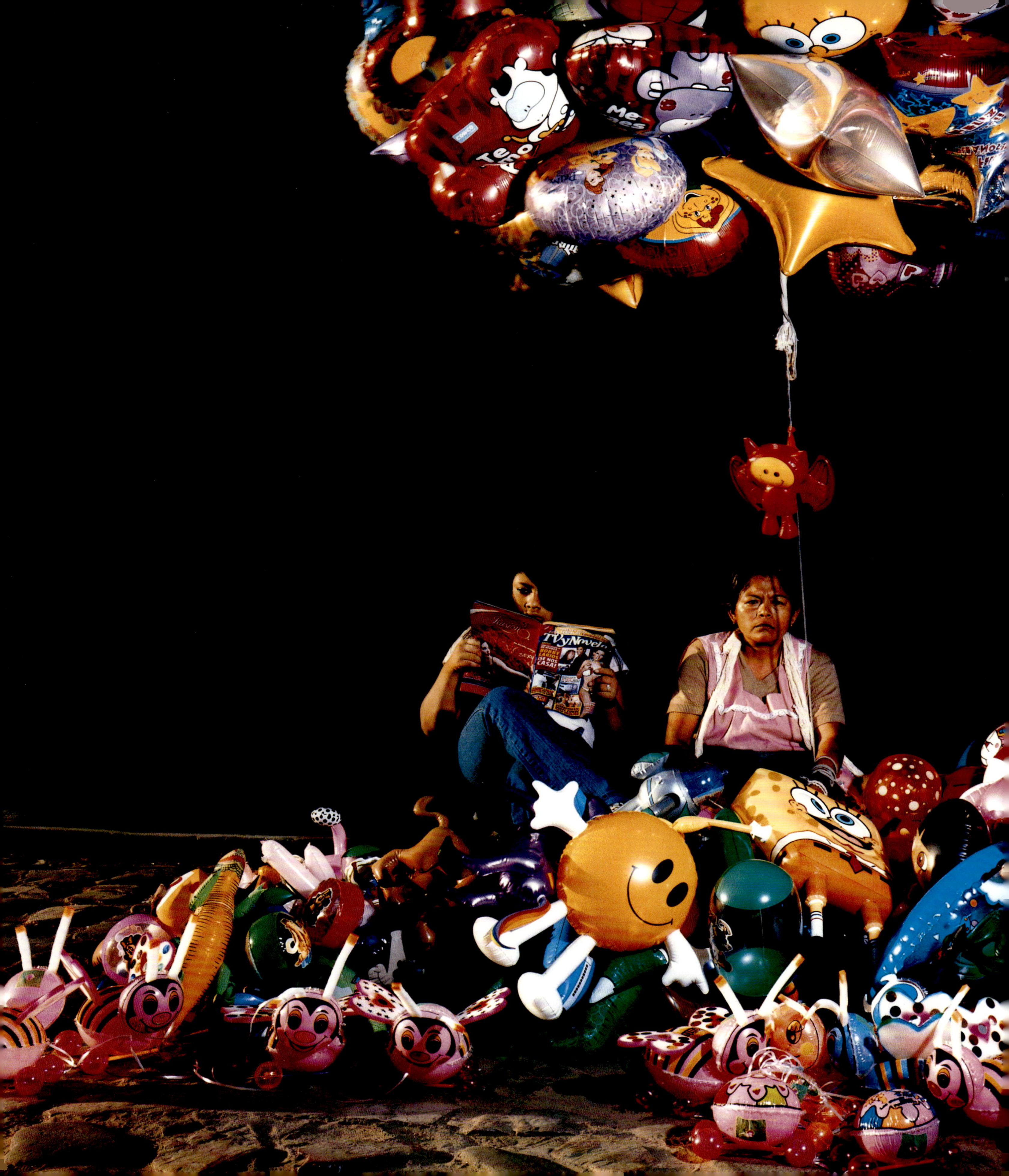
TVyNovelas

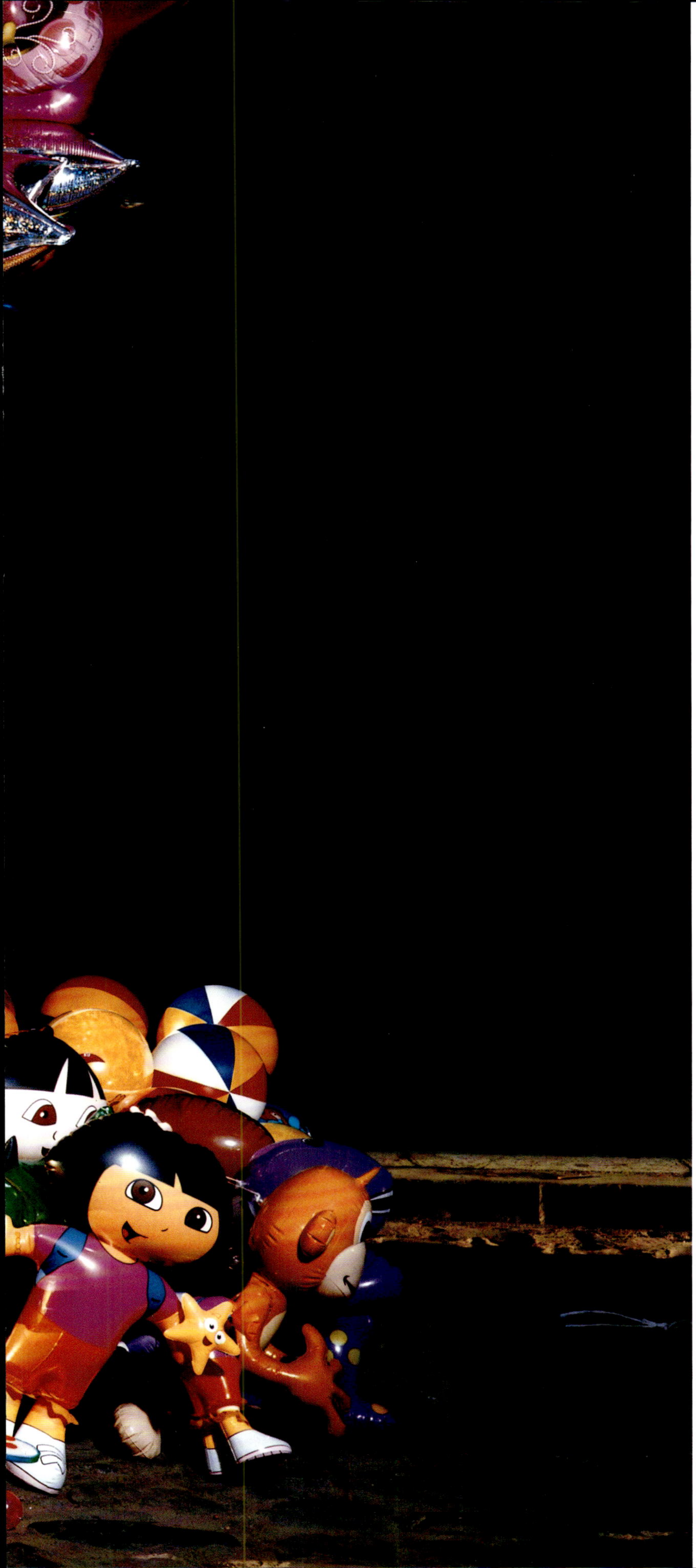

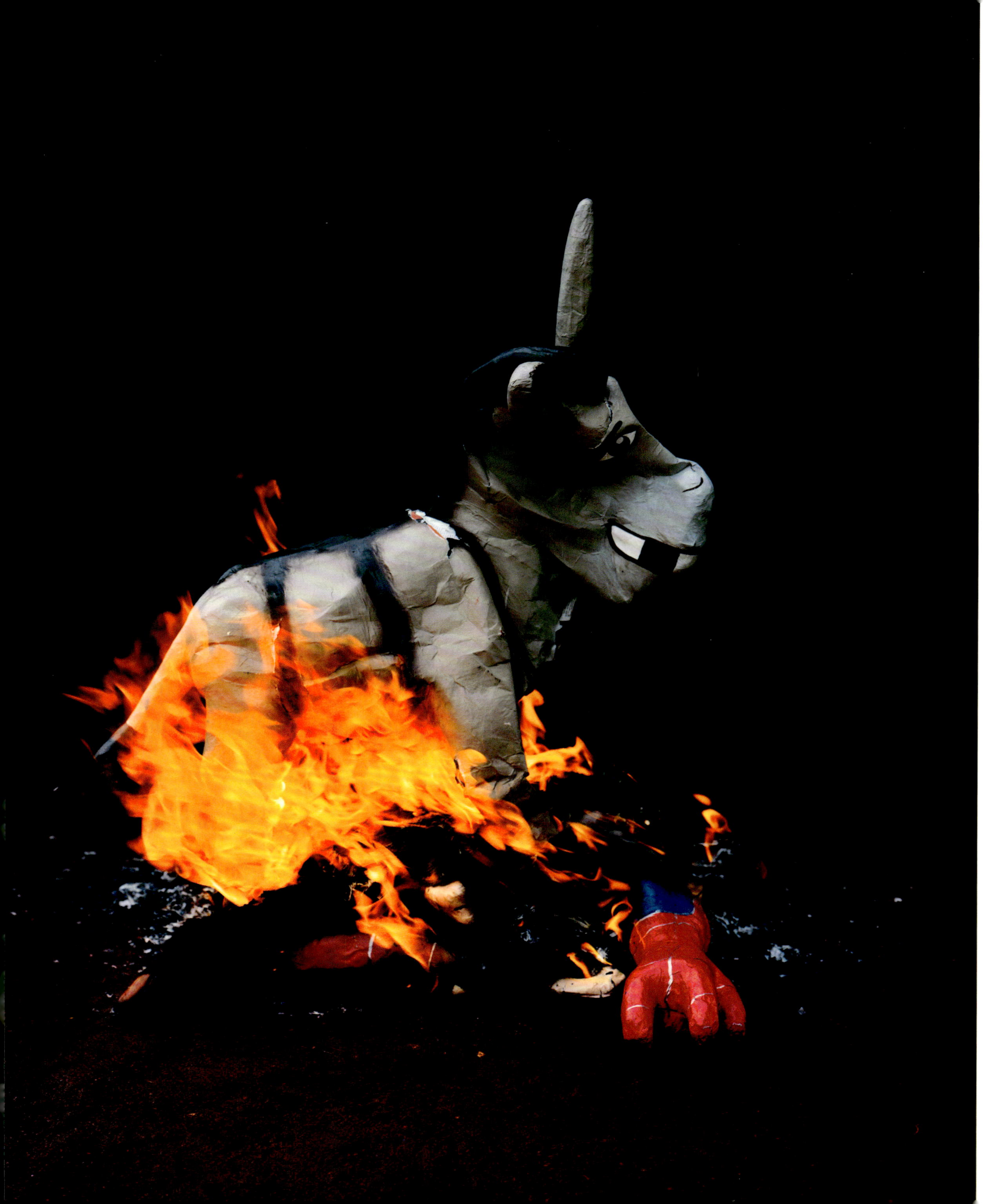

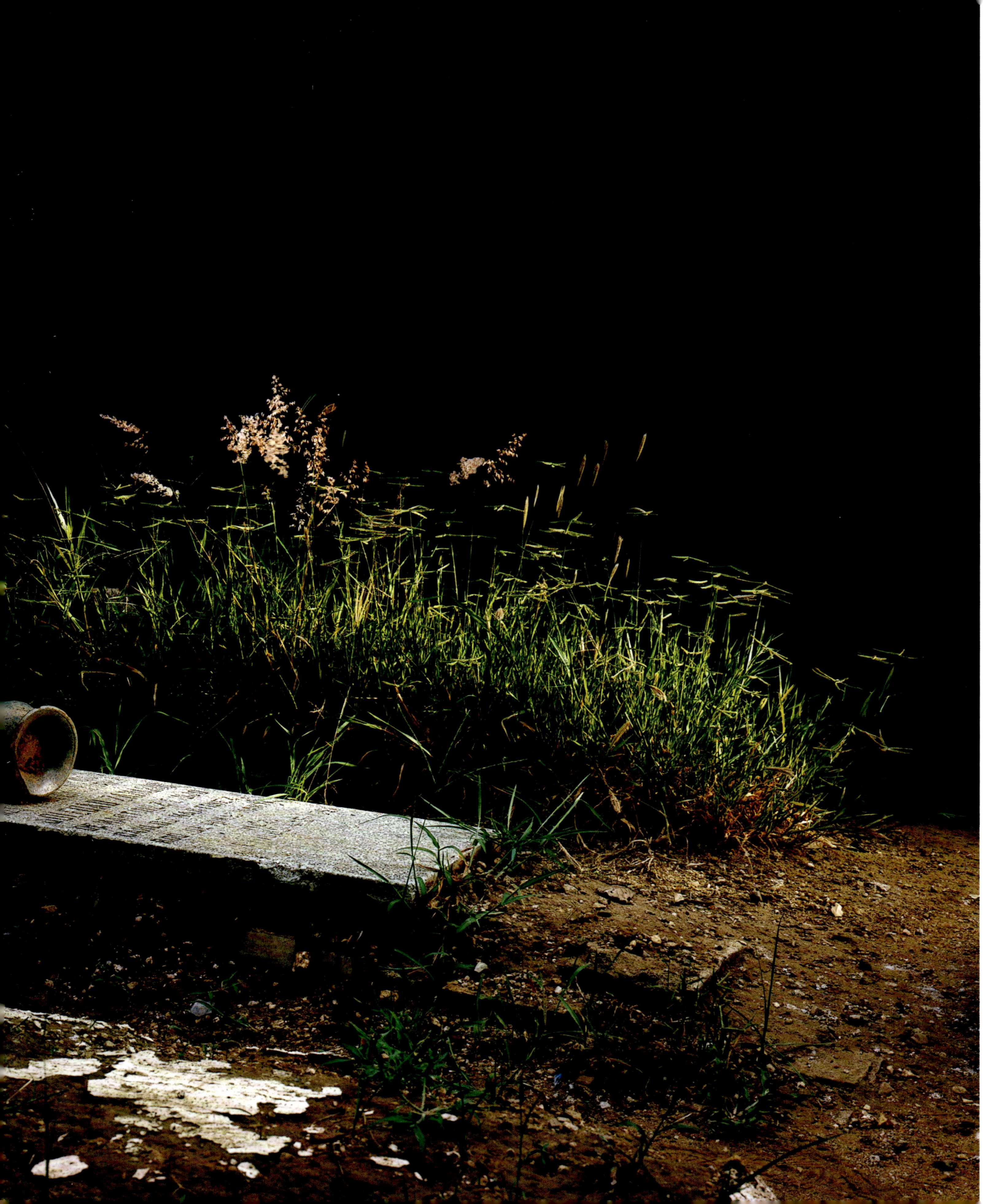

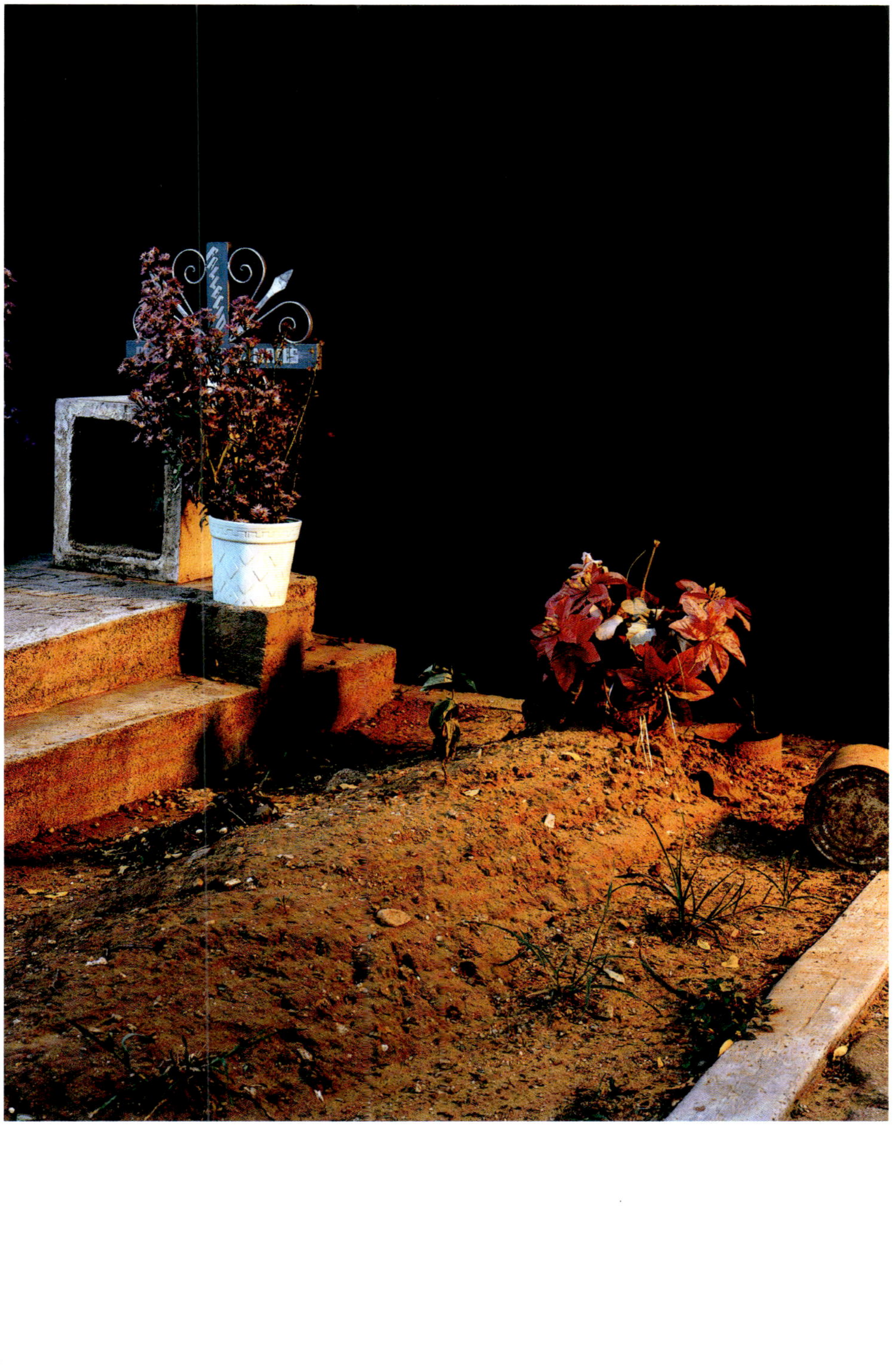

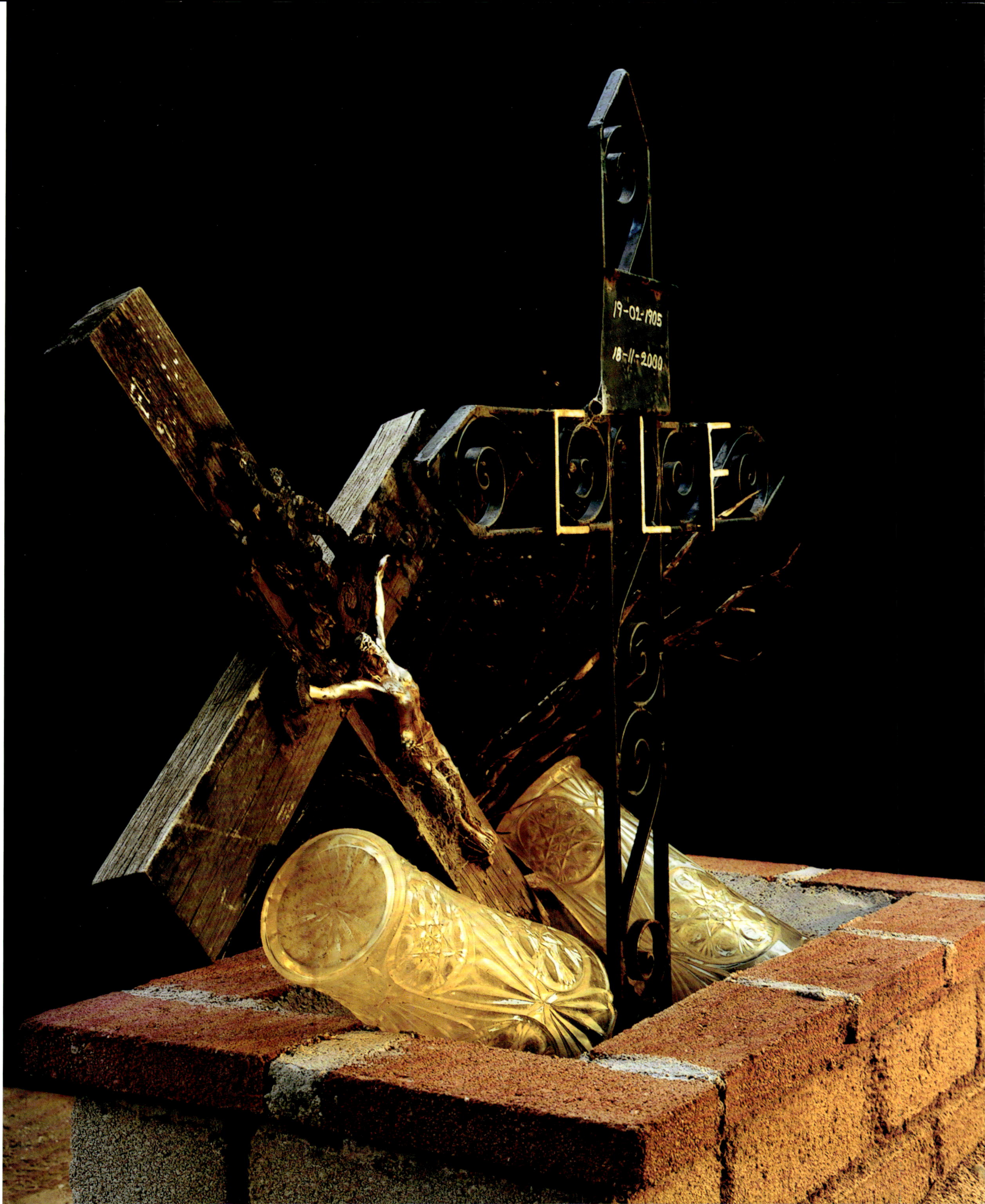
19-02-1905
18-11-2000

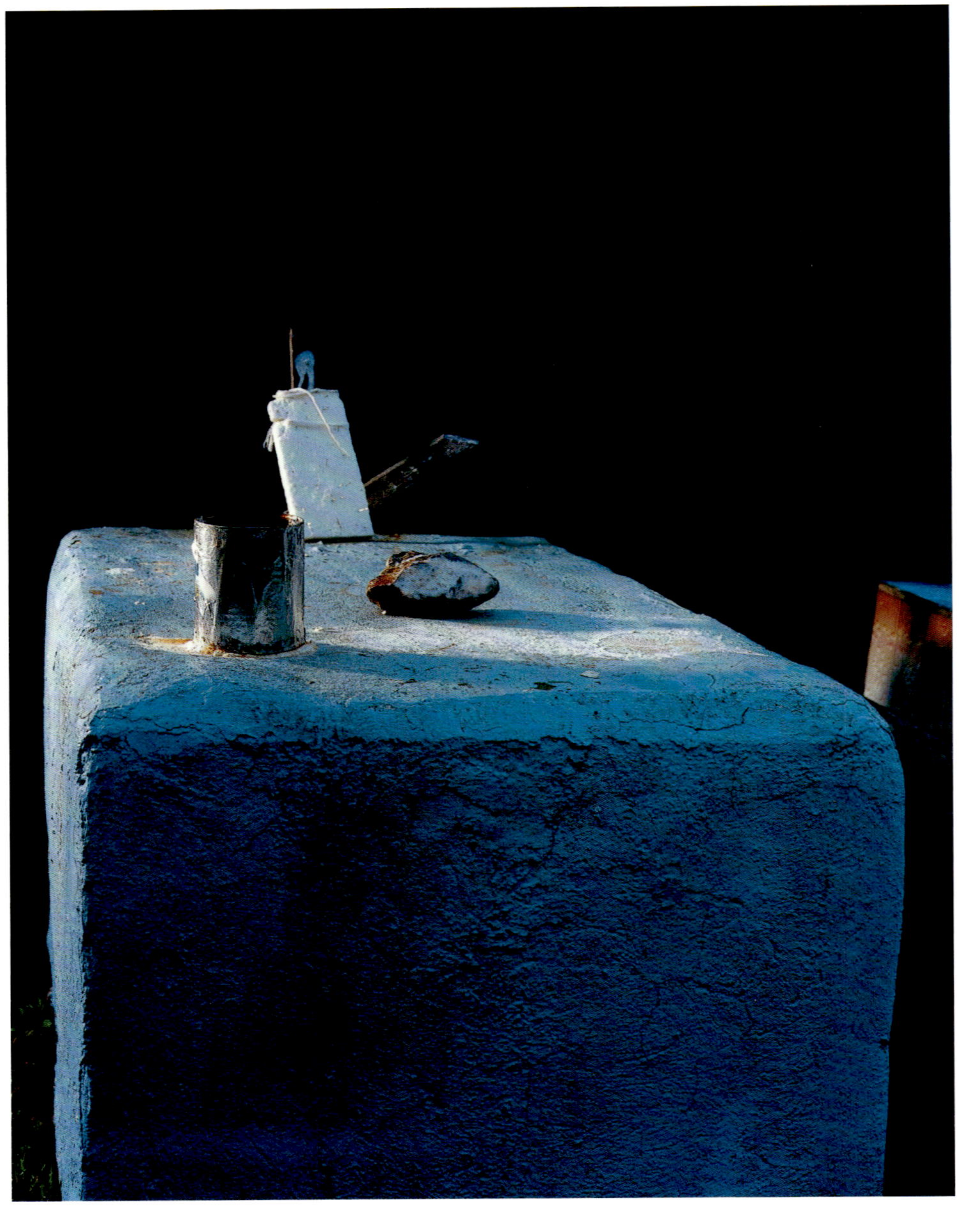

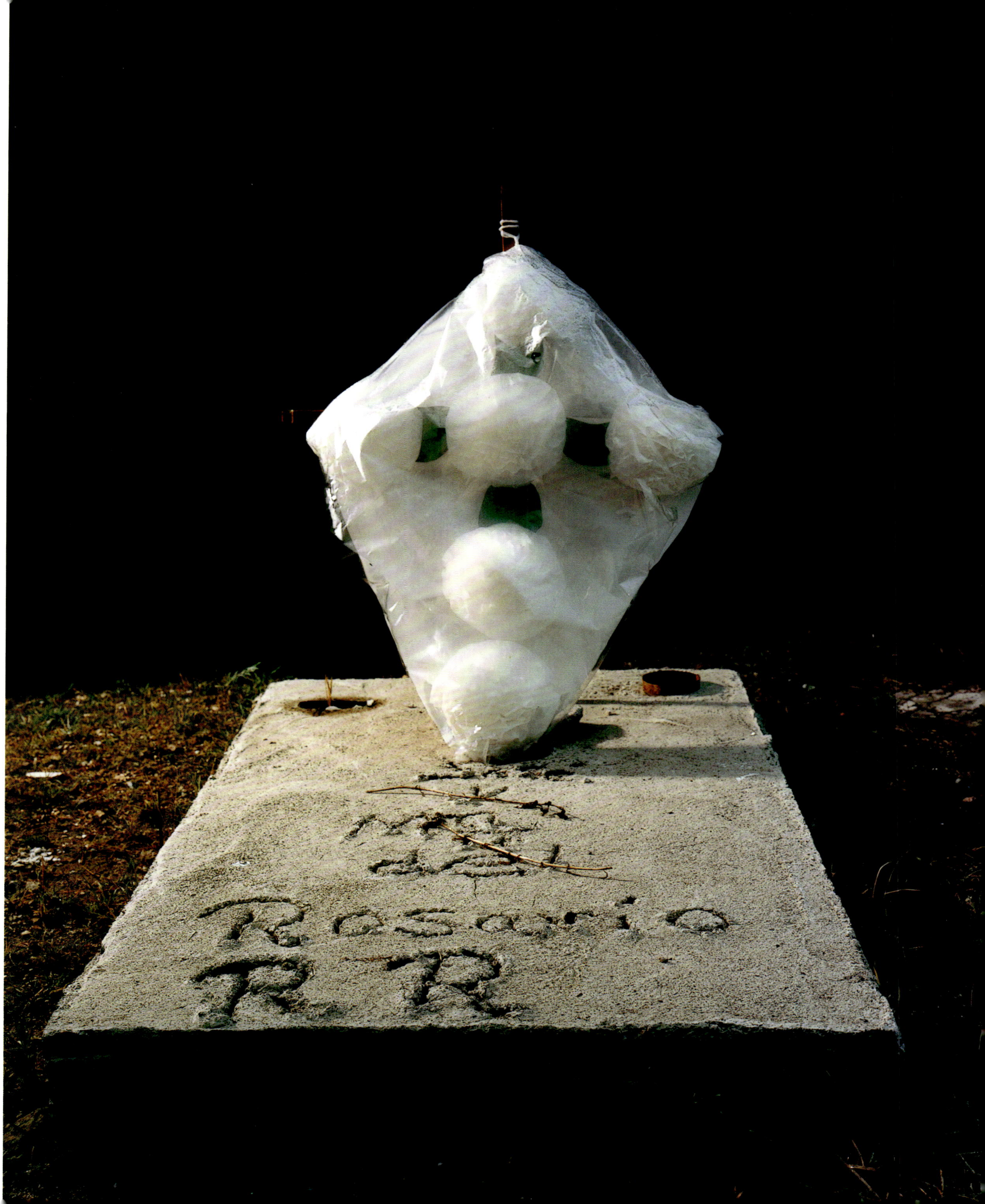
Rosario
R R

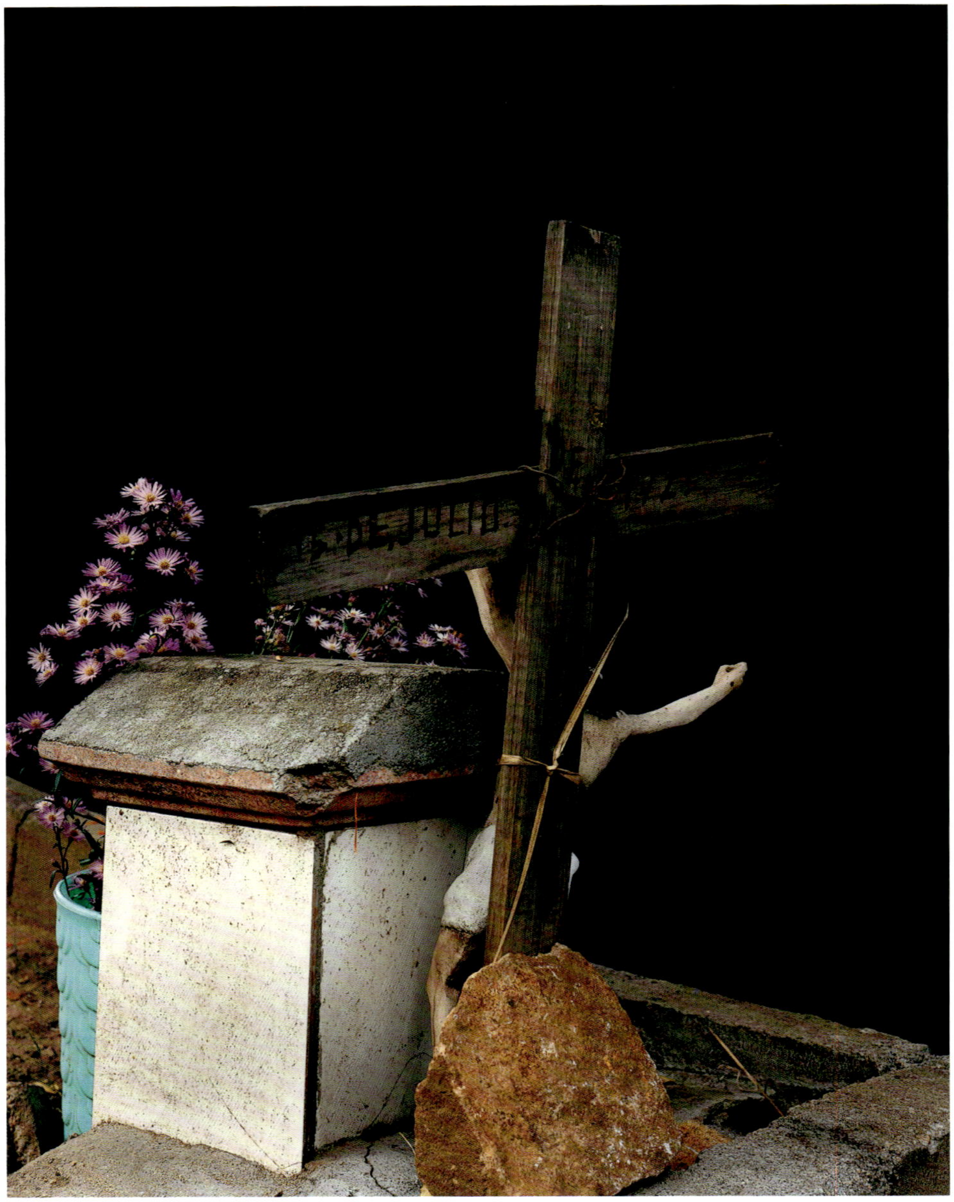

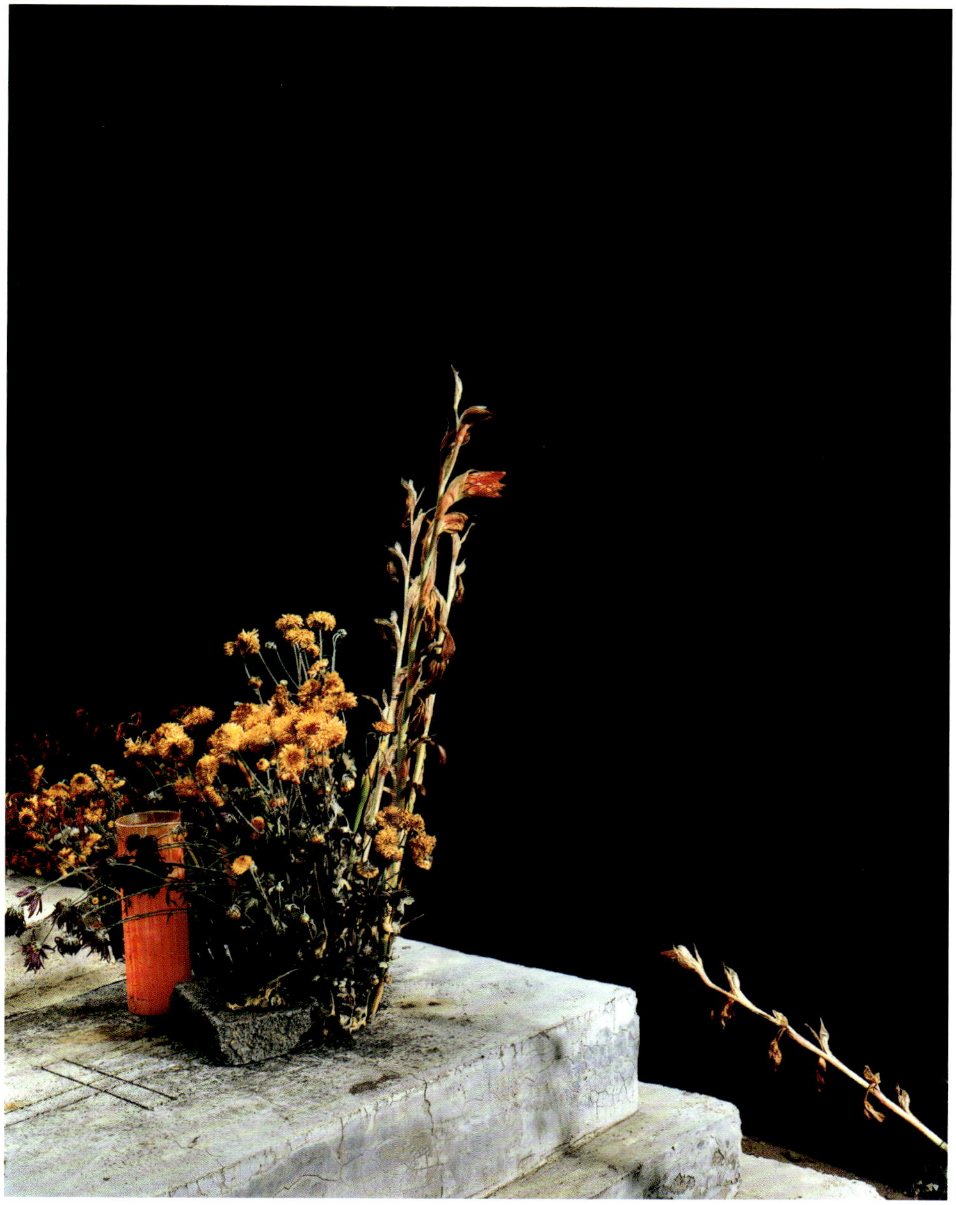

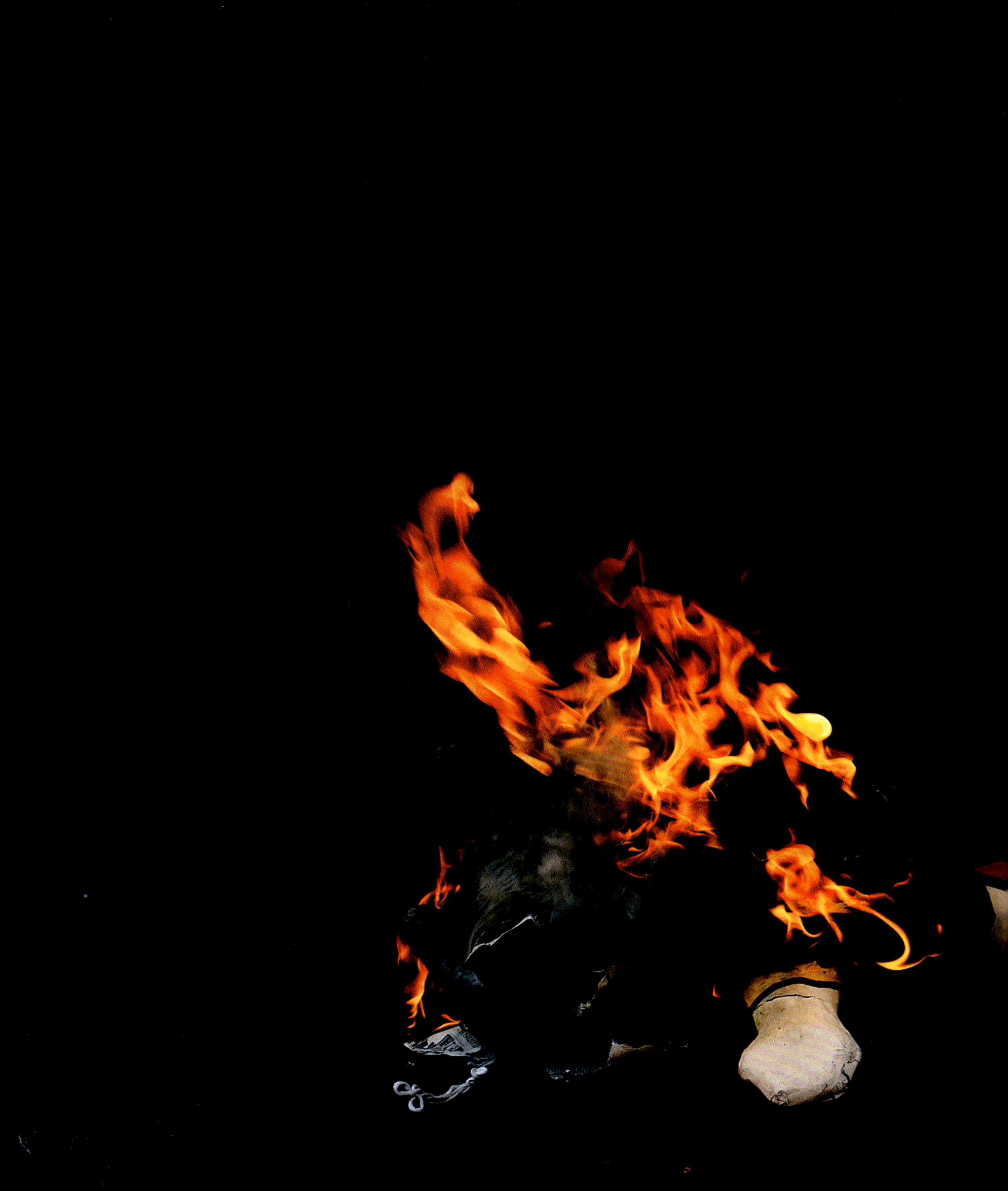

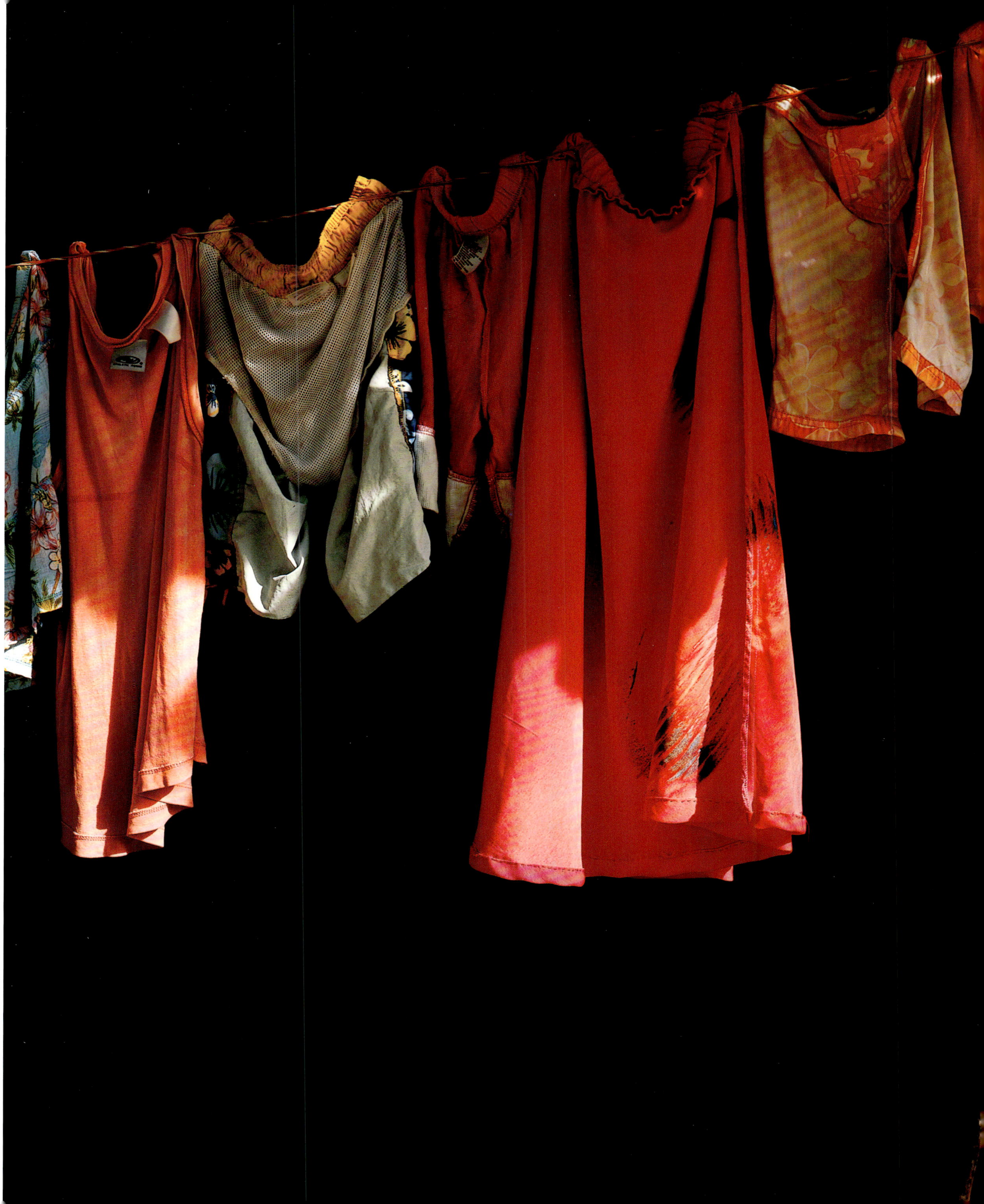

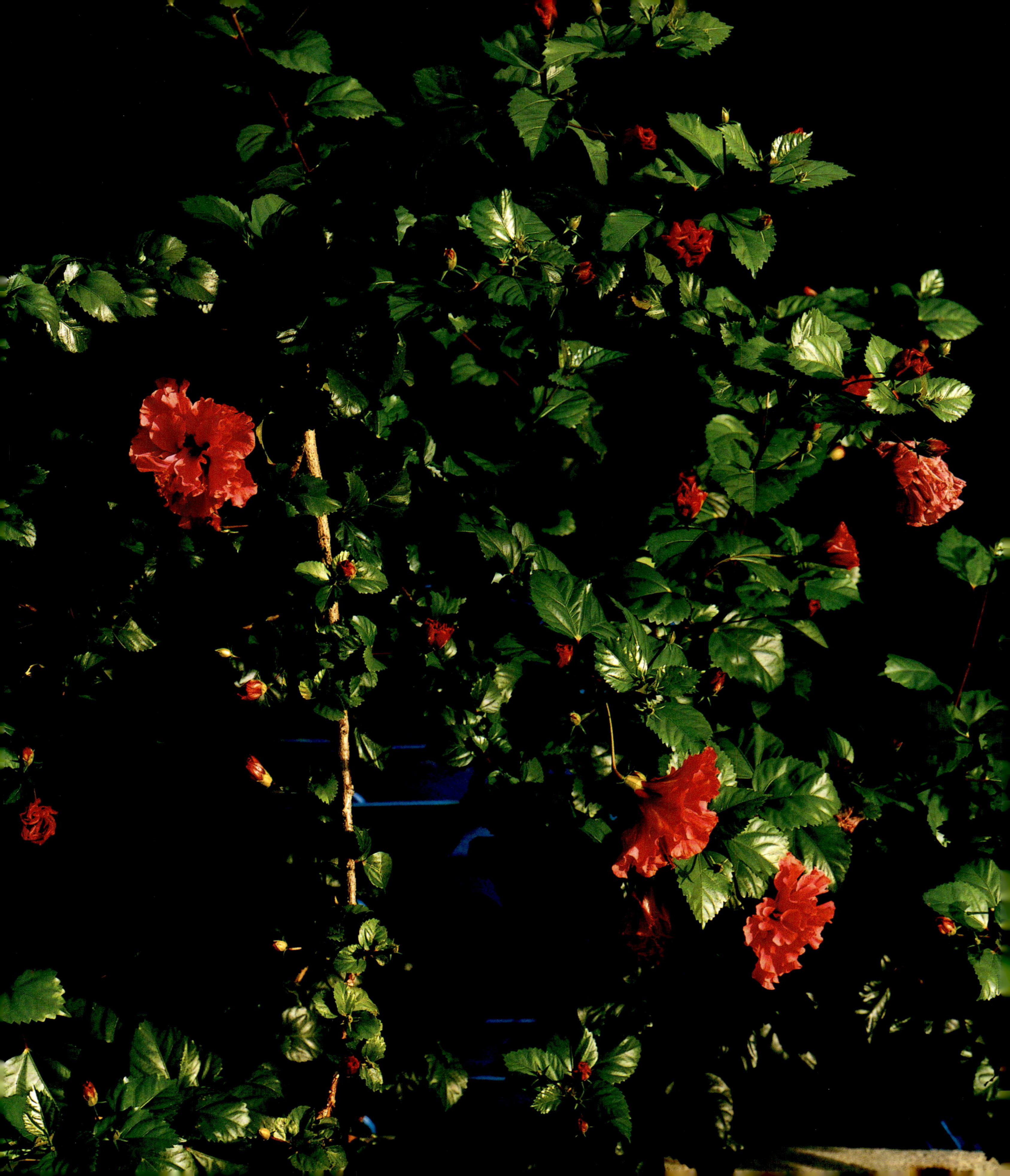

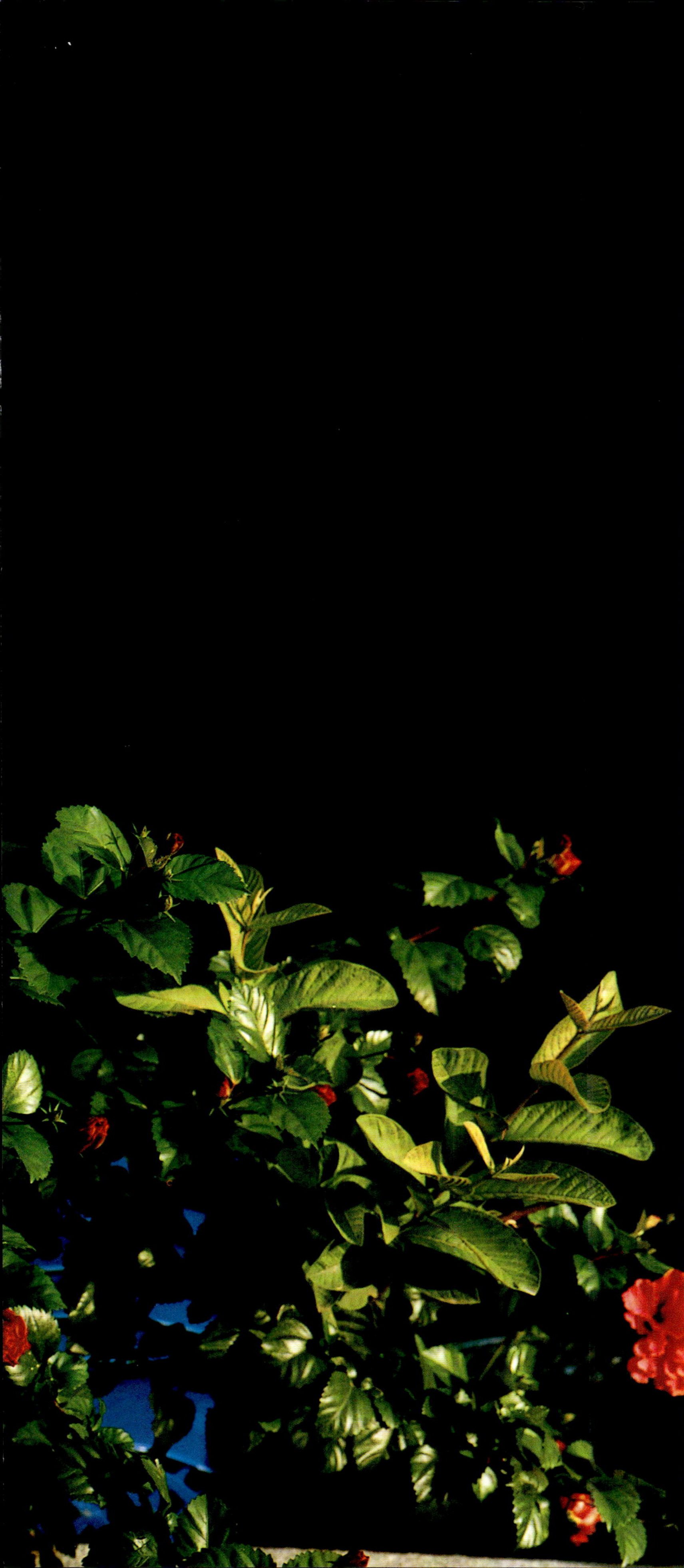

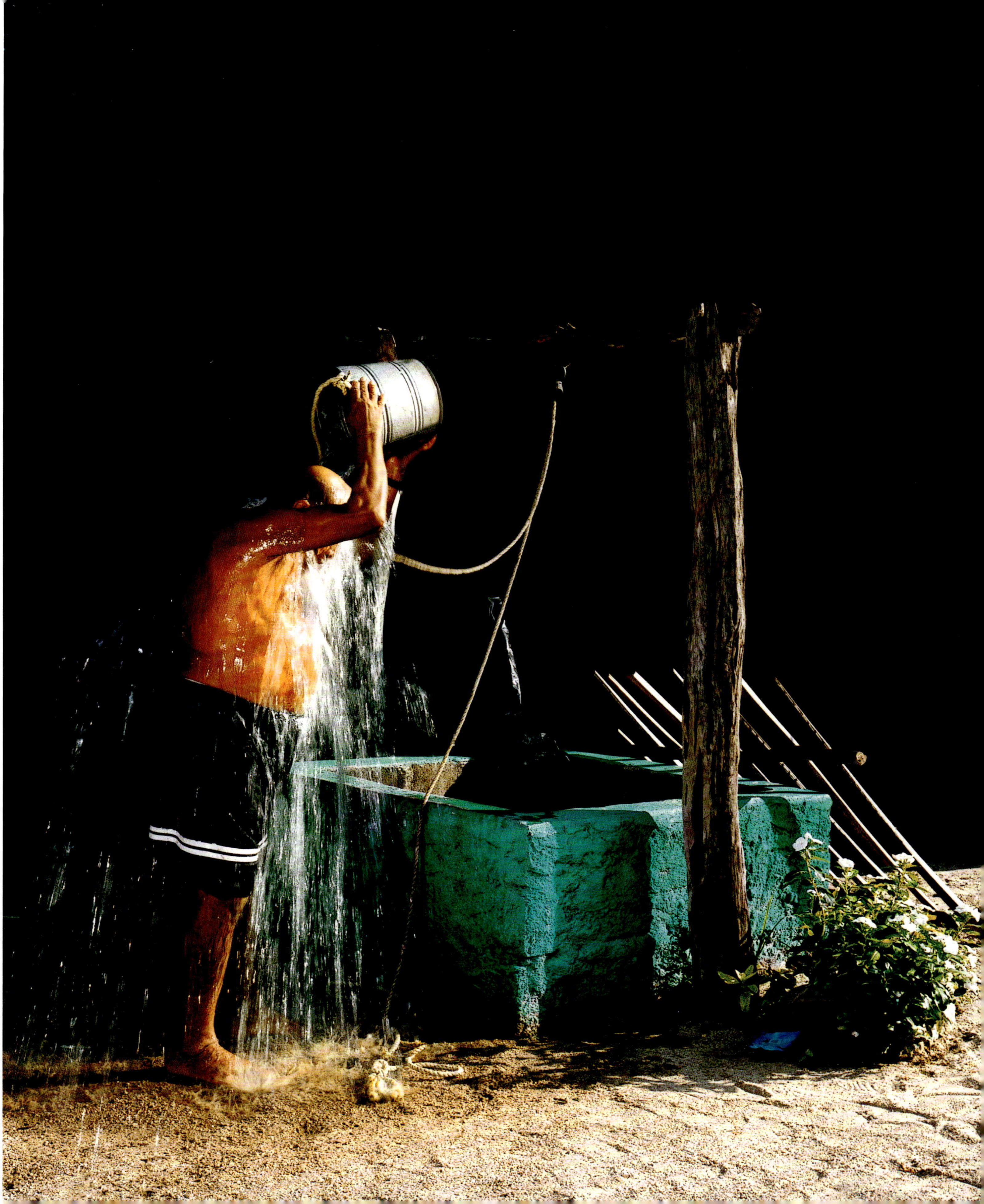

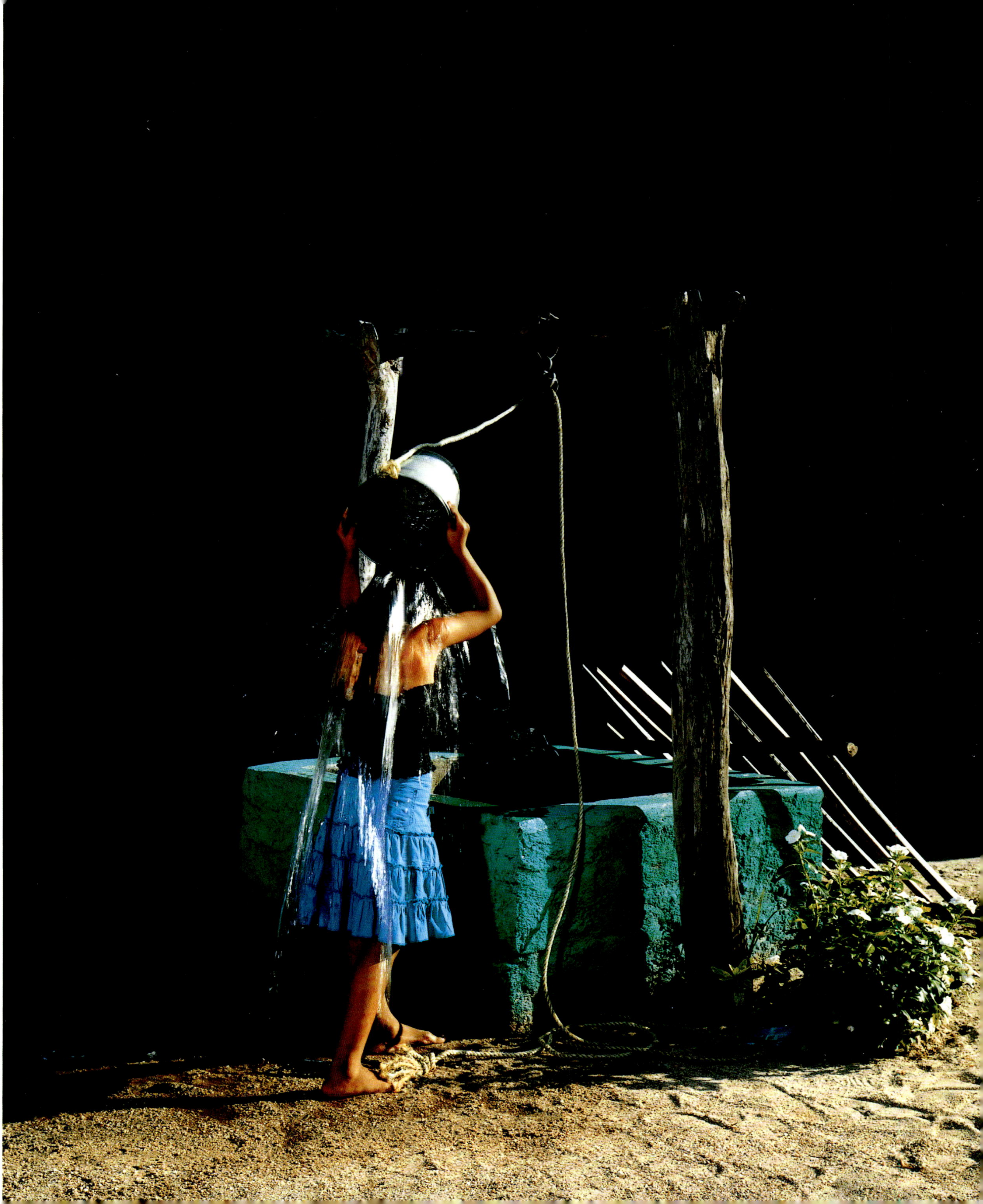

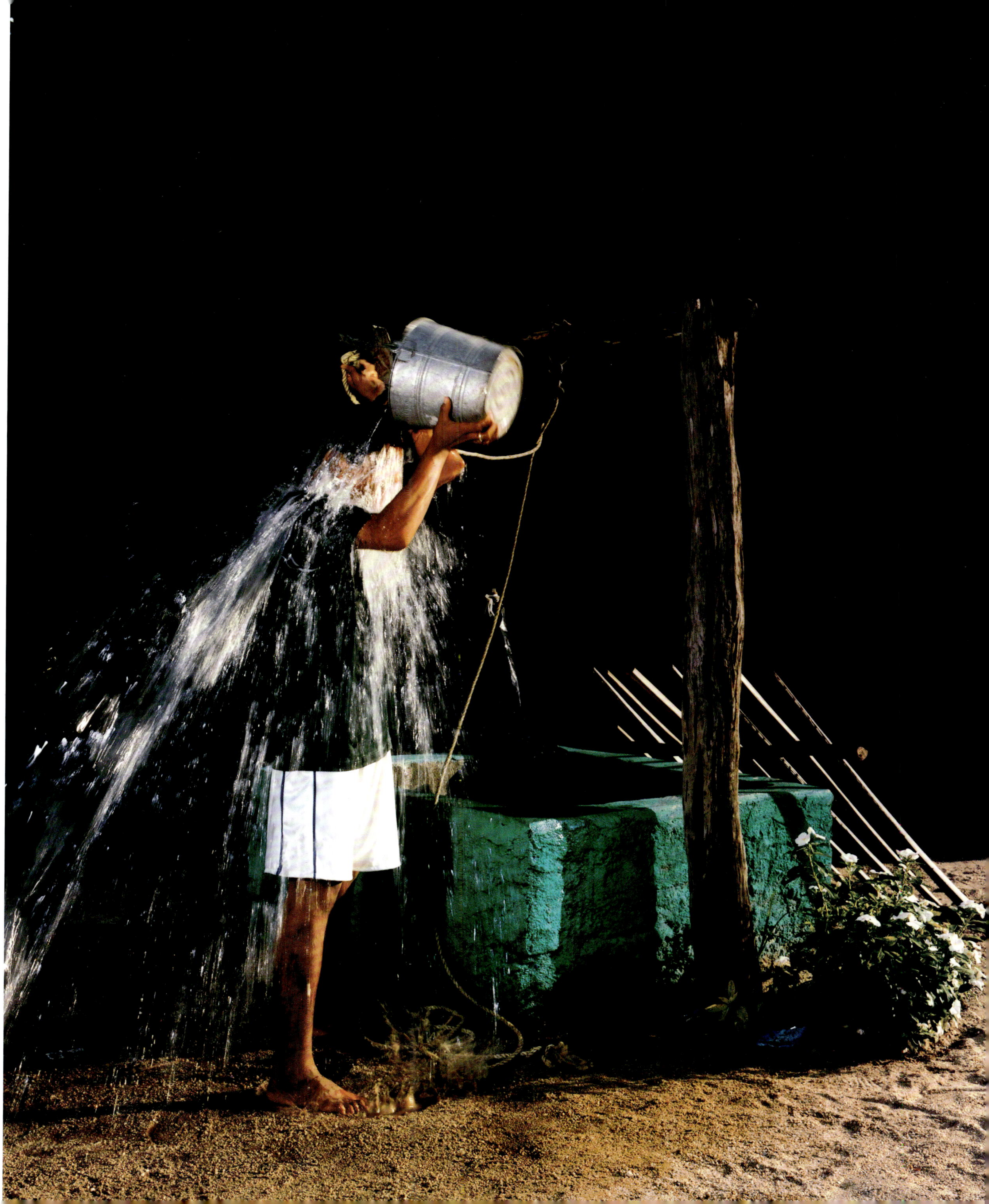

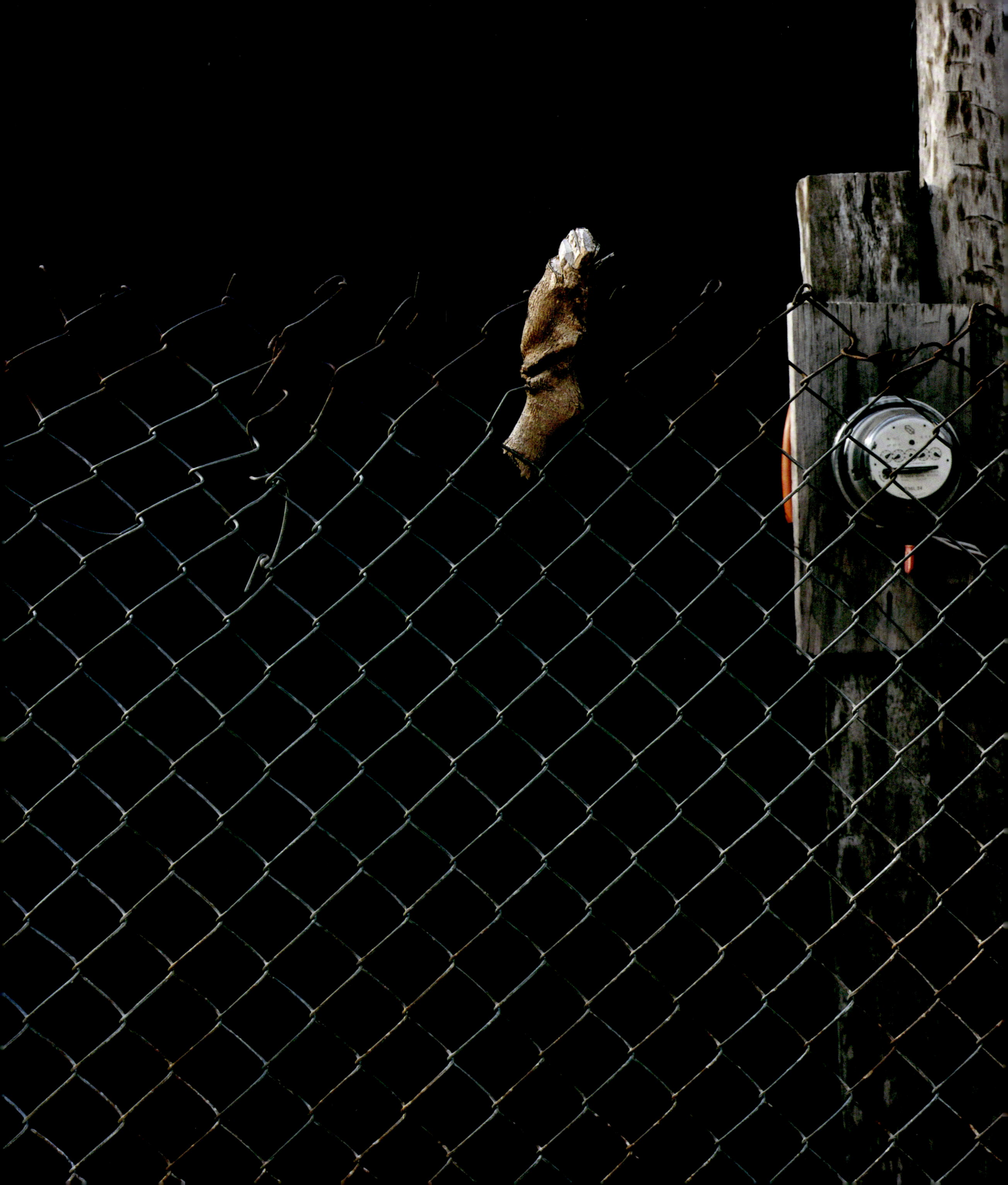

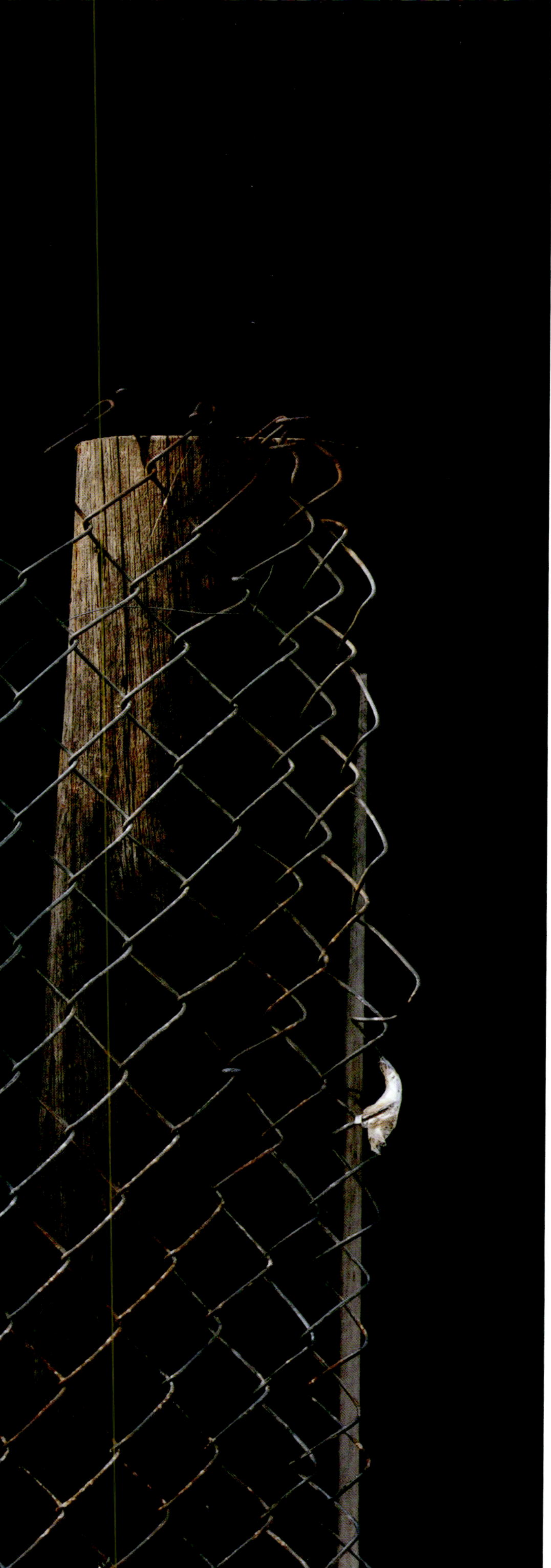

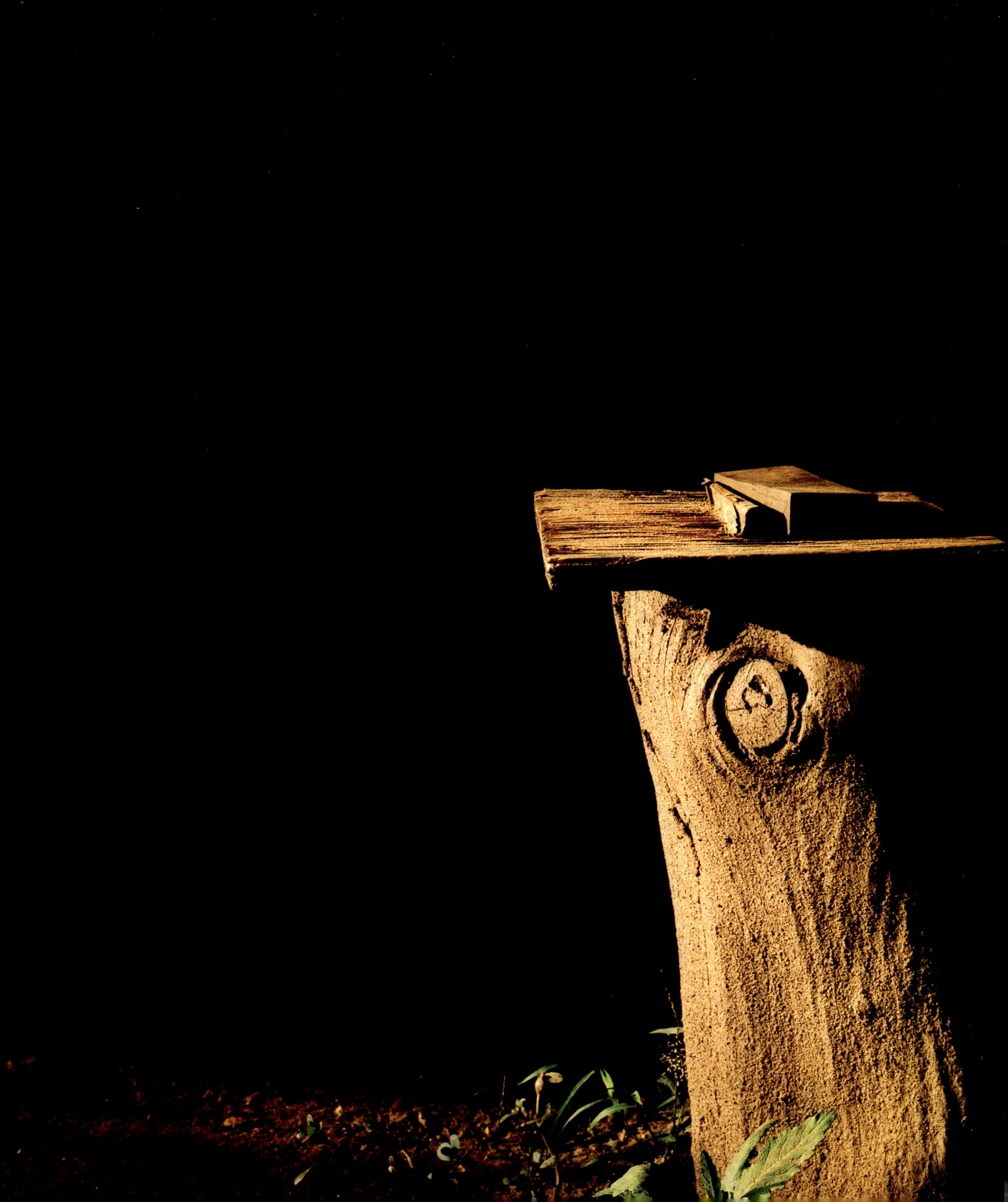

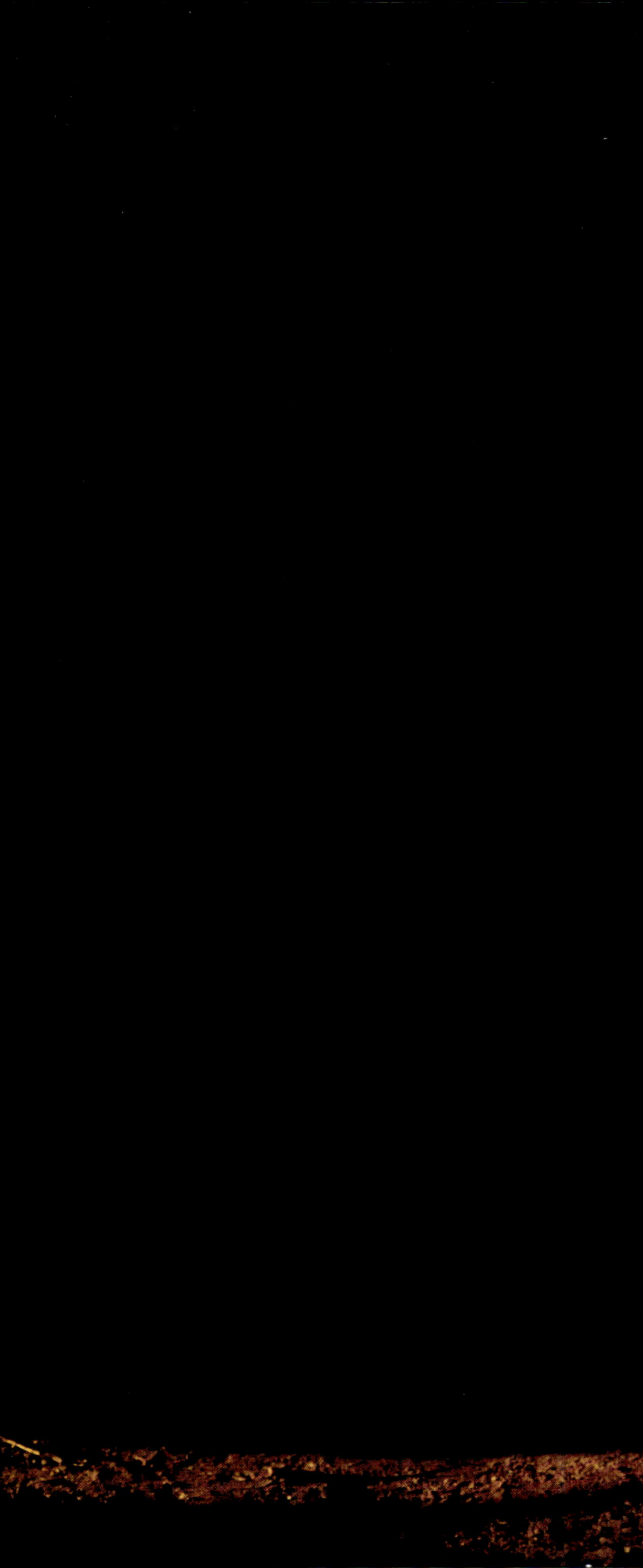

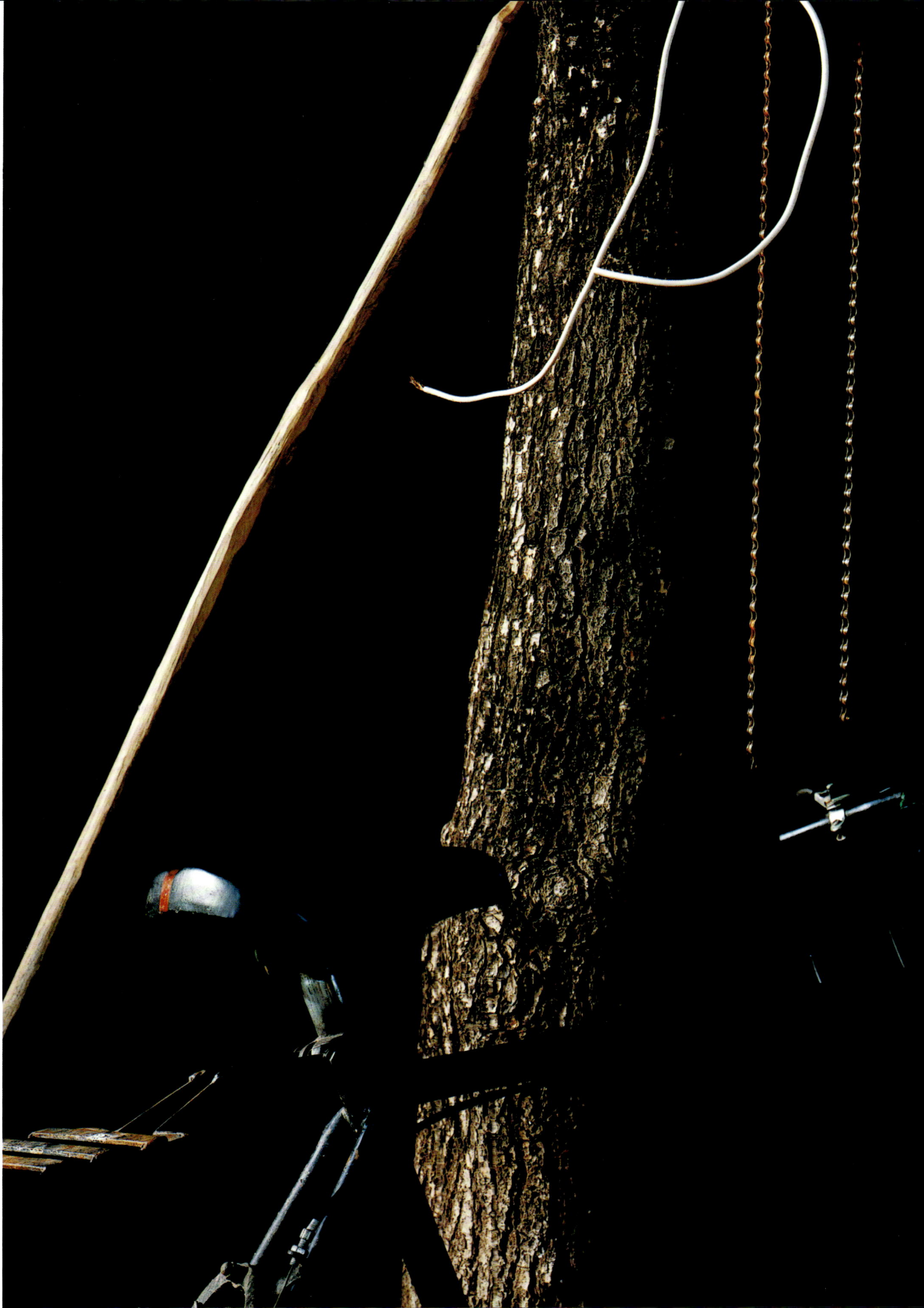

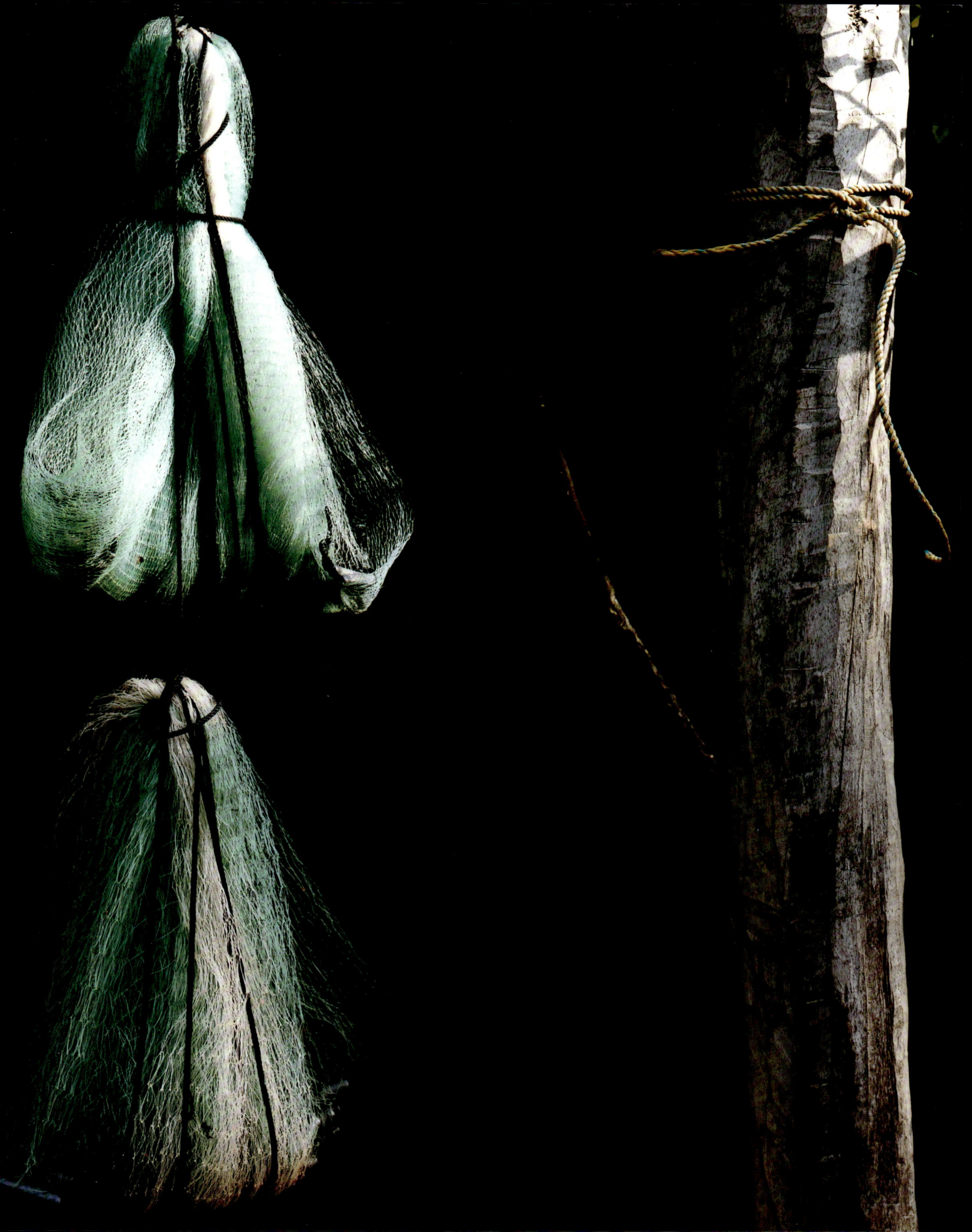

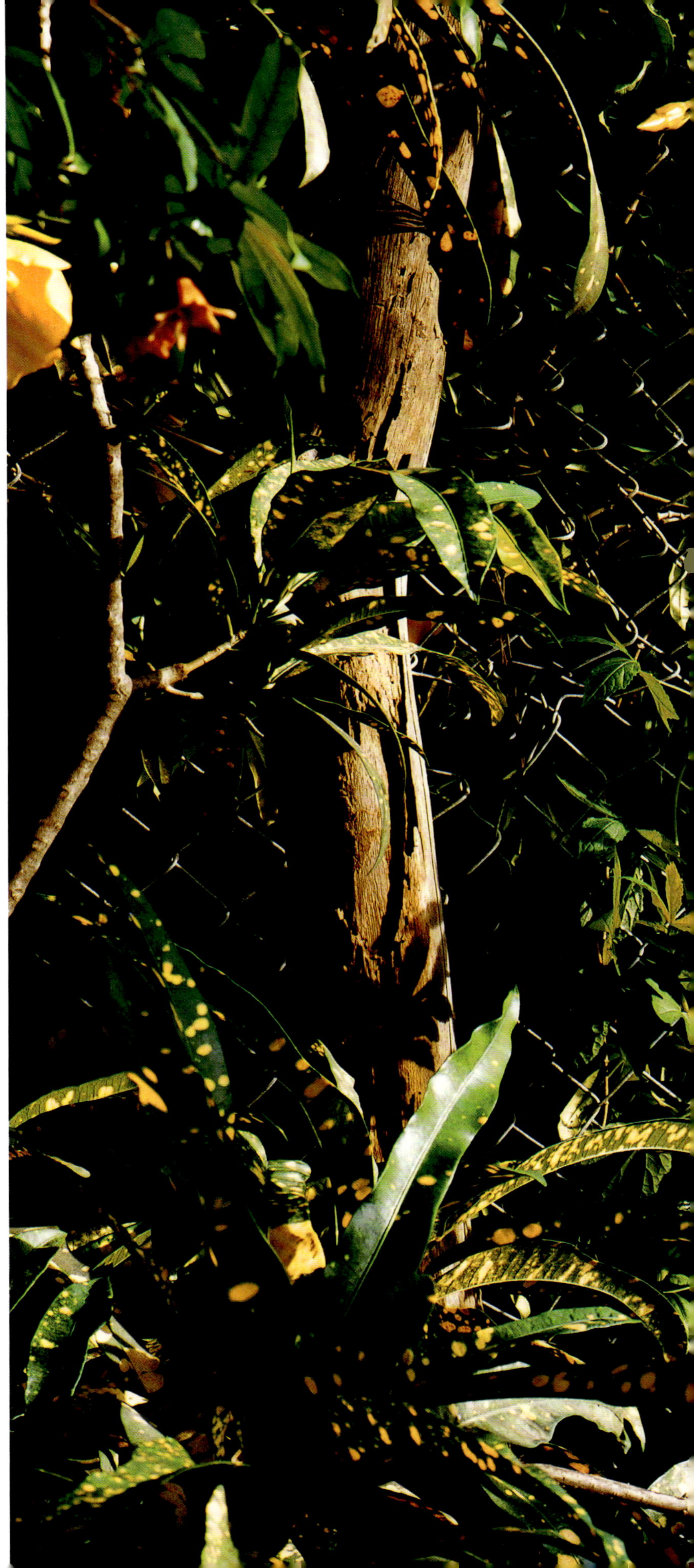

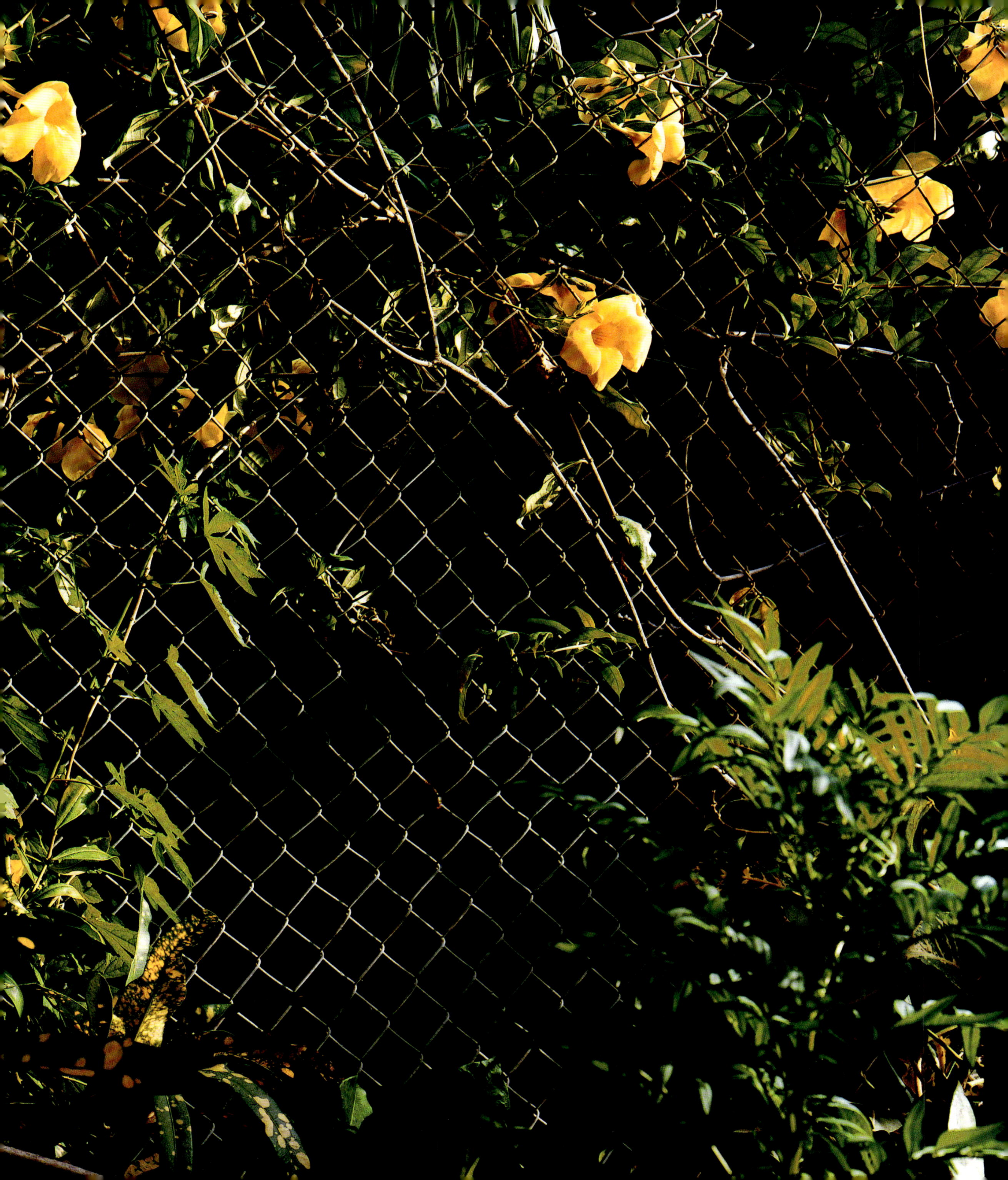

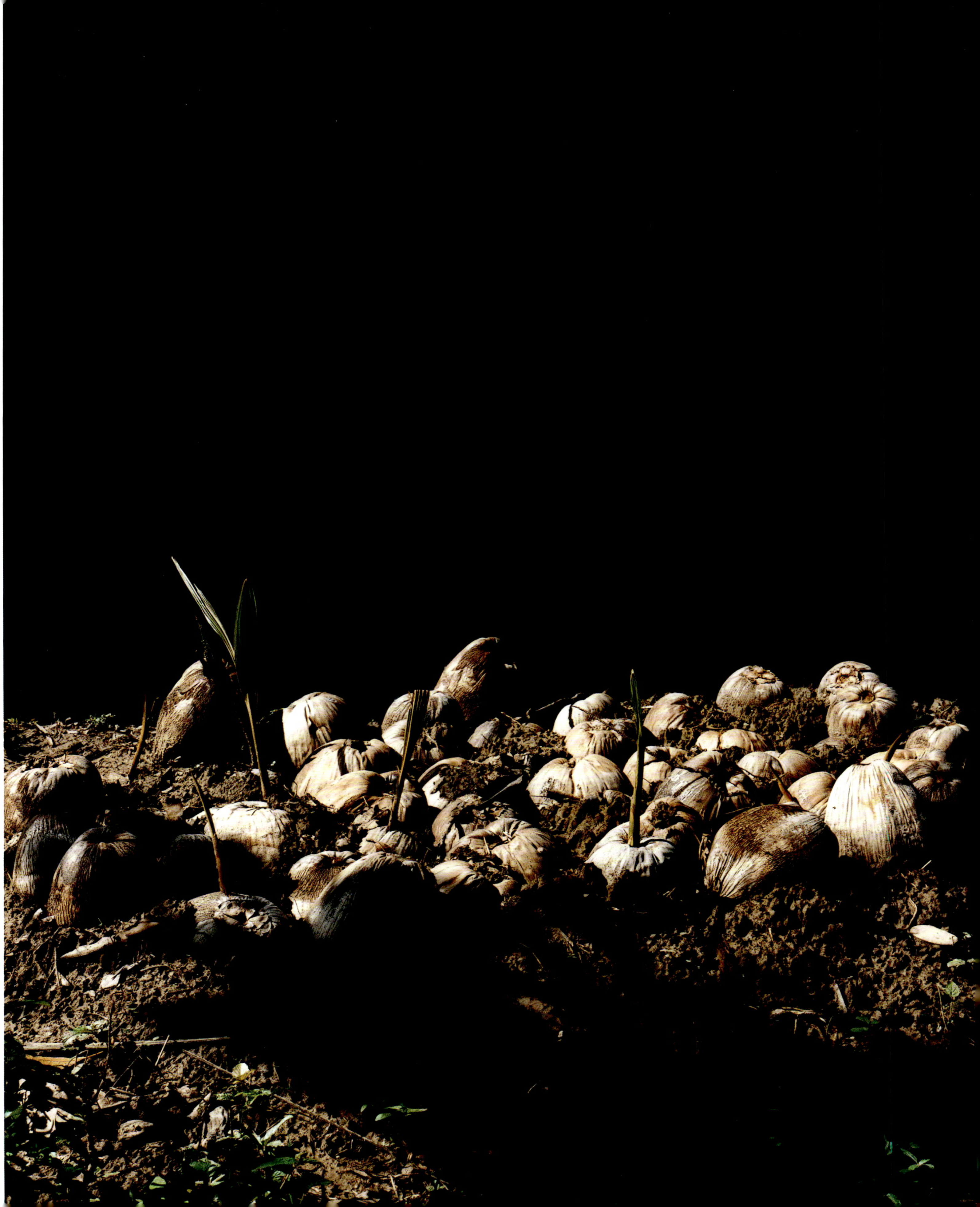

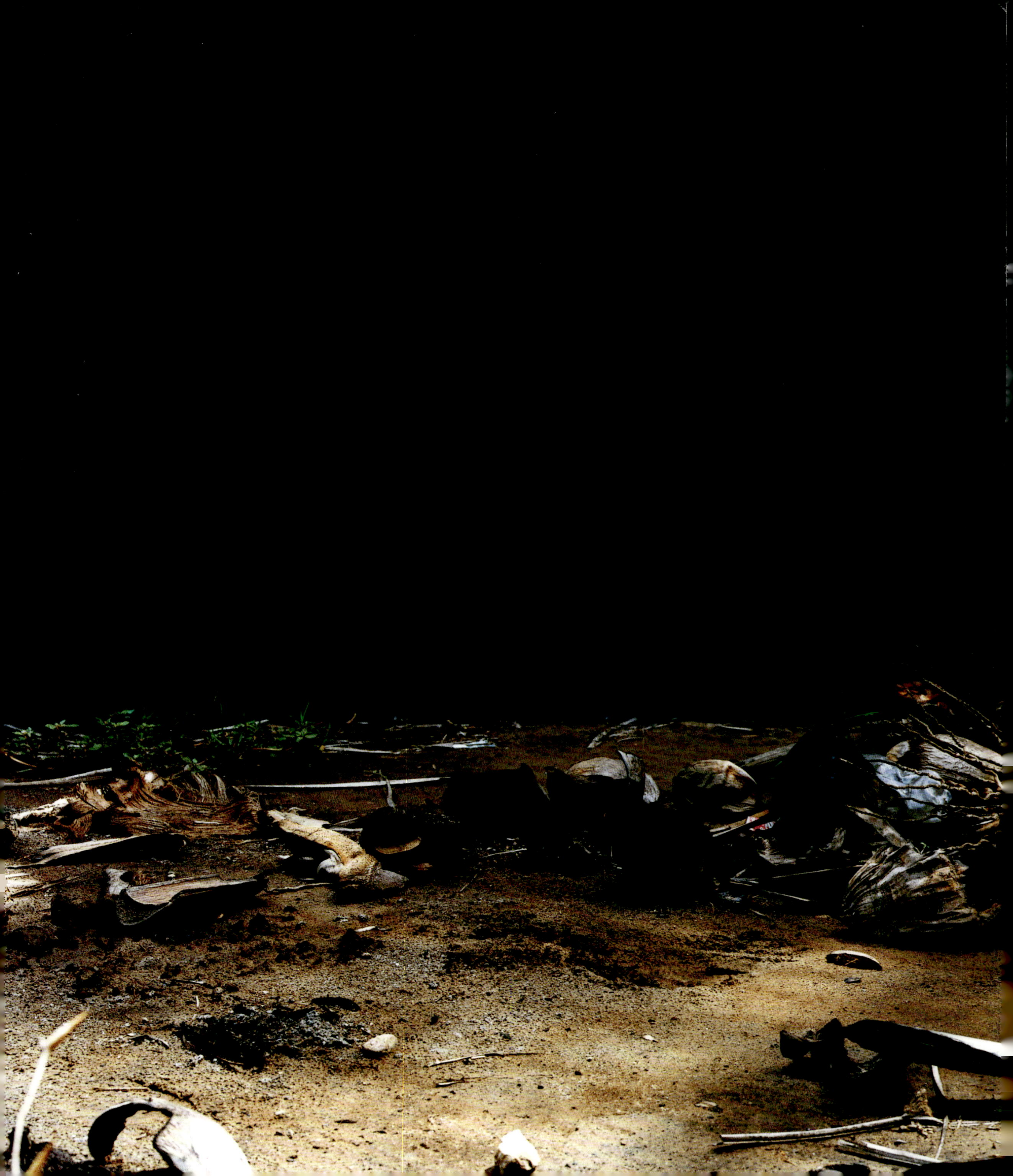

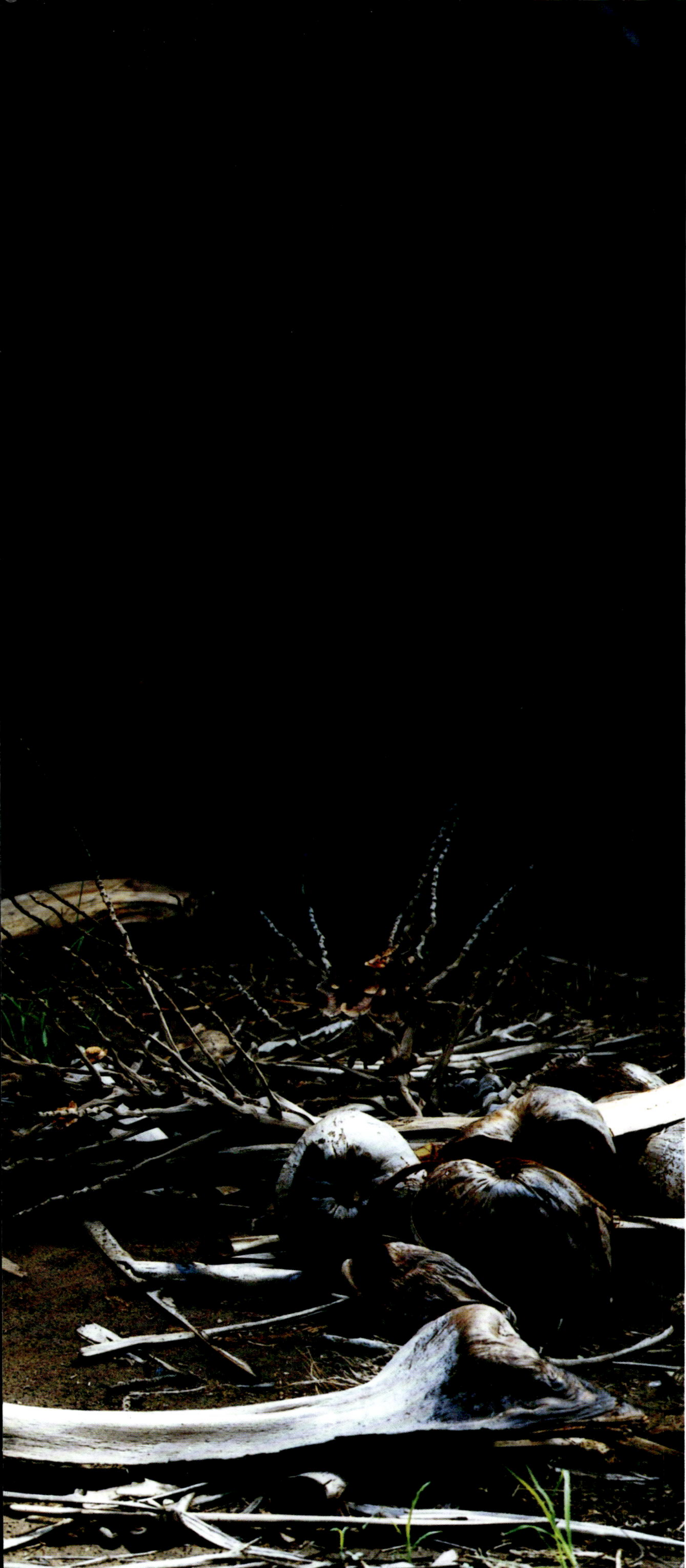

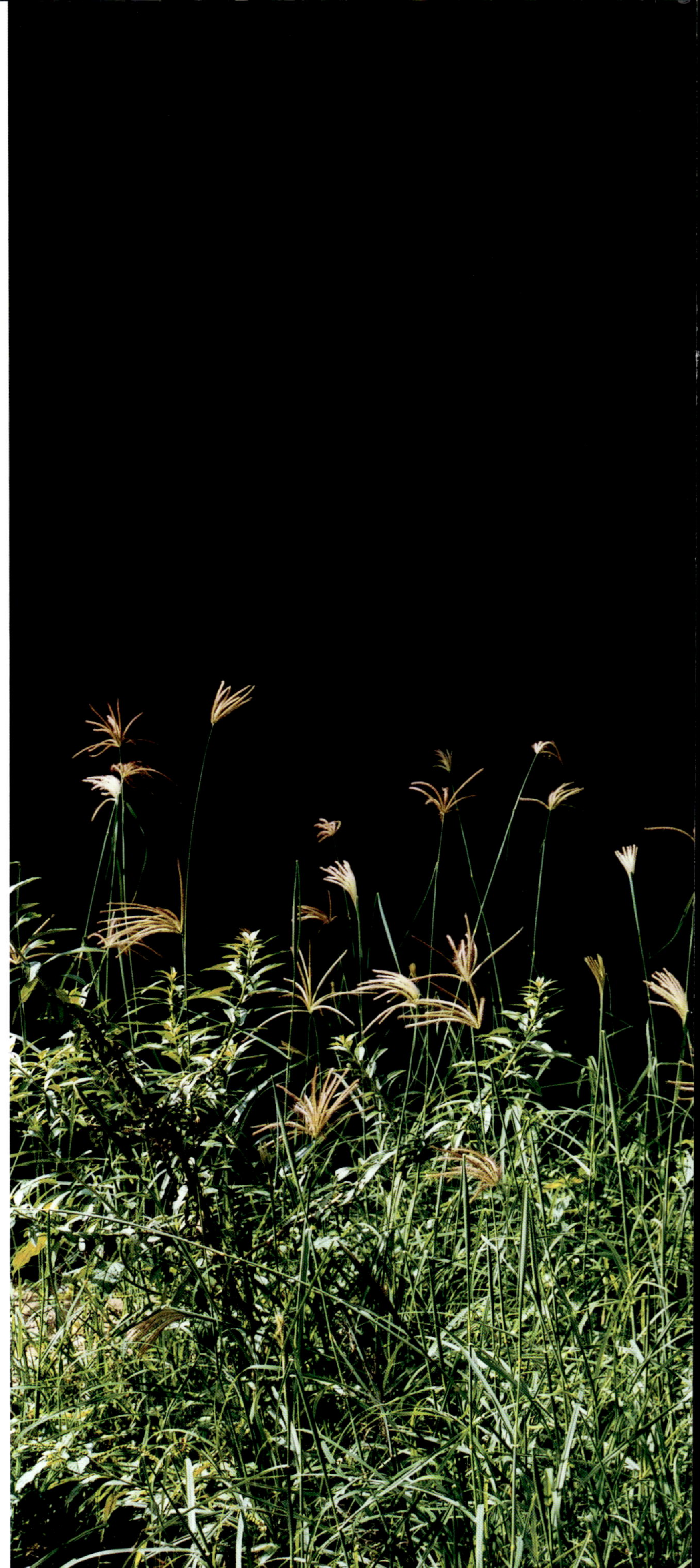

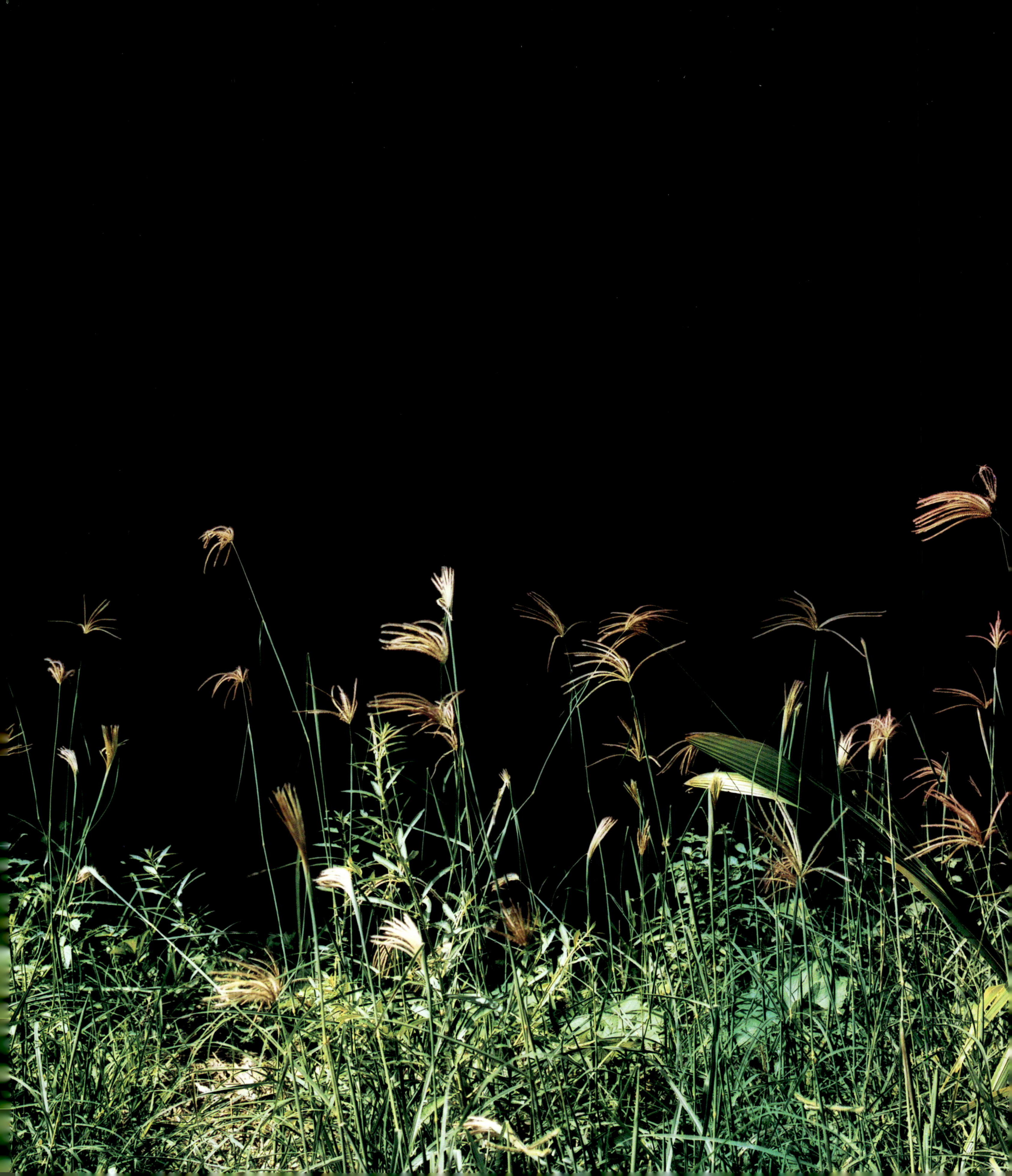

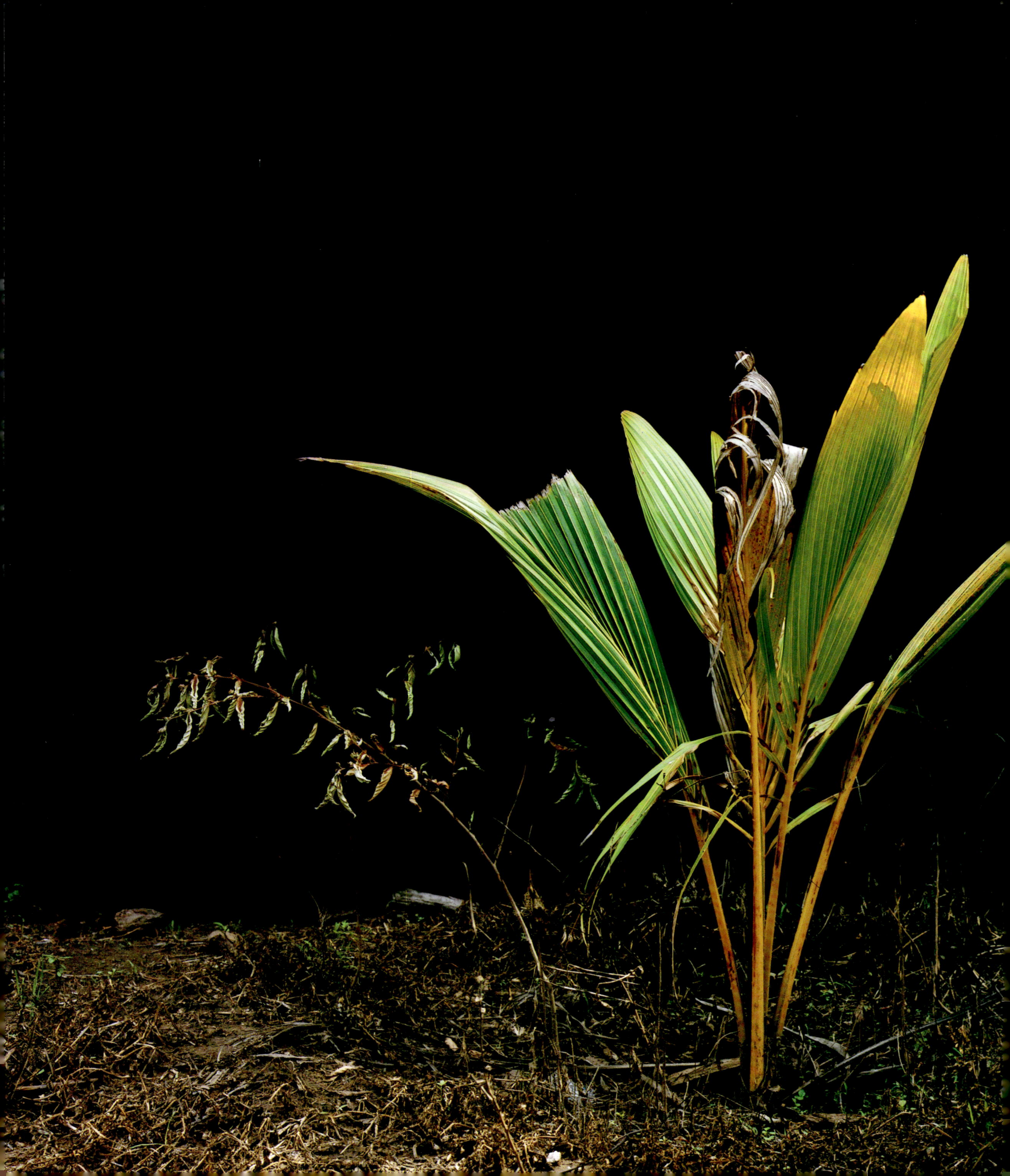

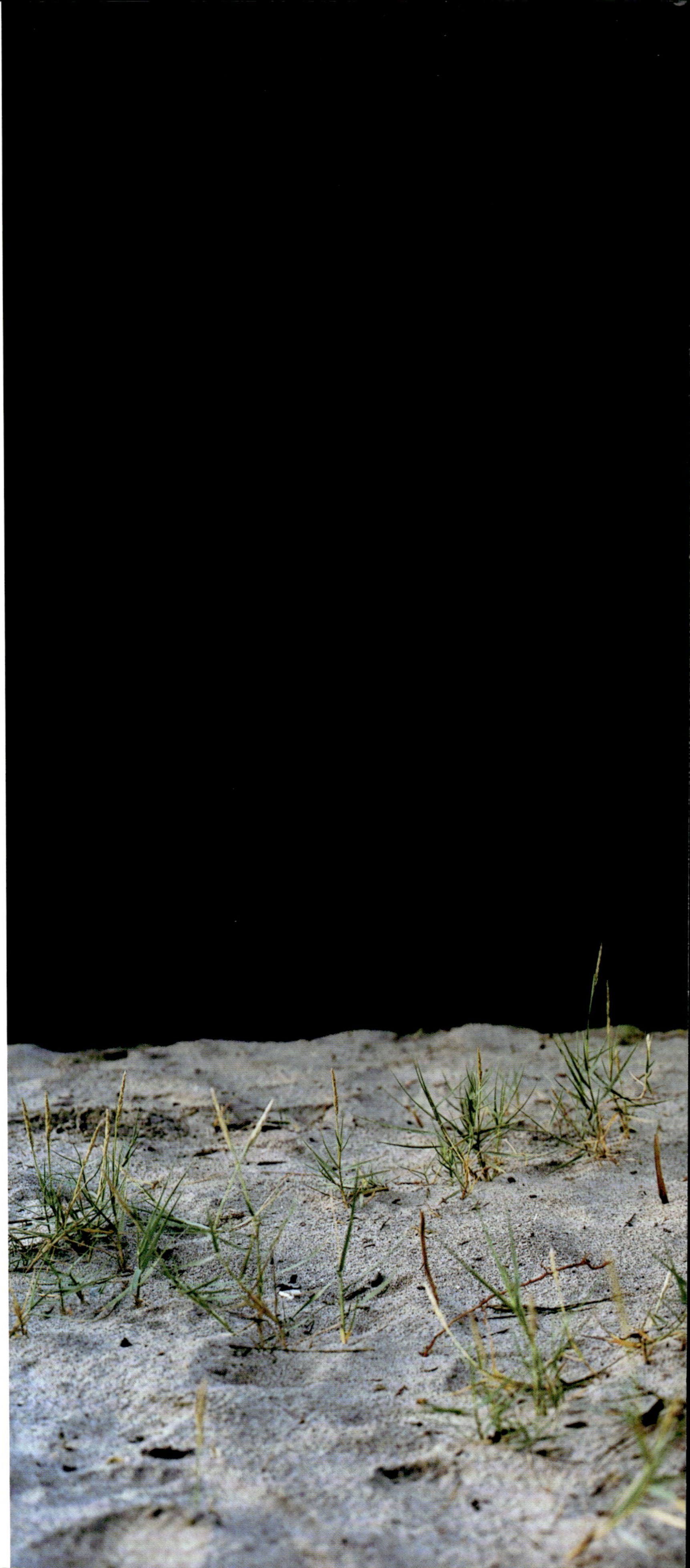

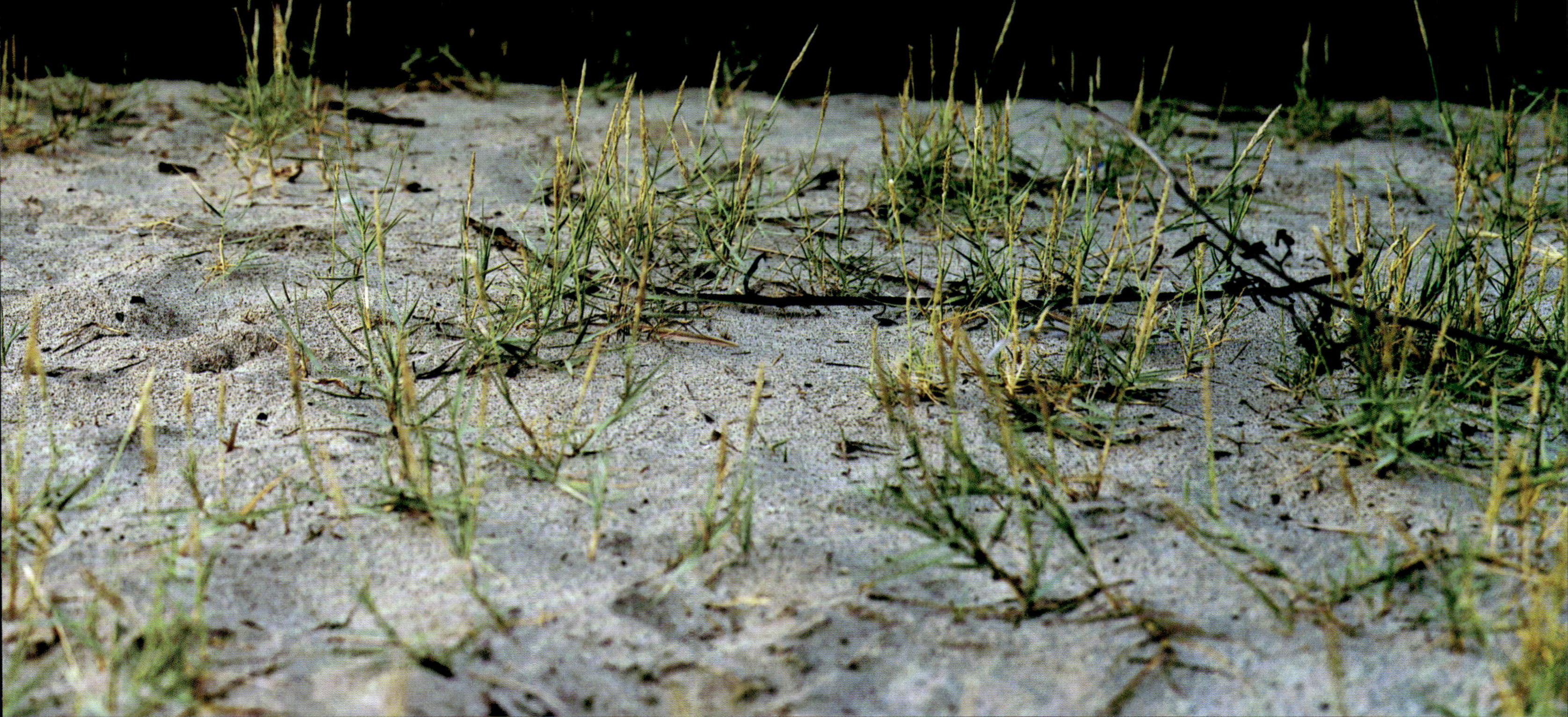

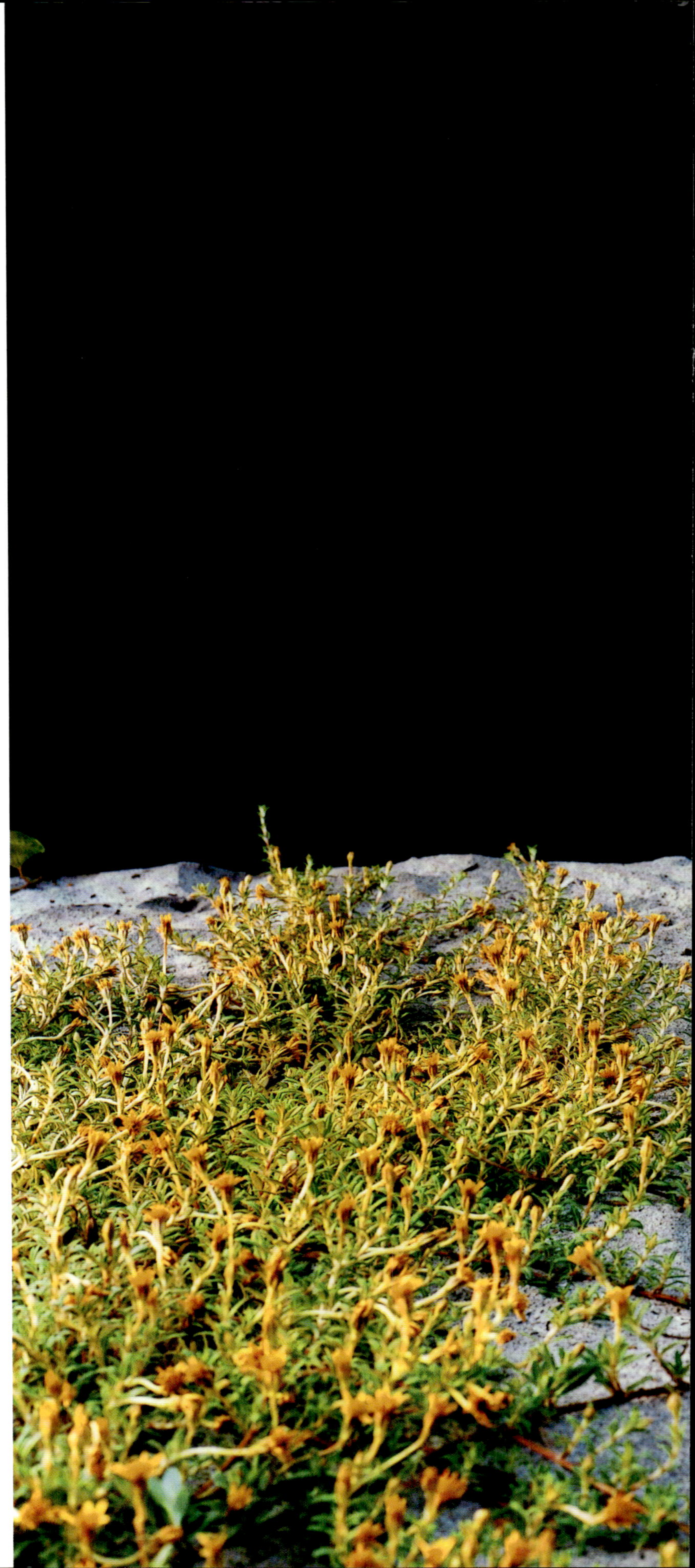

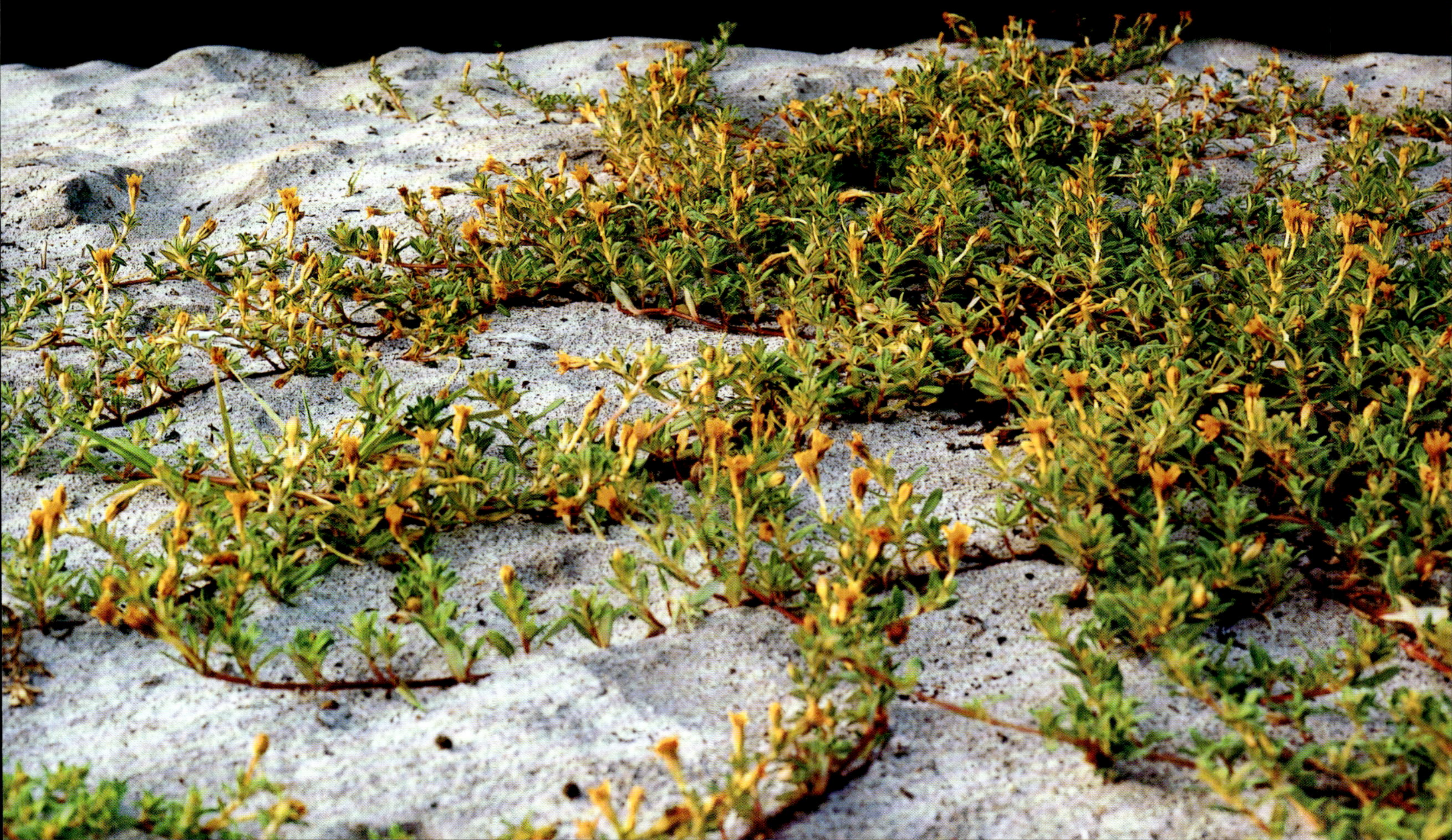

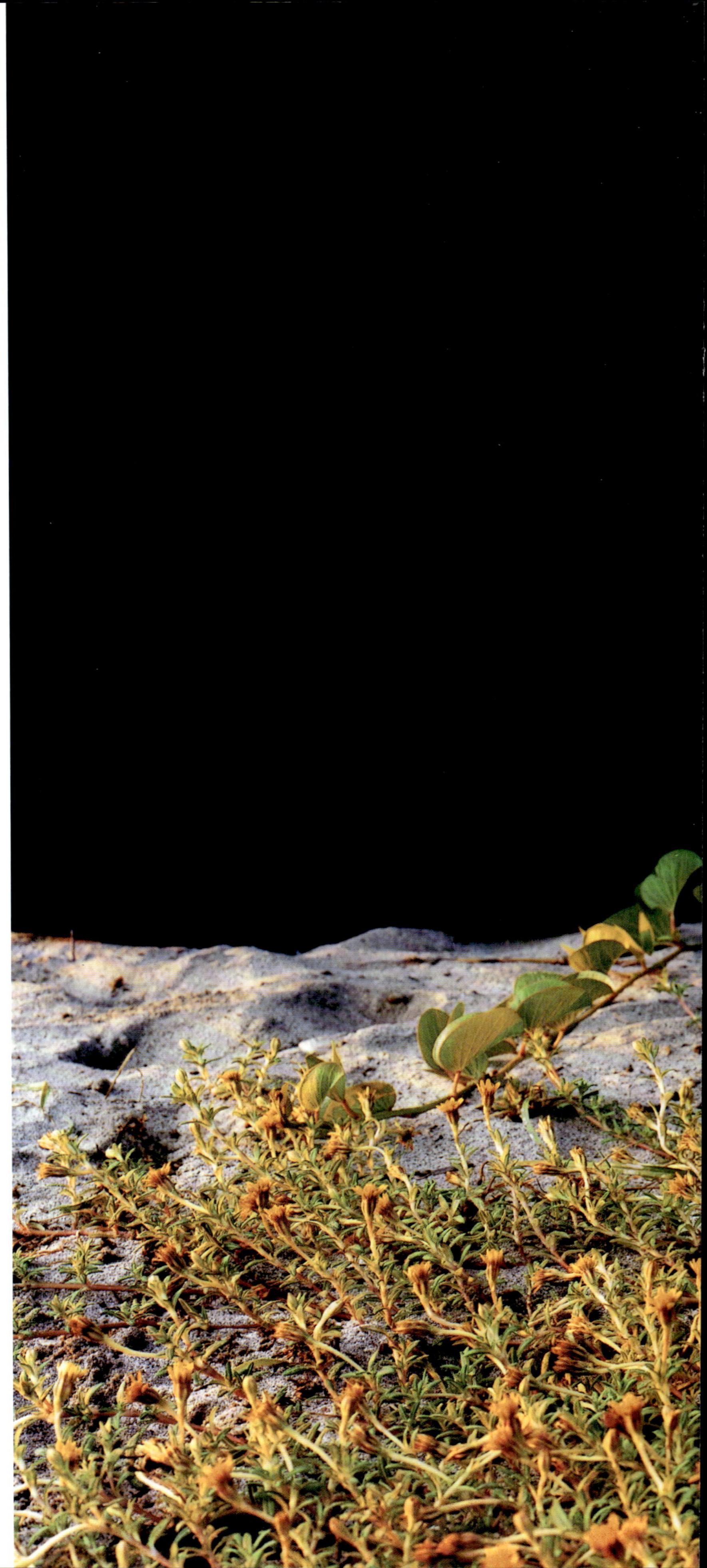

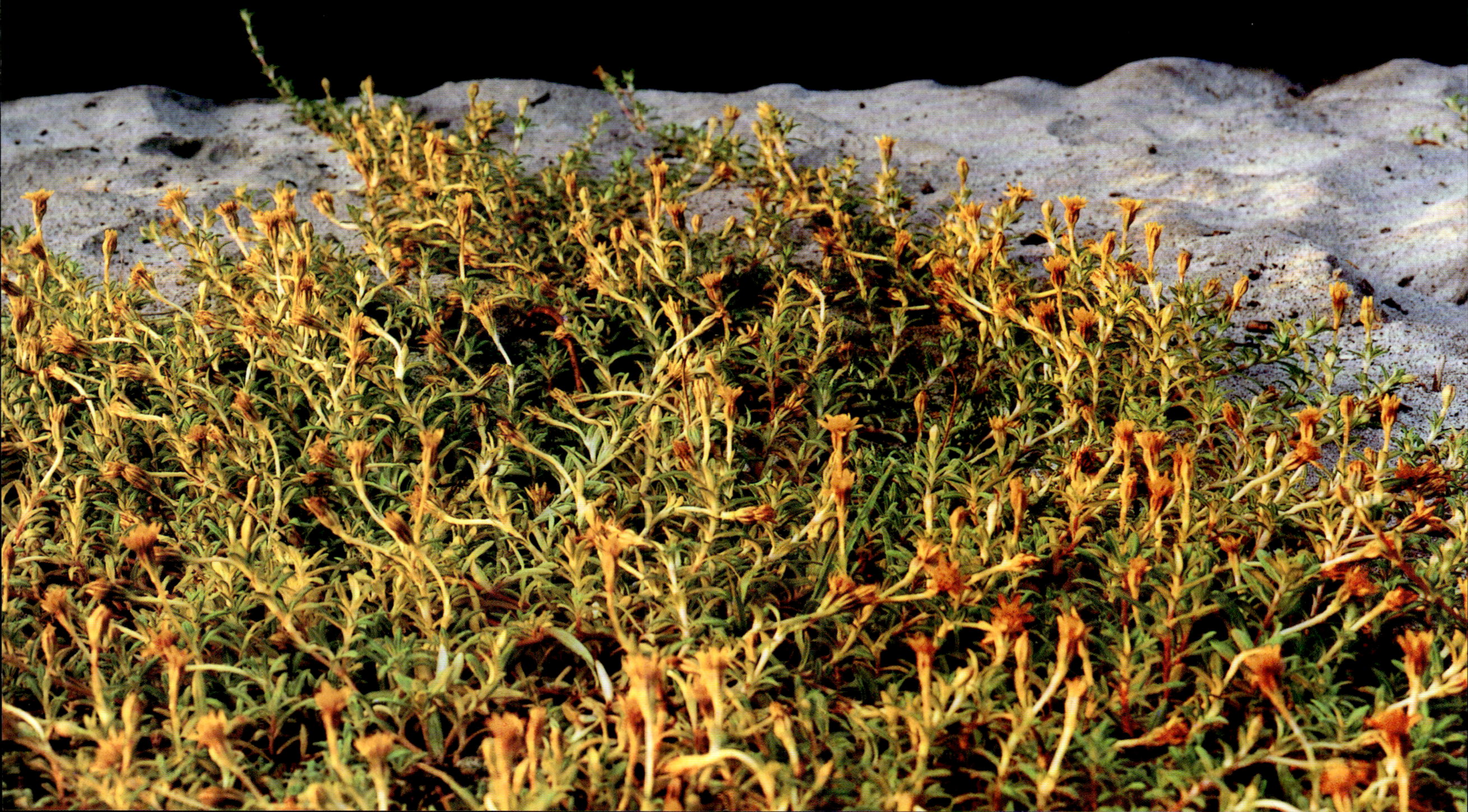

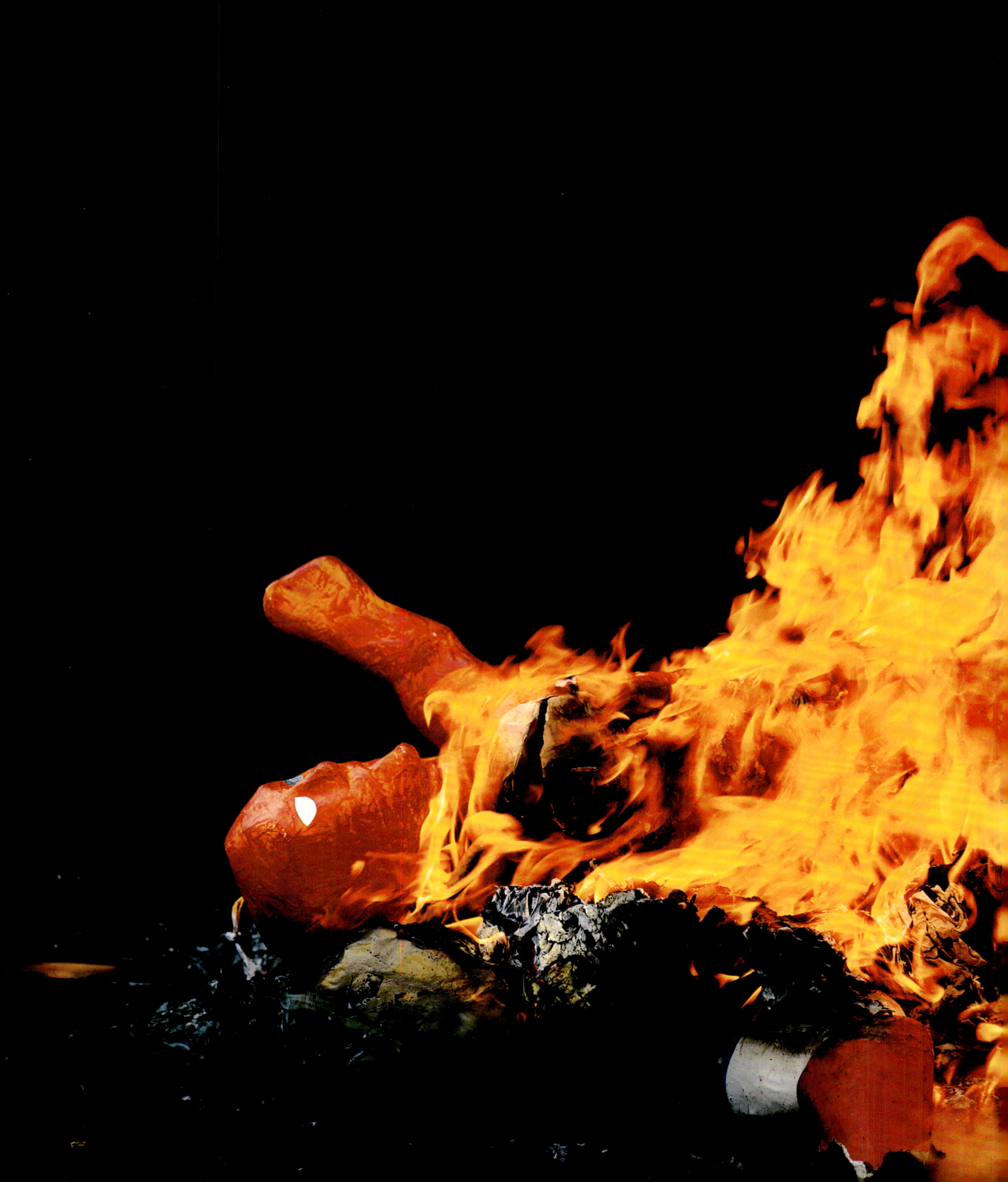

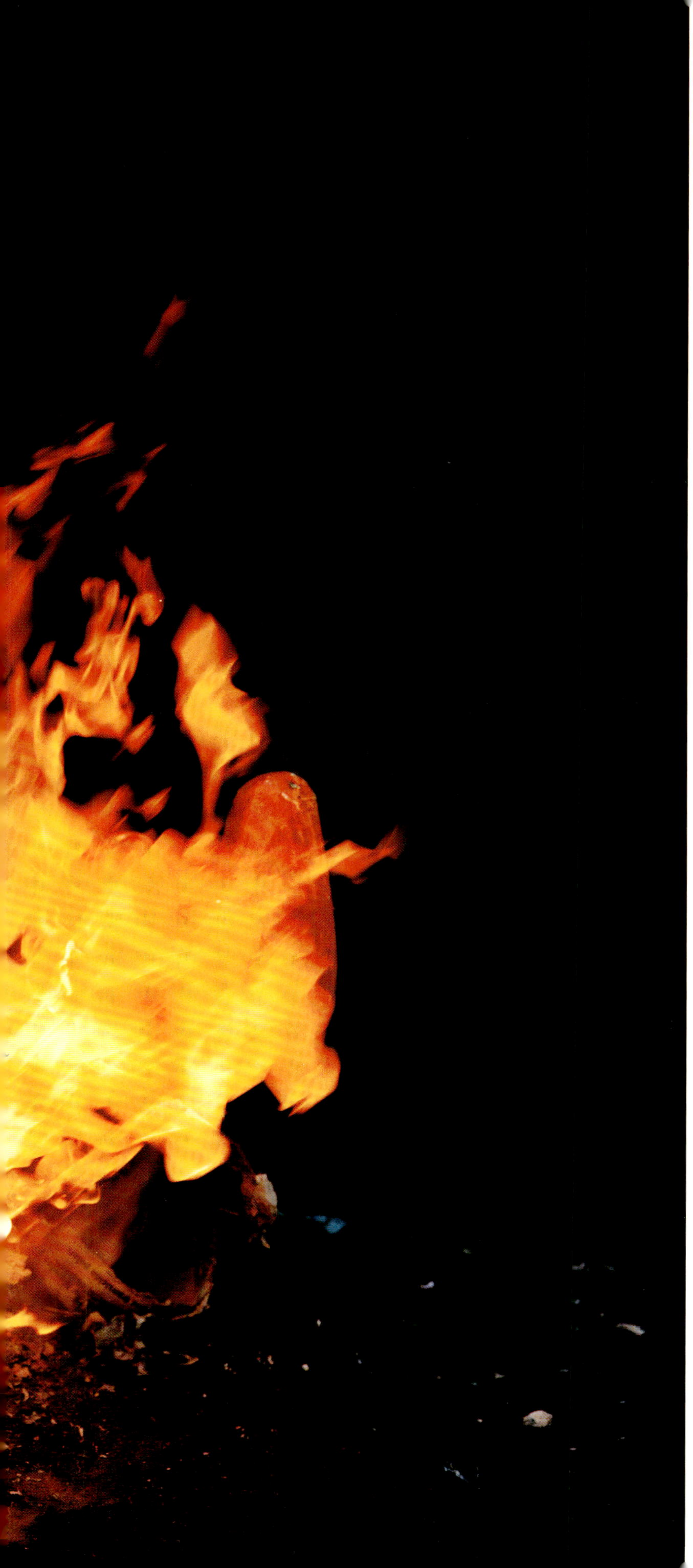

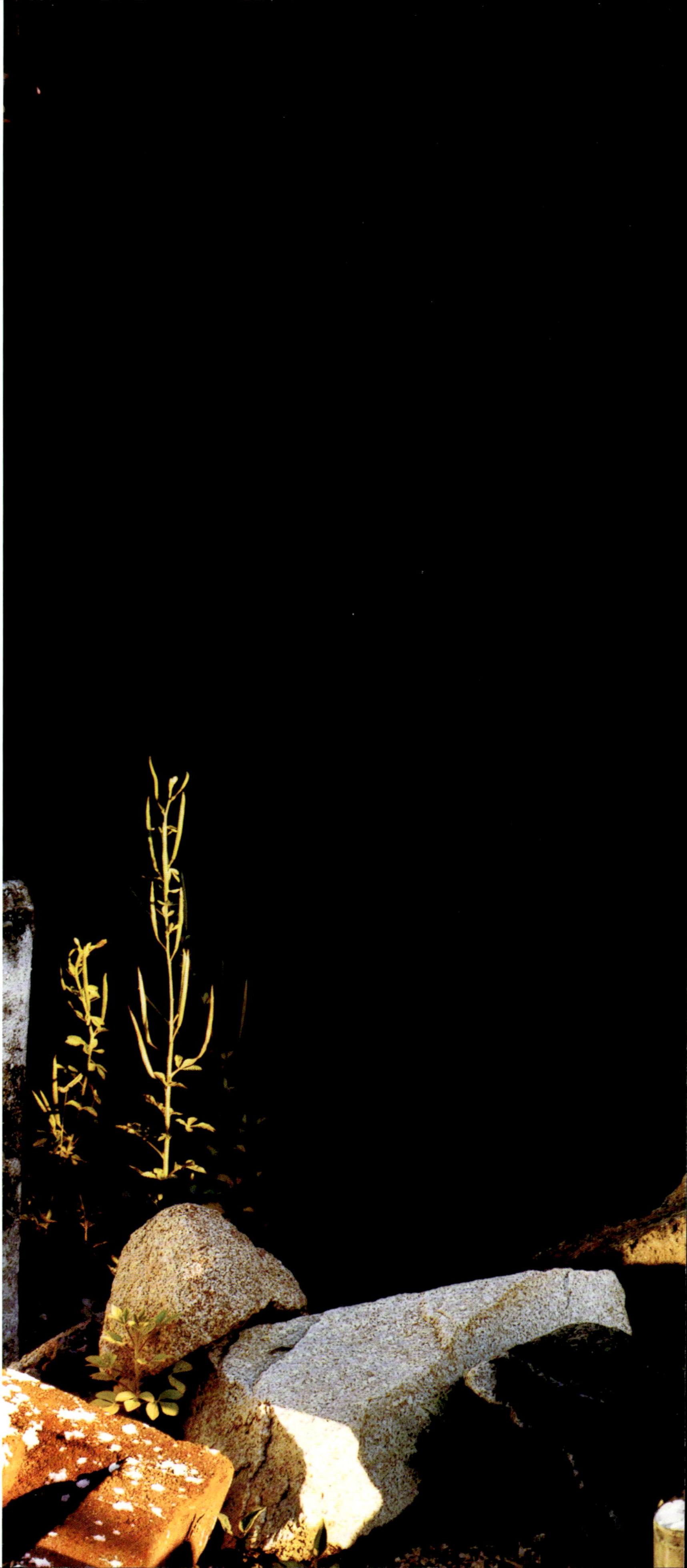

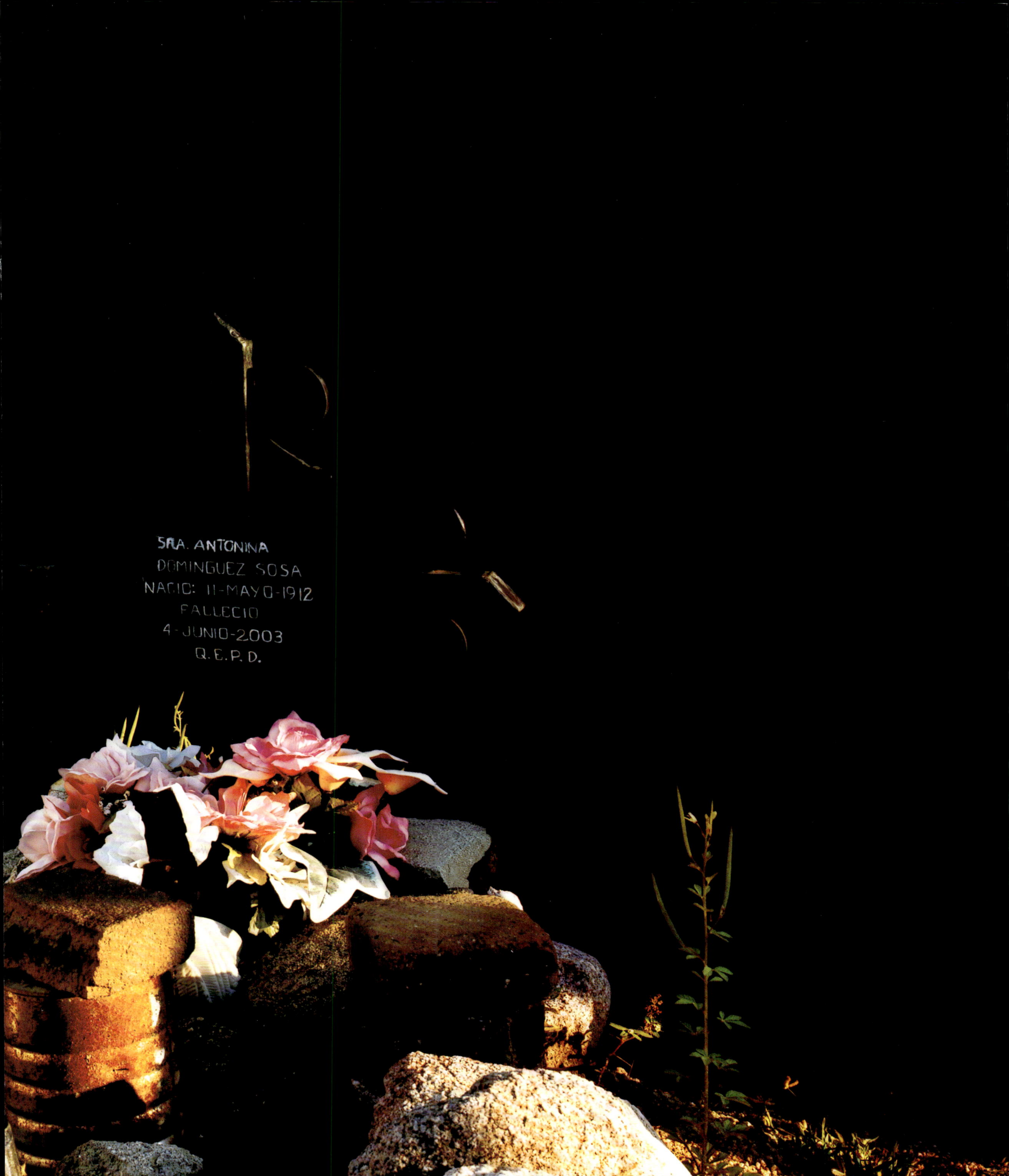
SRA. ANTONINA
DOMINGUEZ SOSA
NACIO: 11-MAYO-1912
FALLECIO
4-JUNIO-2003
Q.E.P.D.

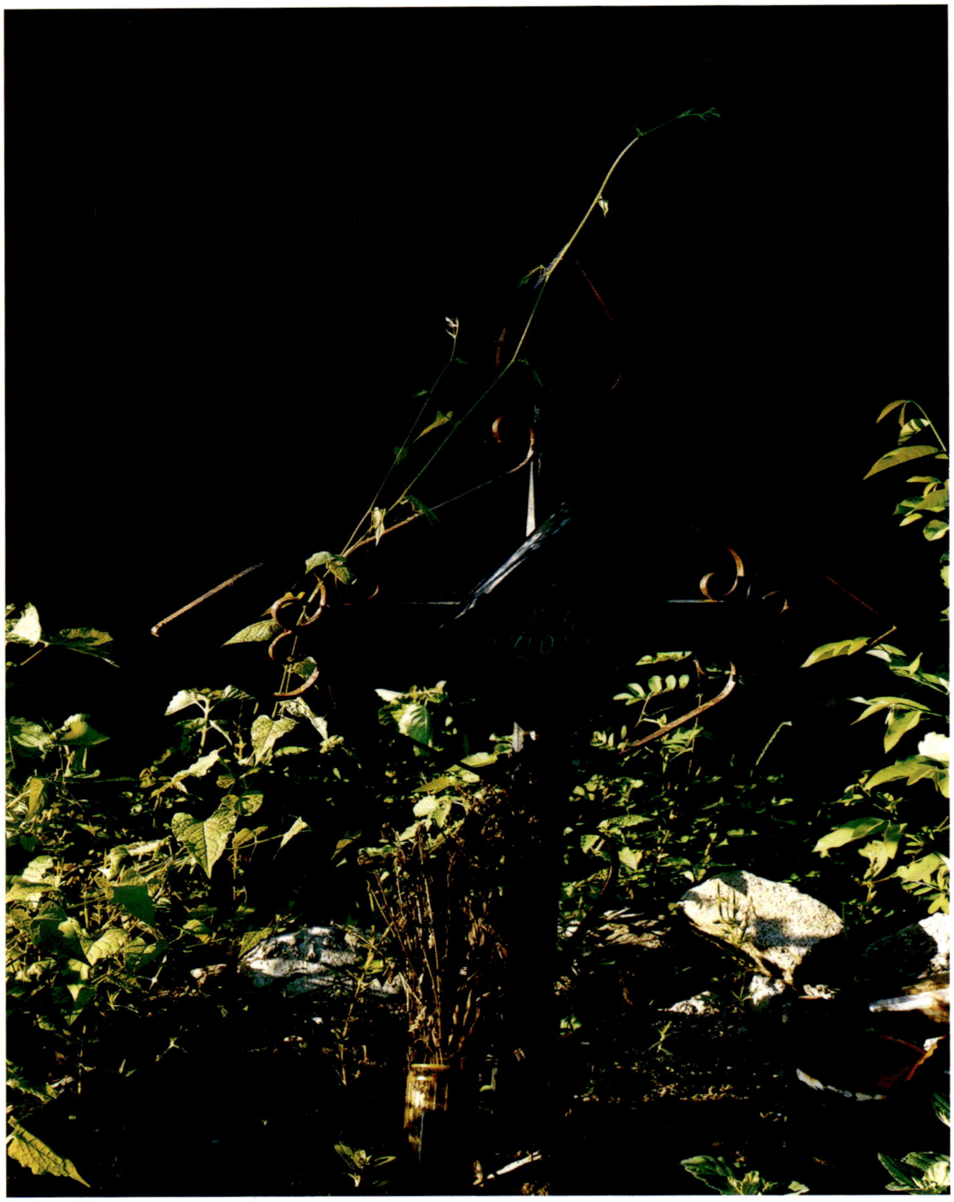

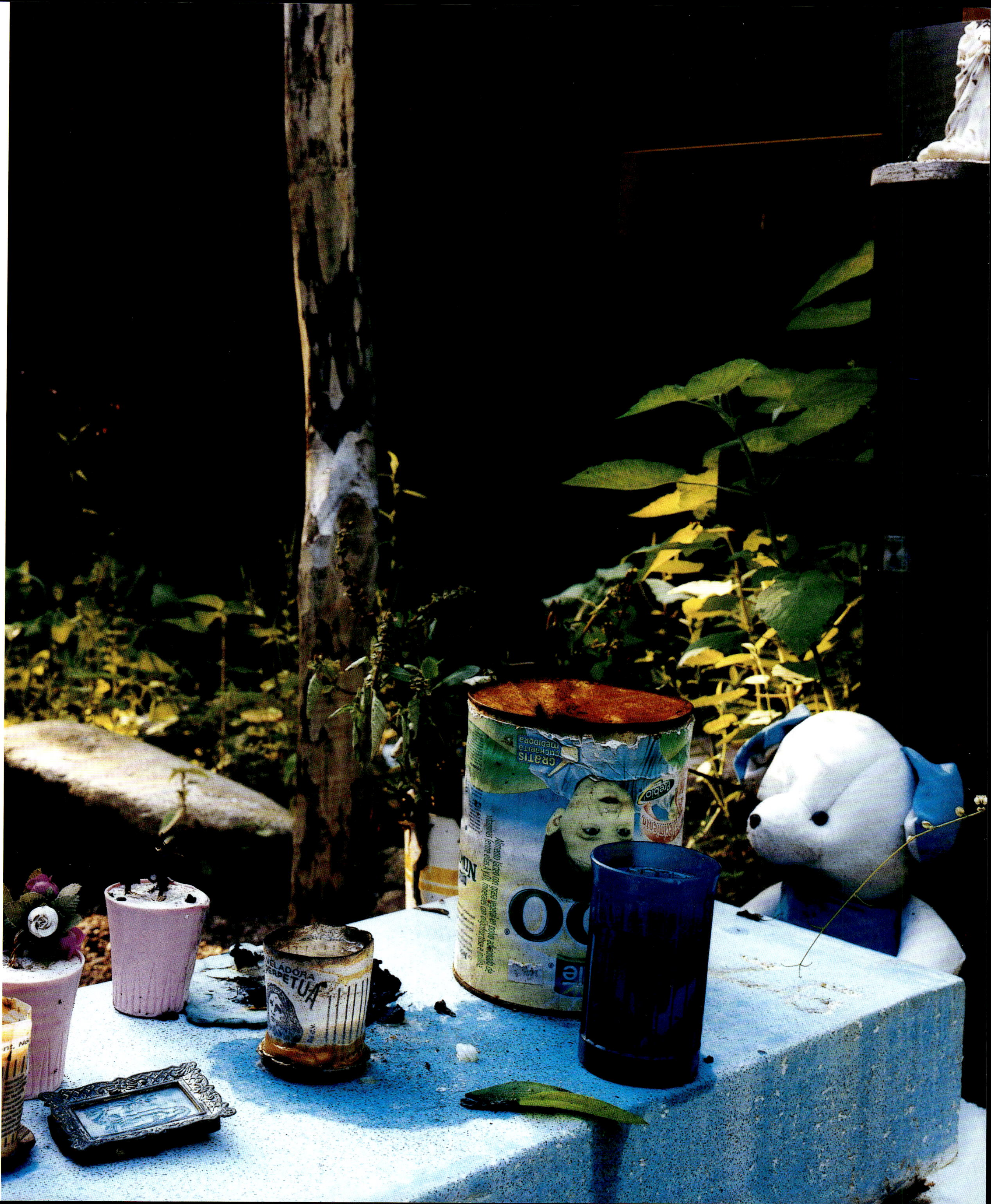

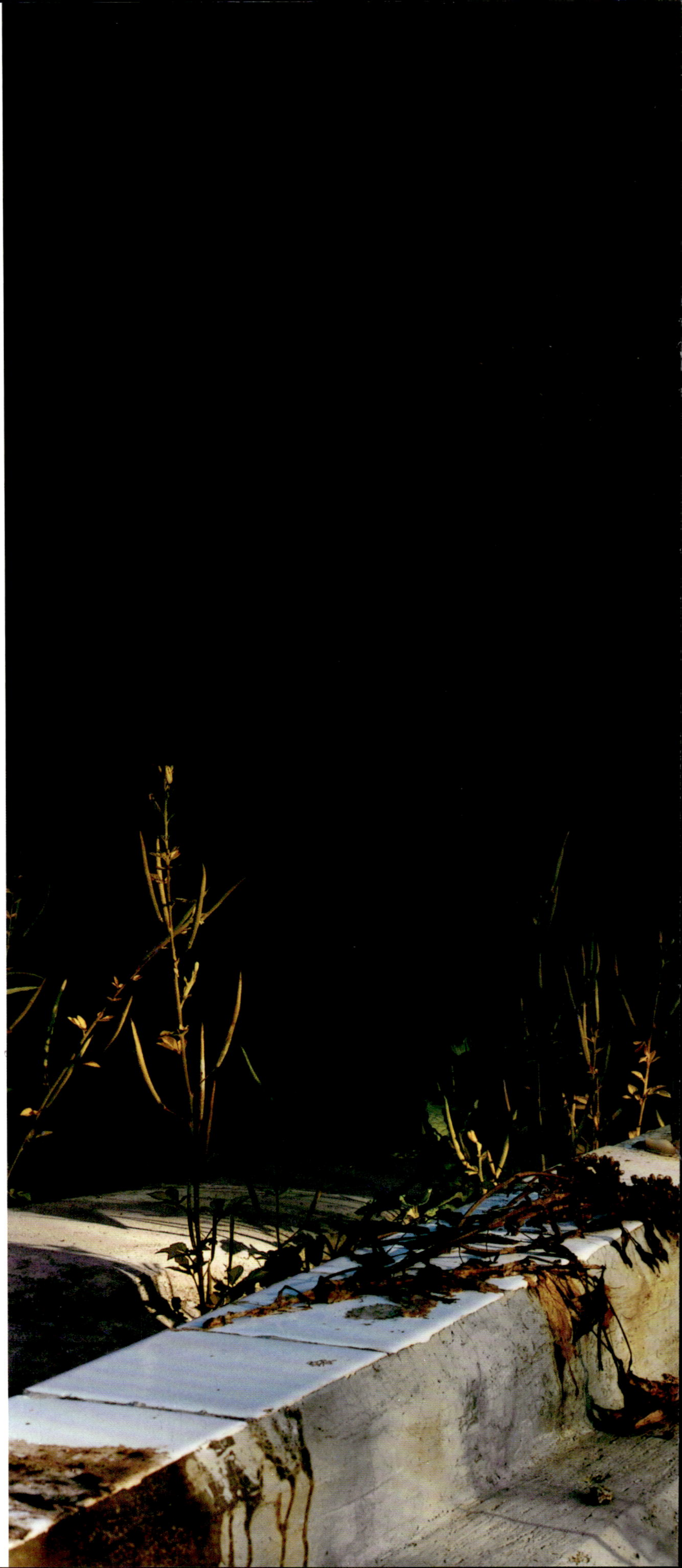

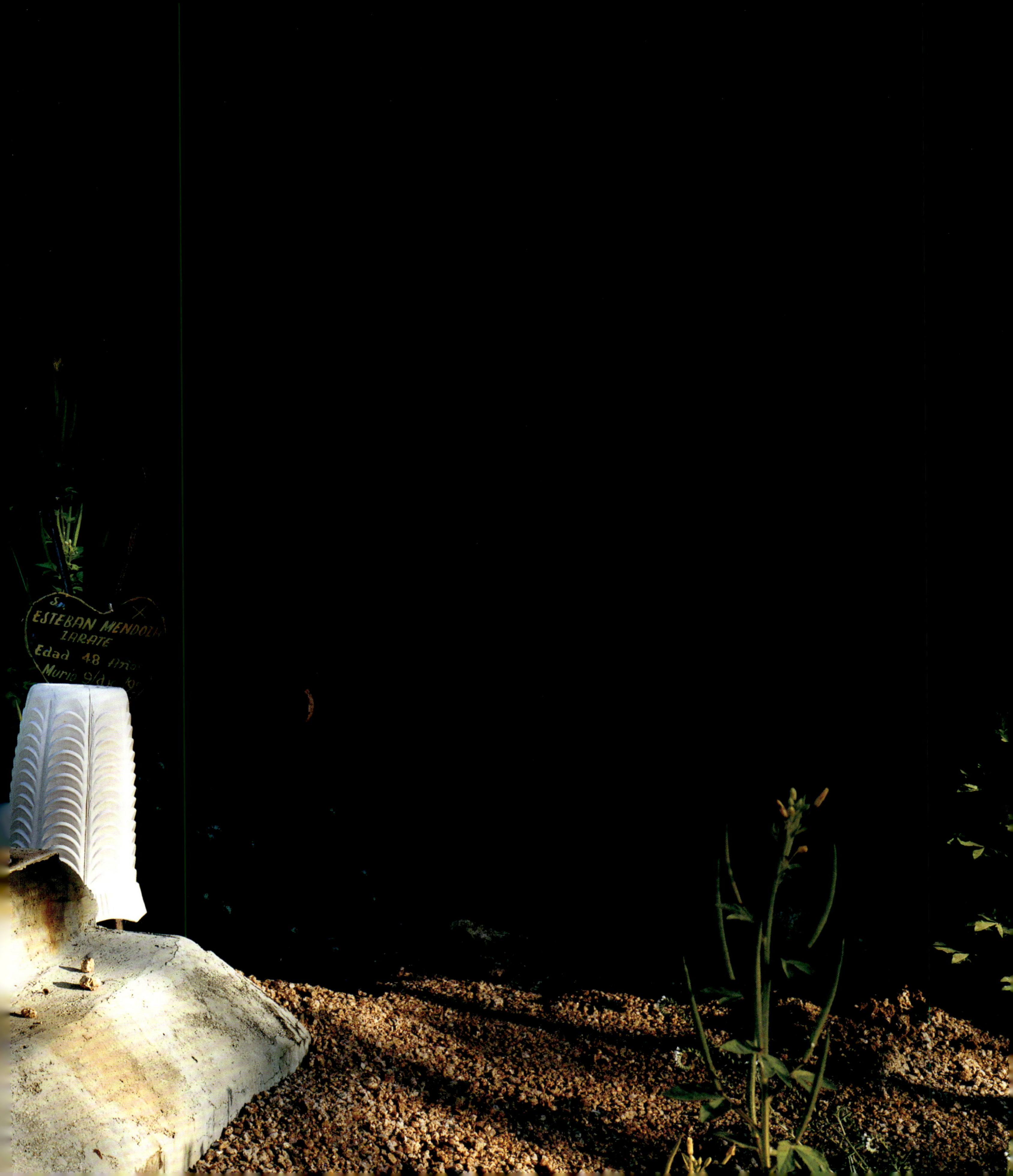
Sr.
ESTEBAN
ZARATE
Edad 48

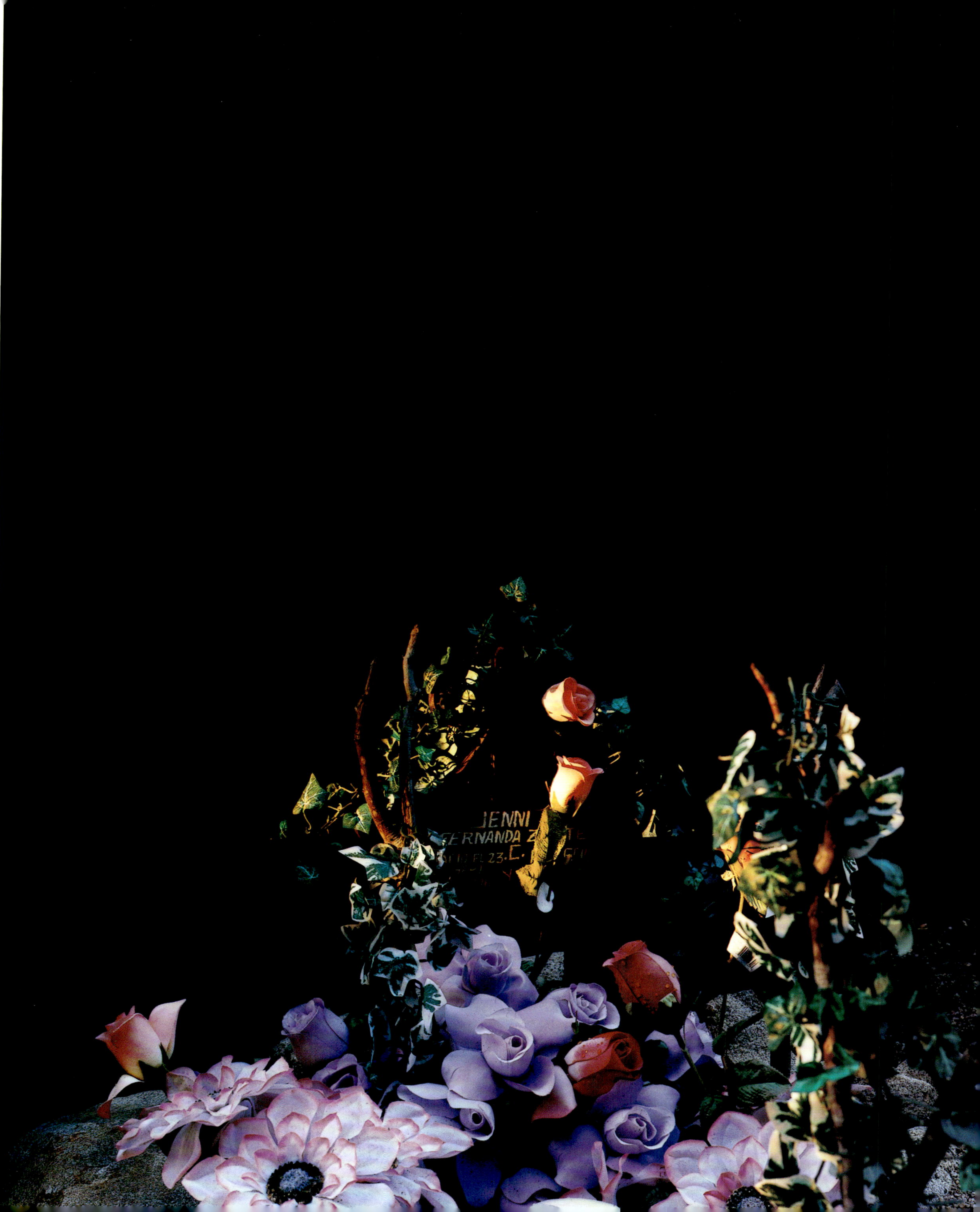
JENNI
FERNANDA

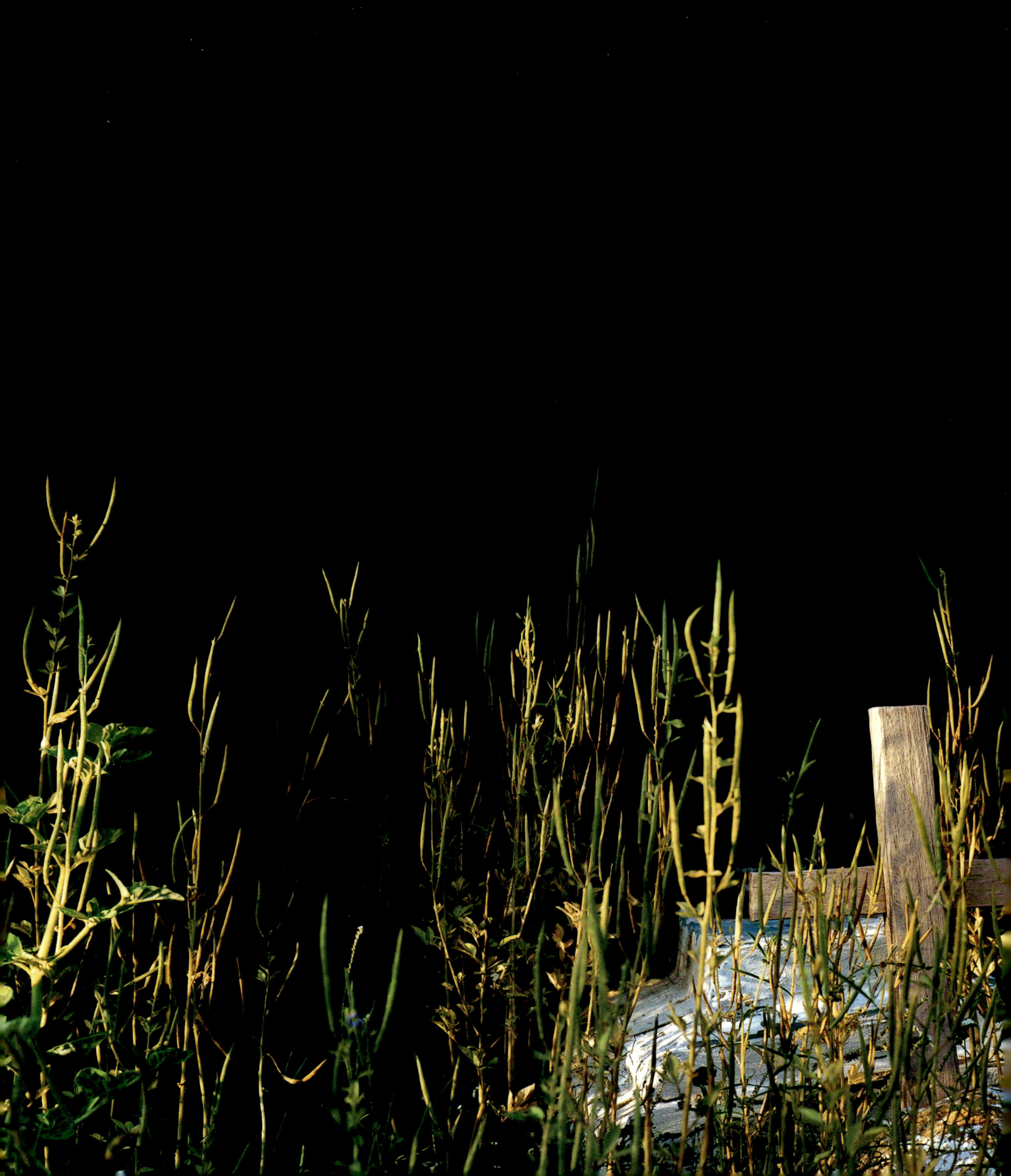

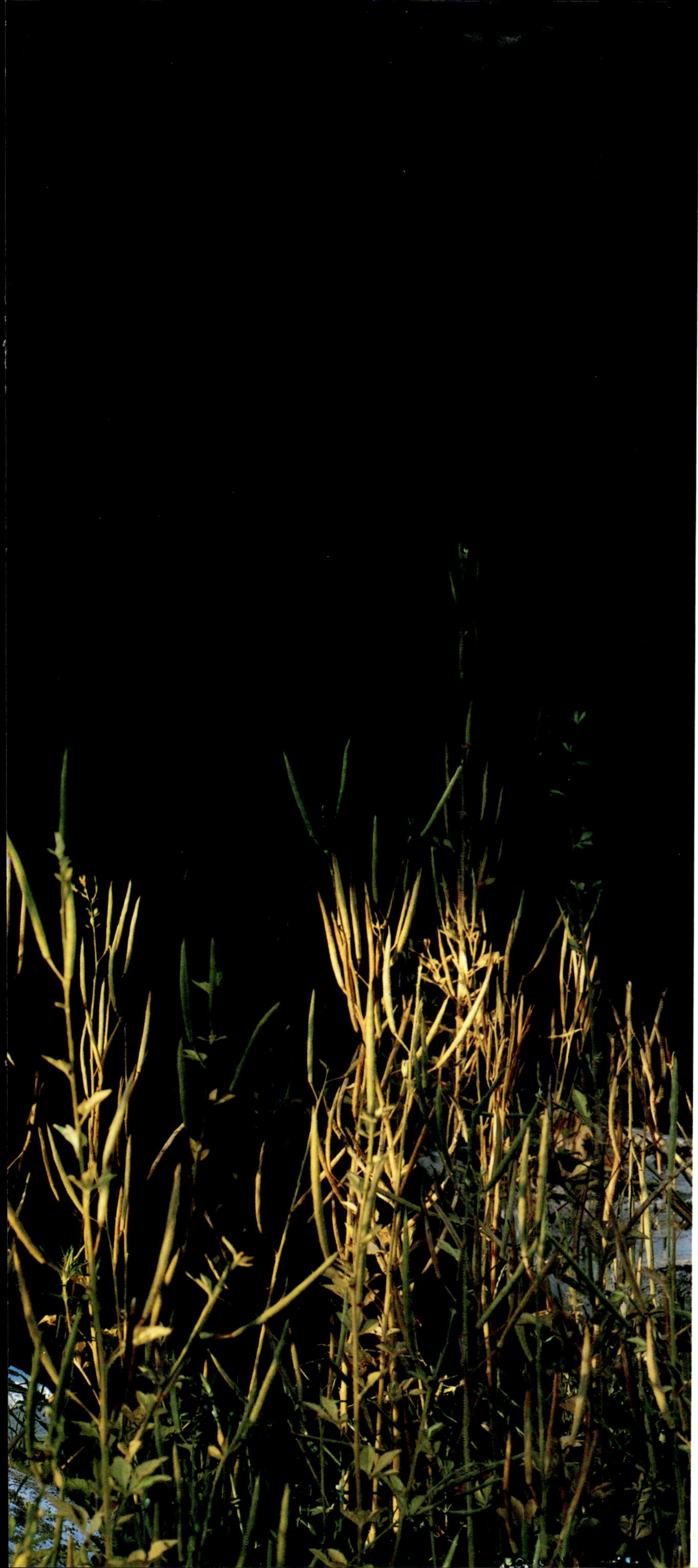

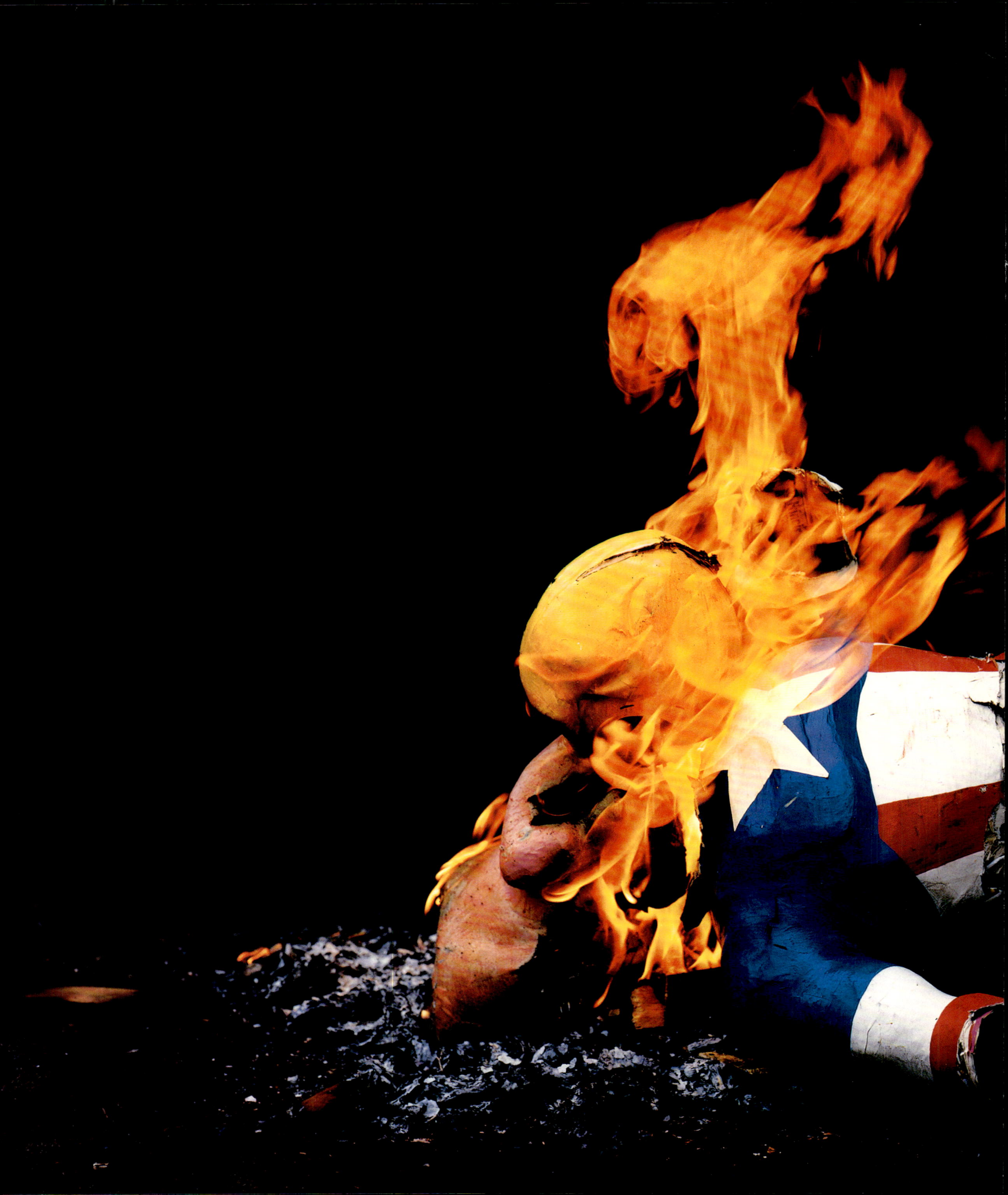

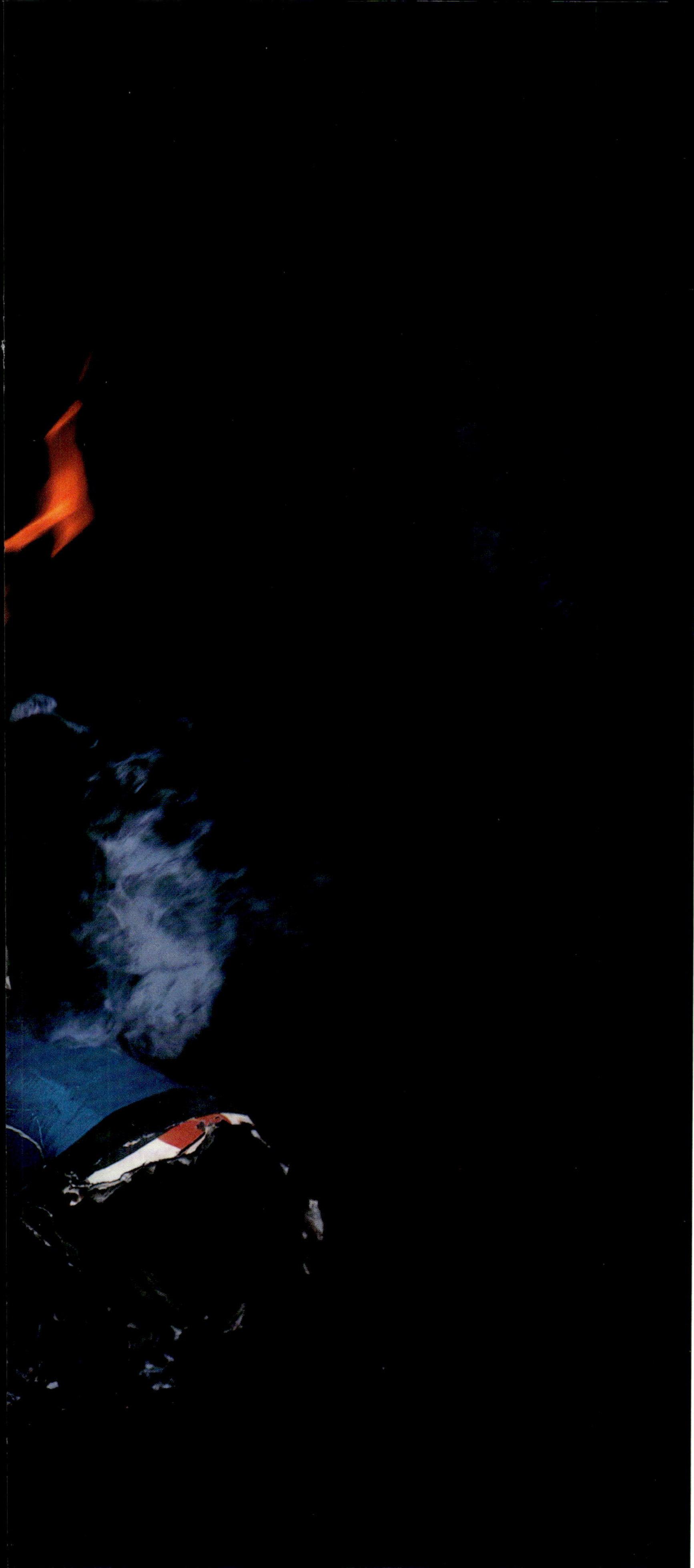

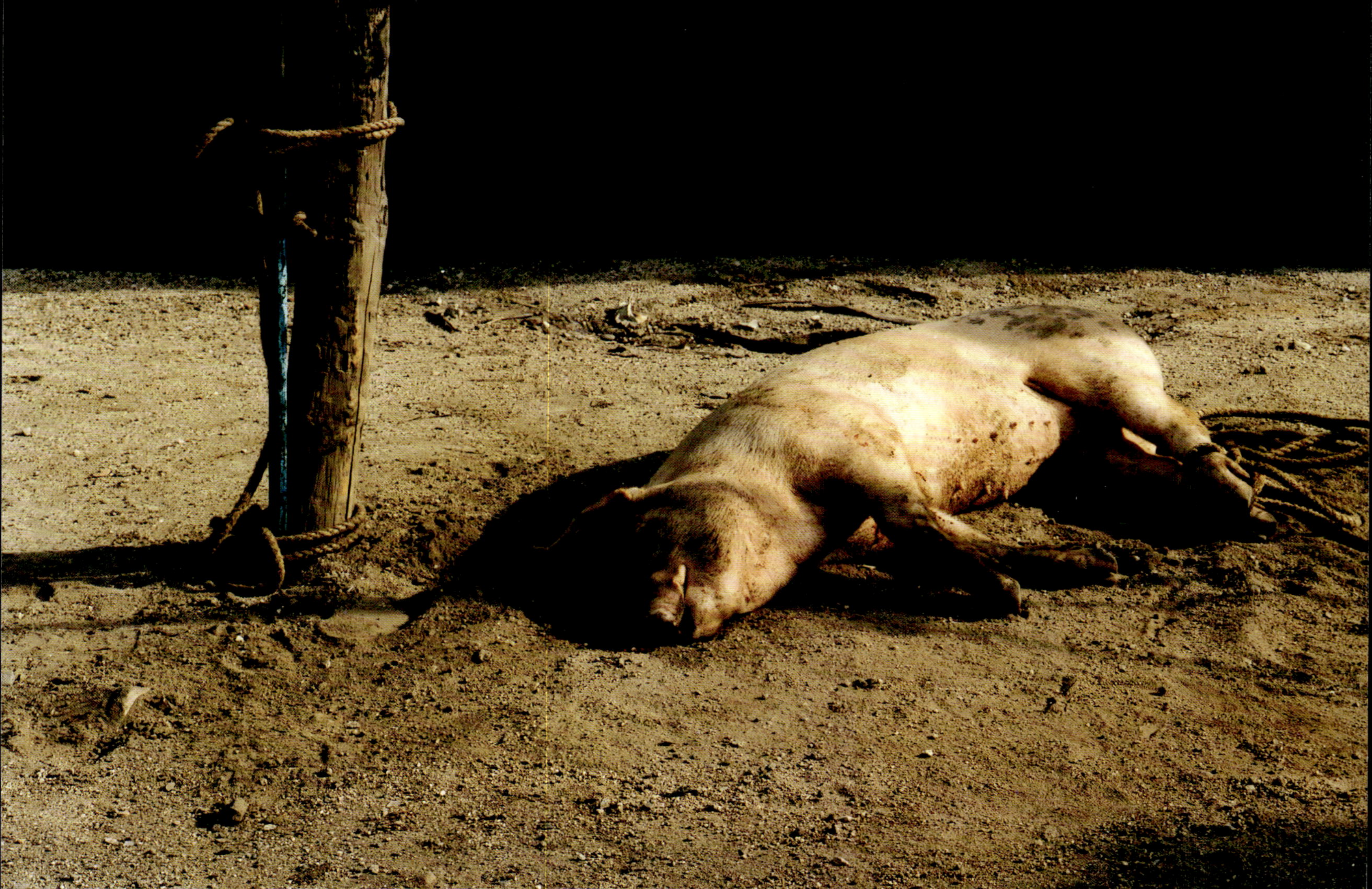

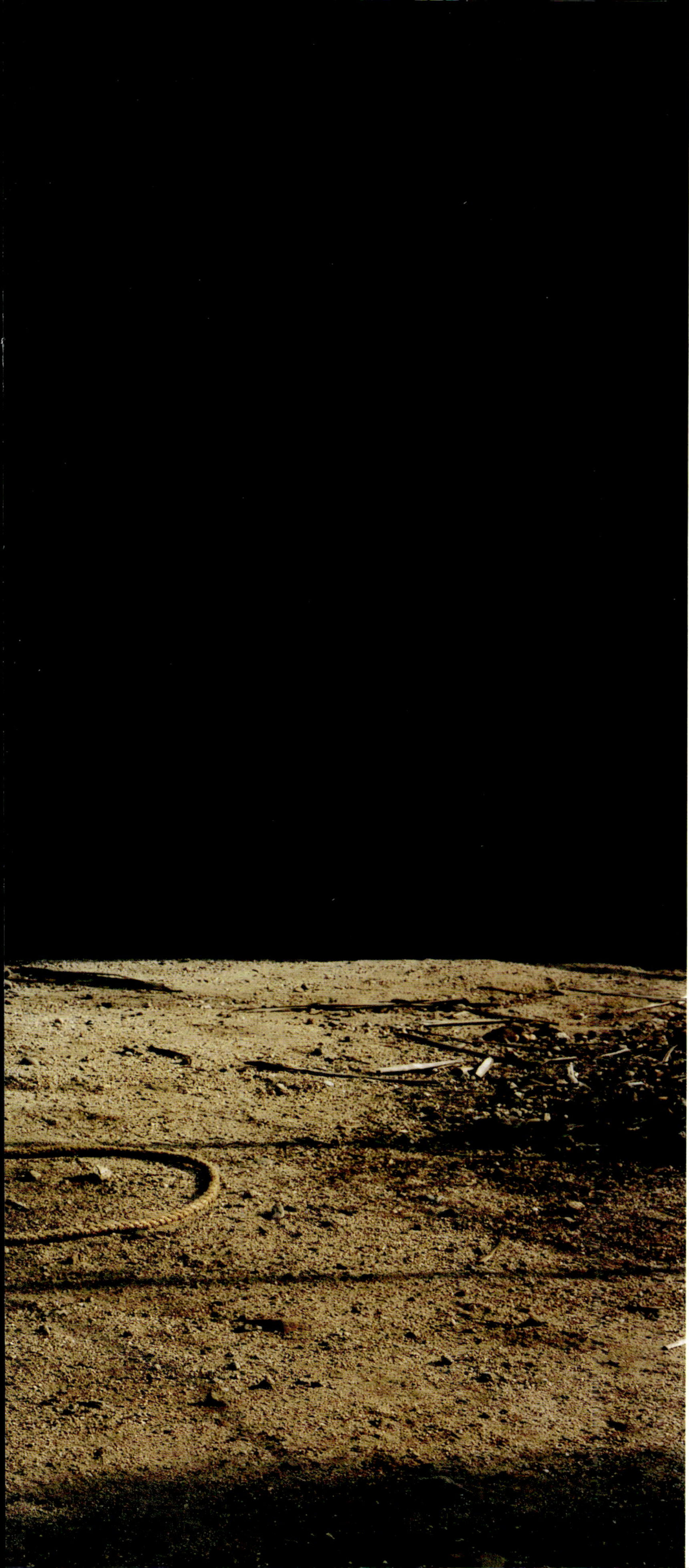

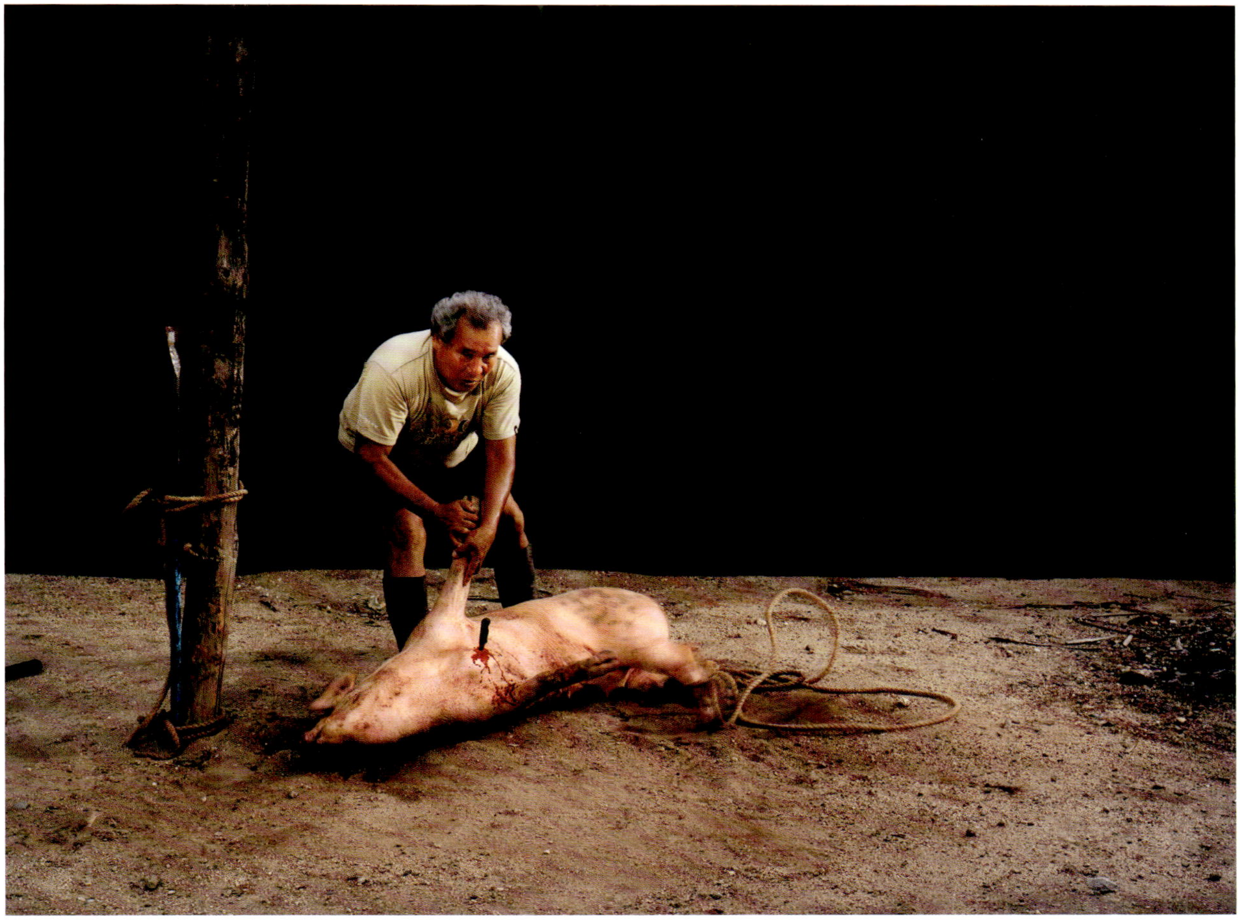

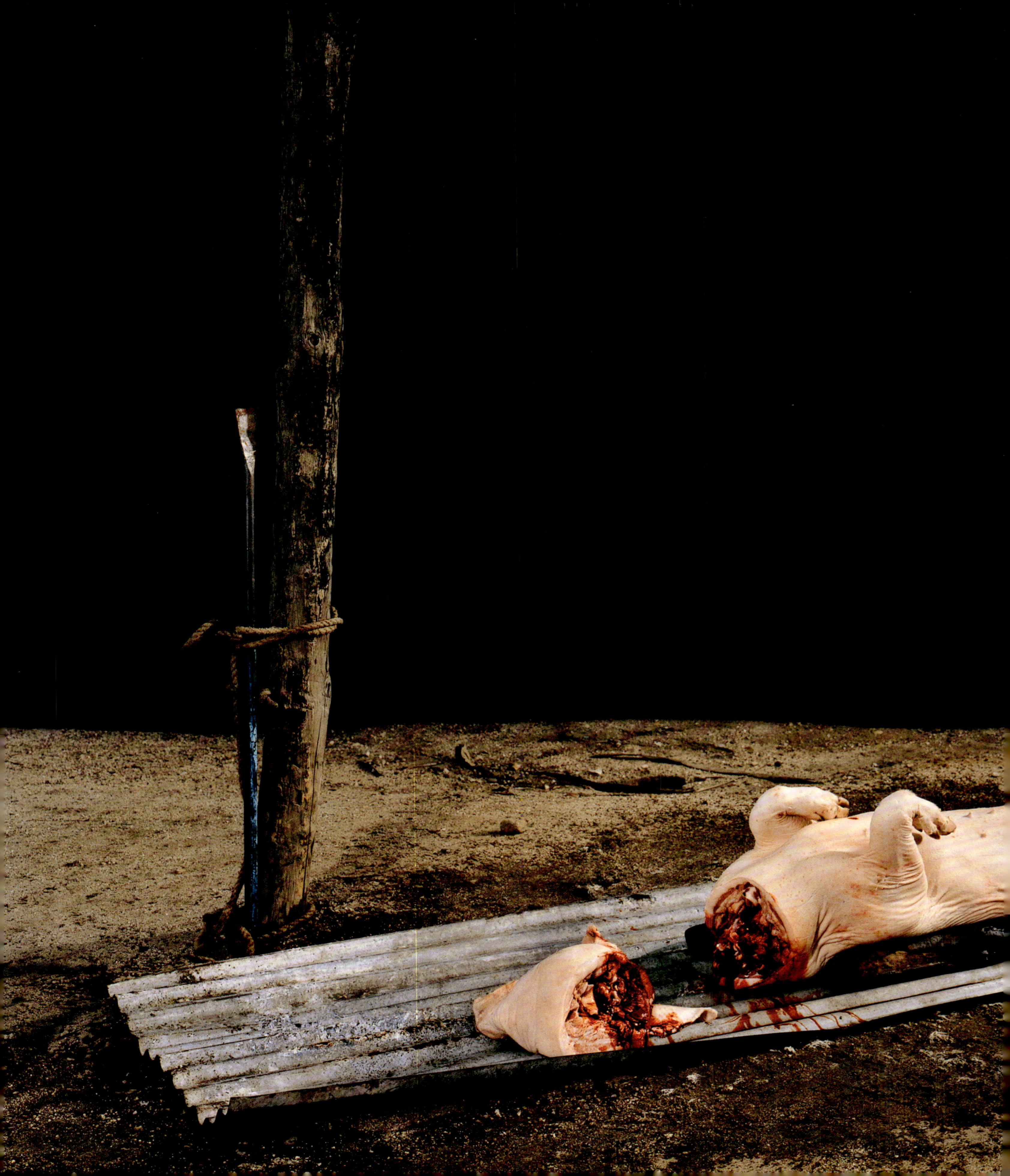

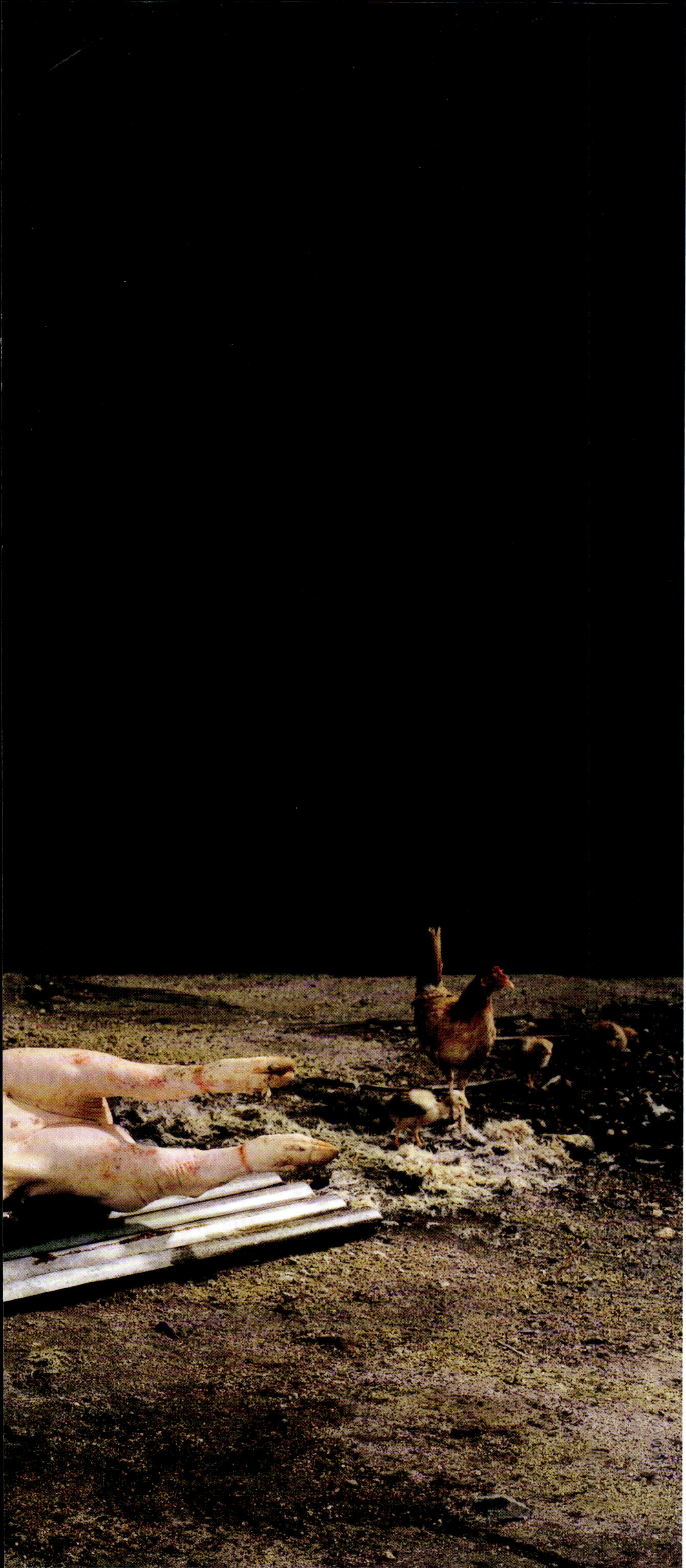

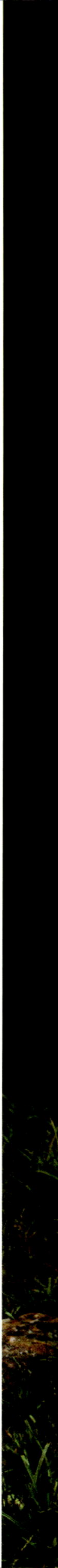

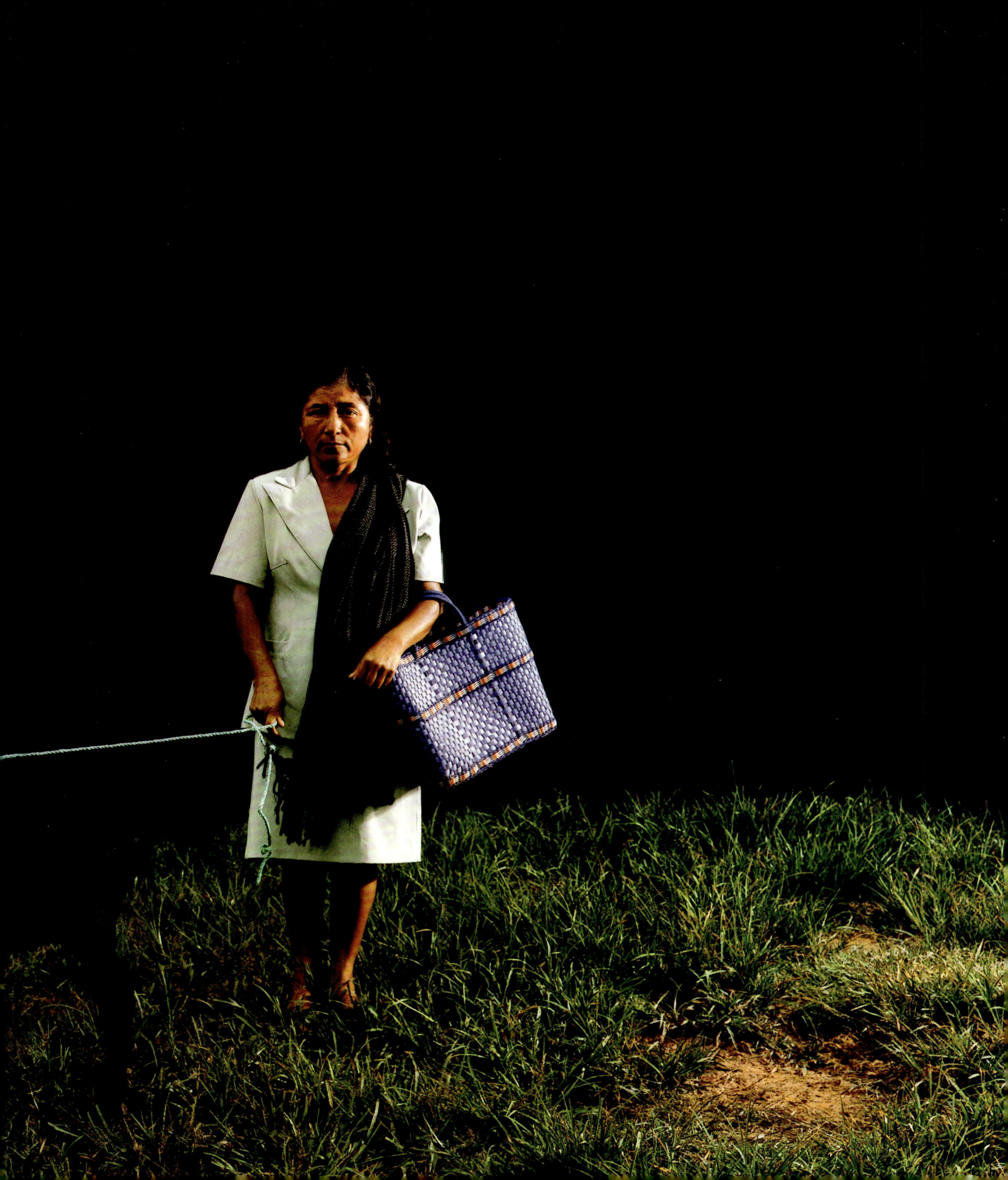

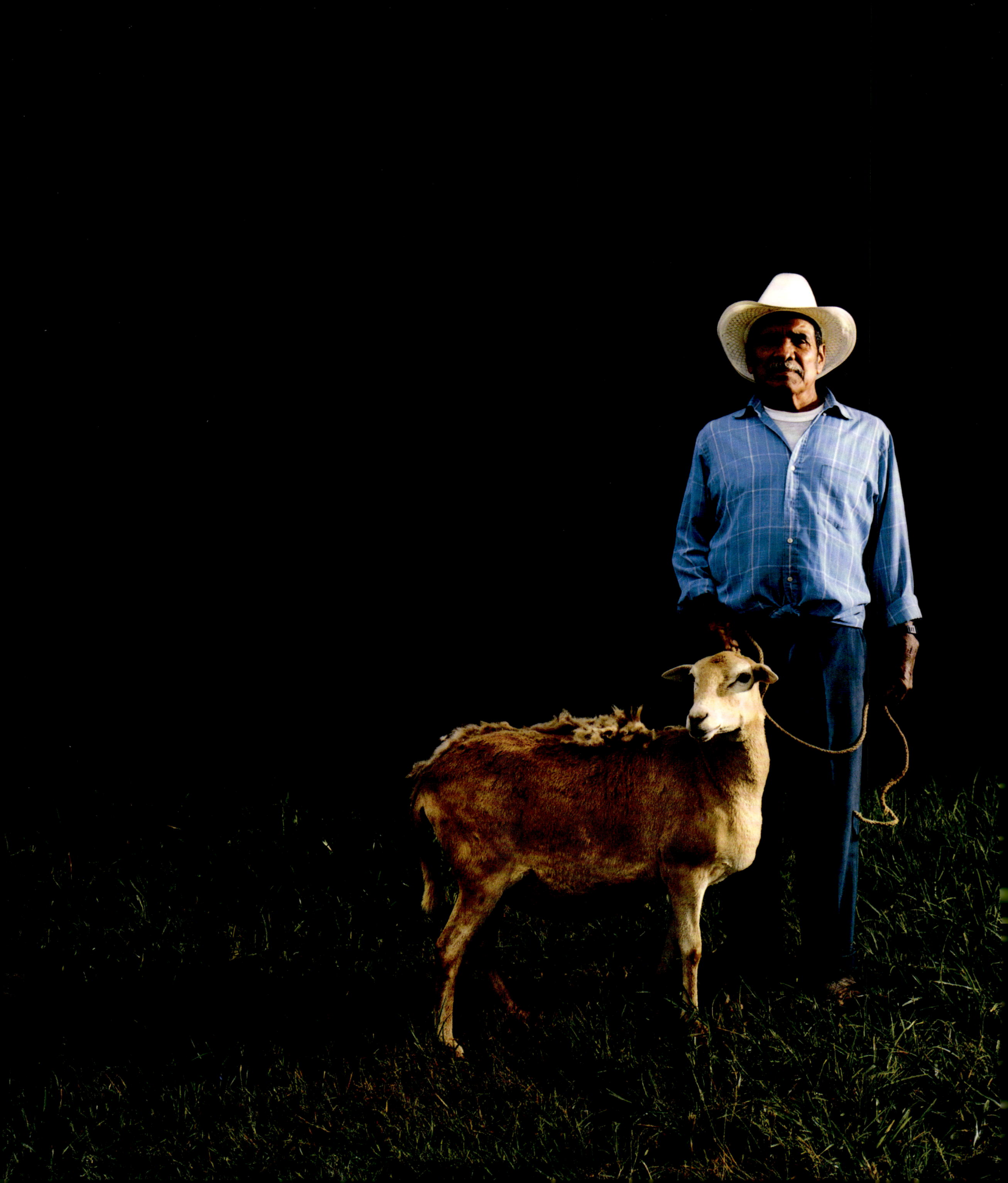

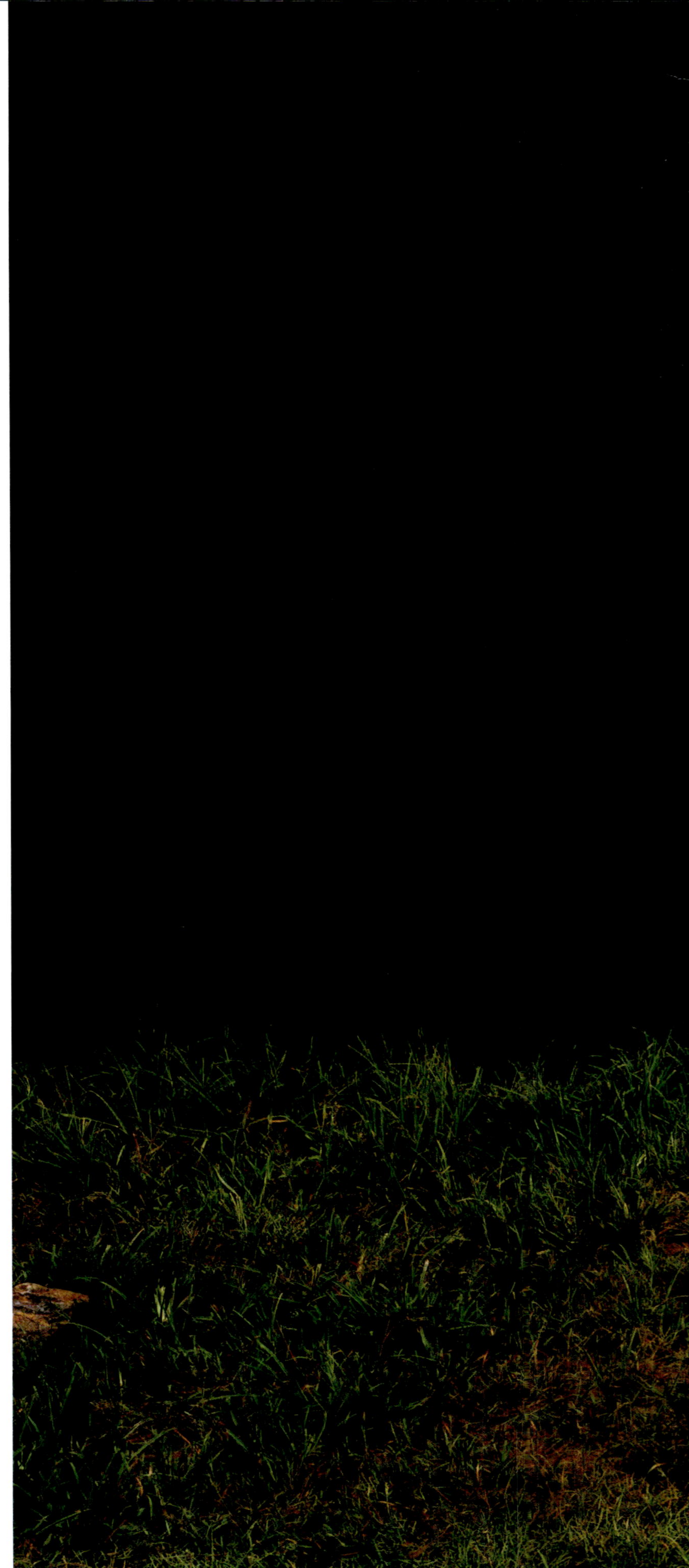

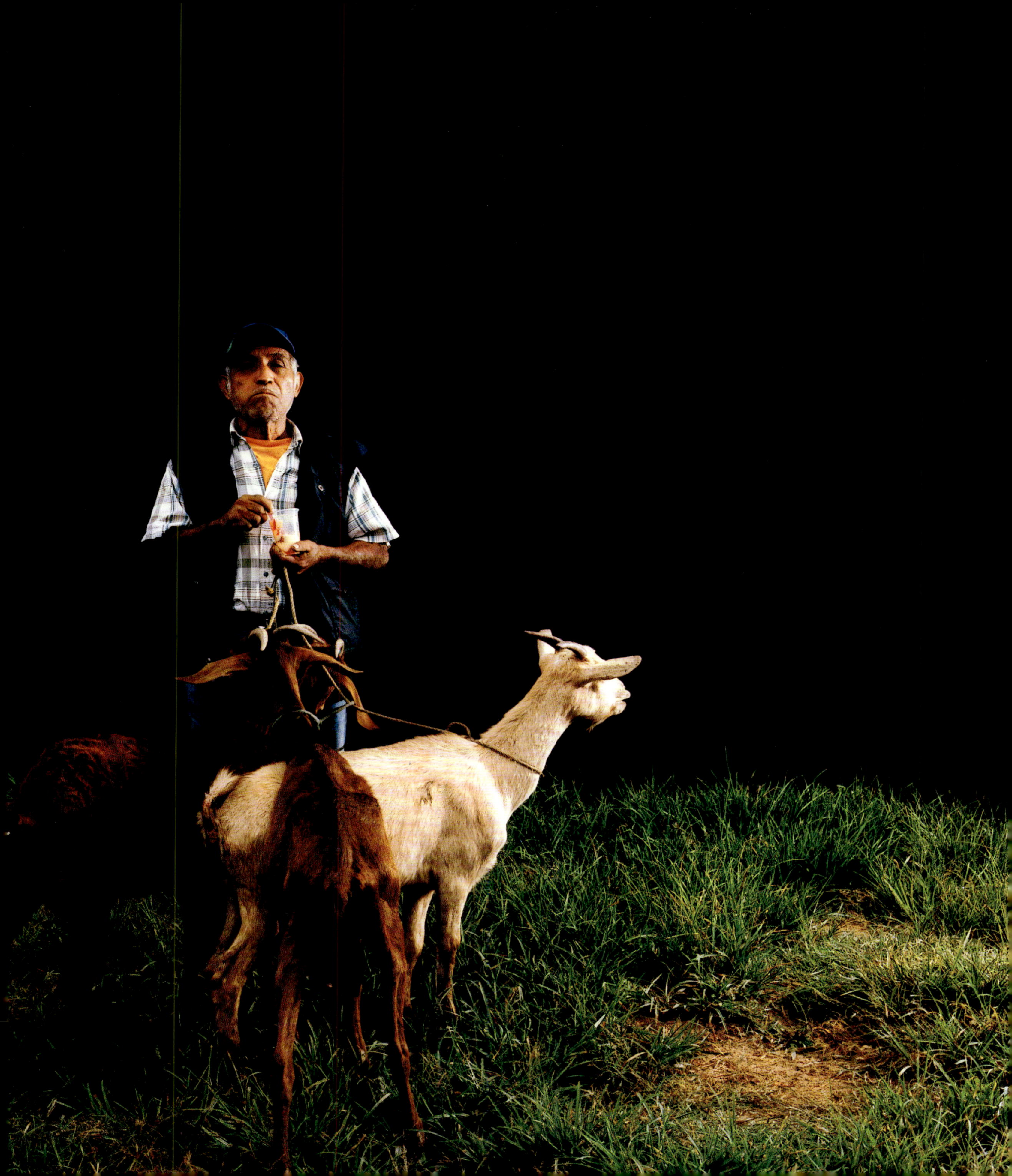

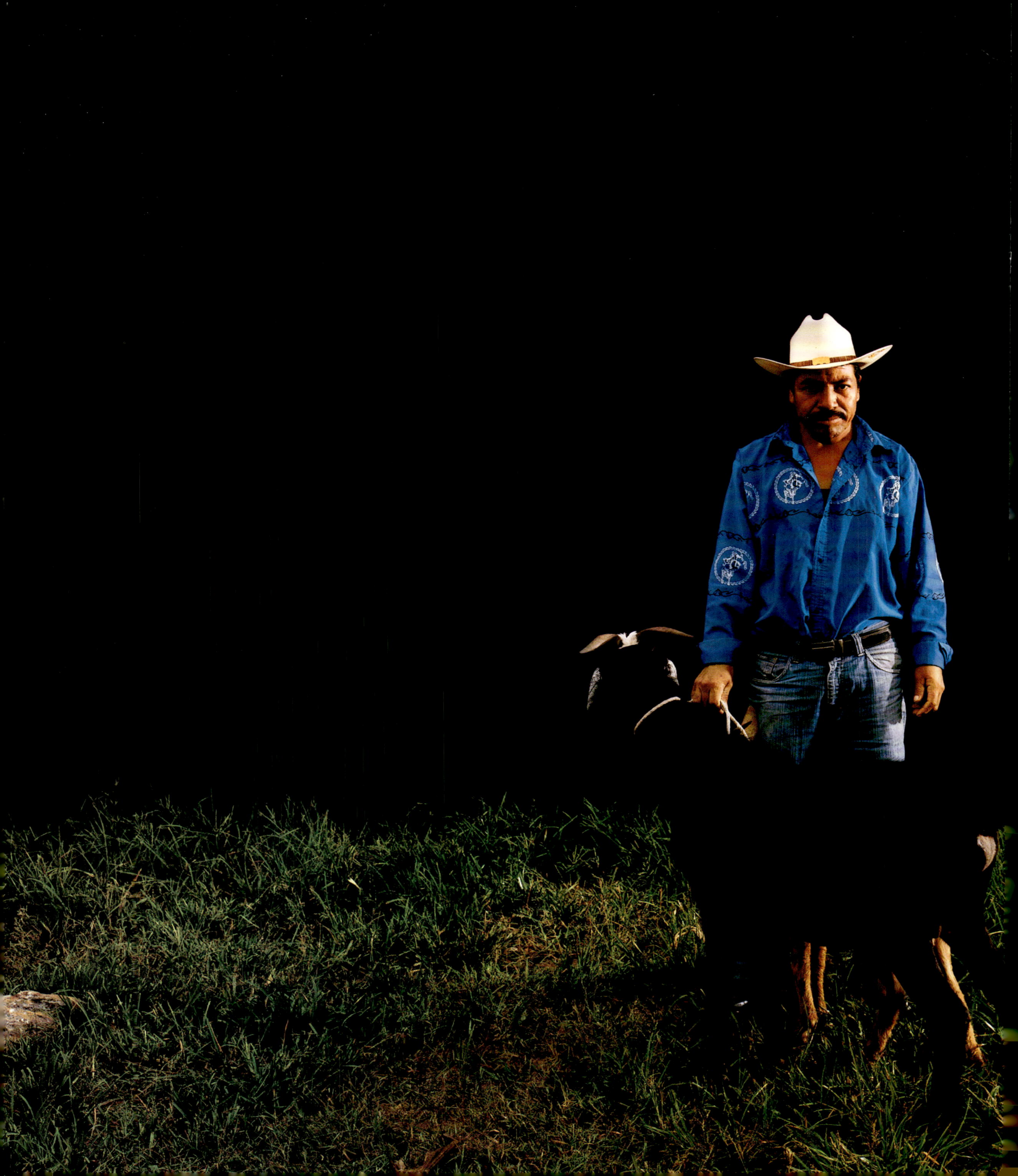

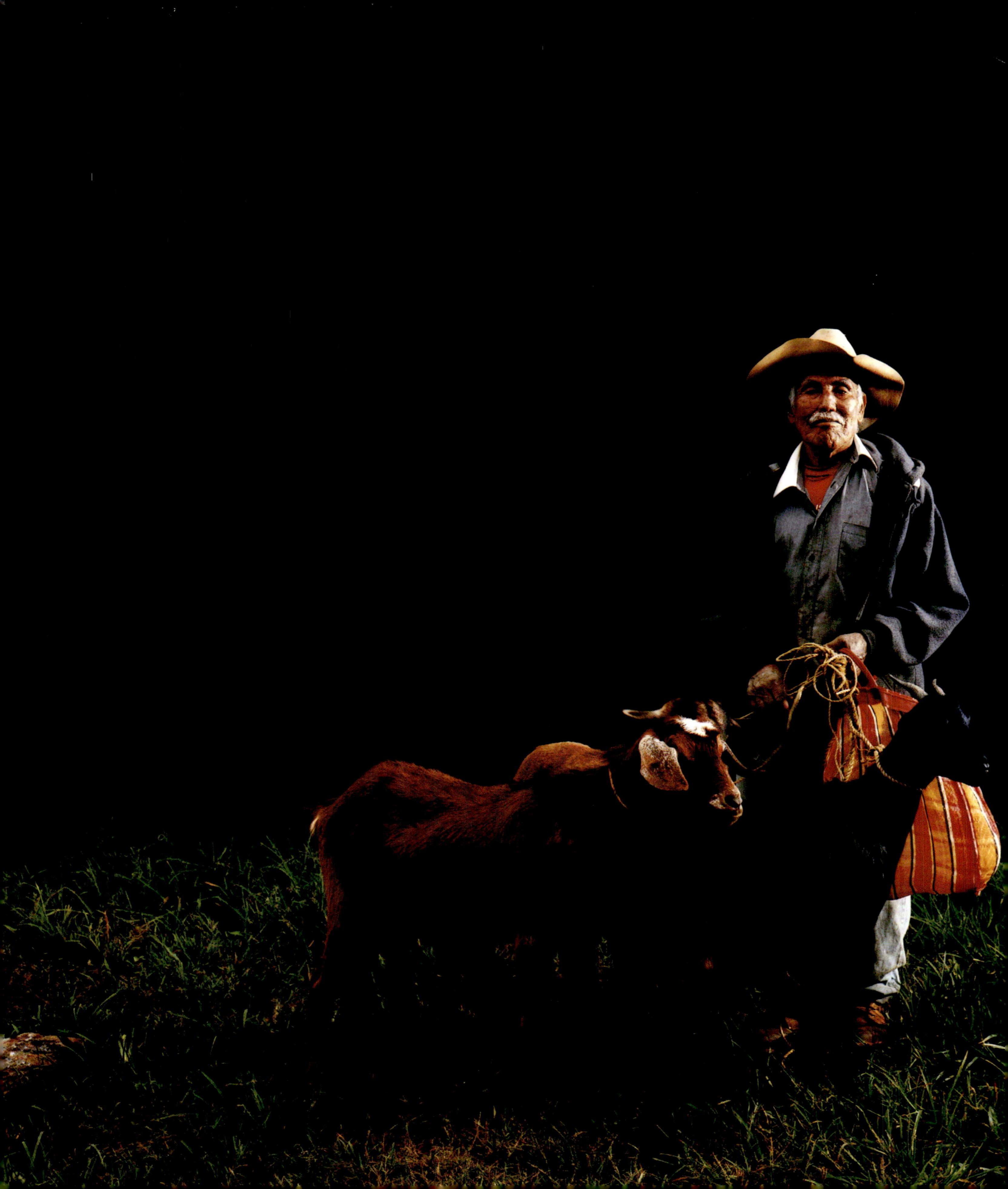

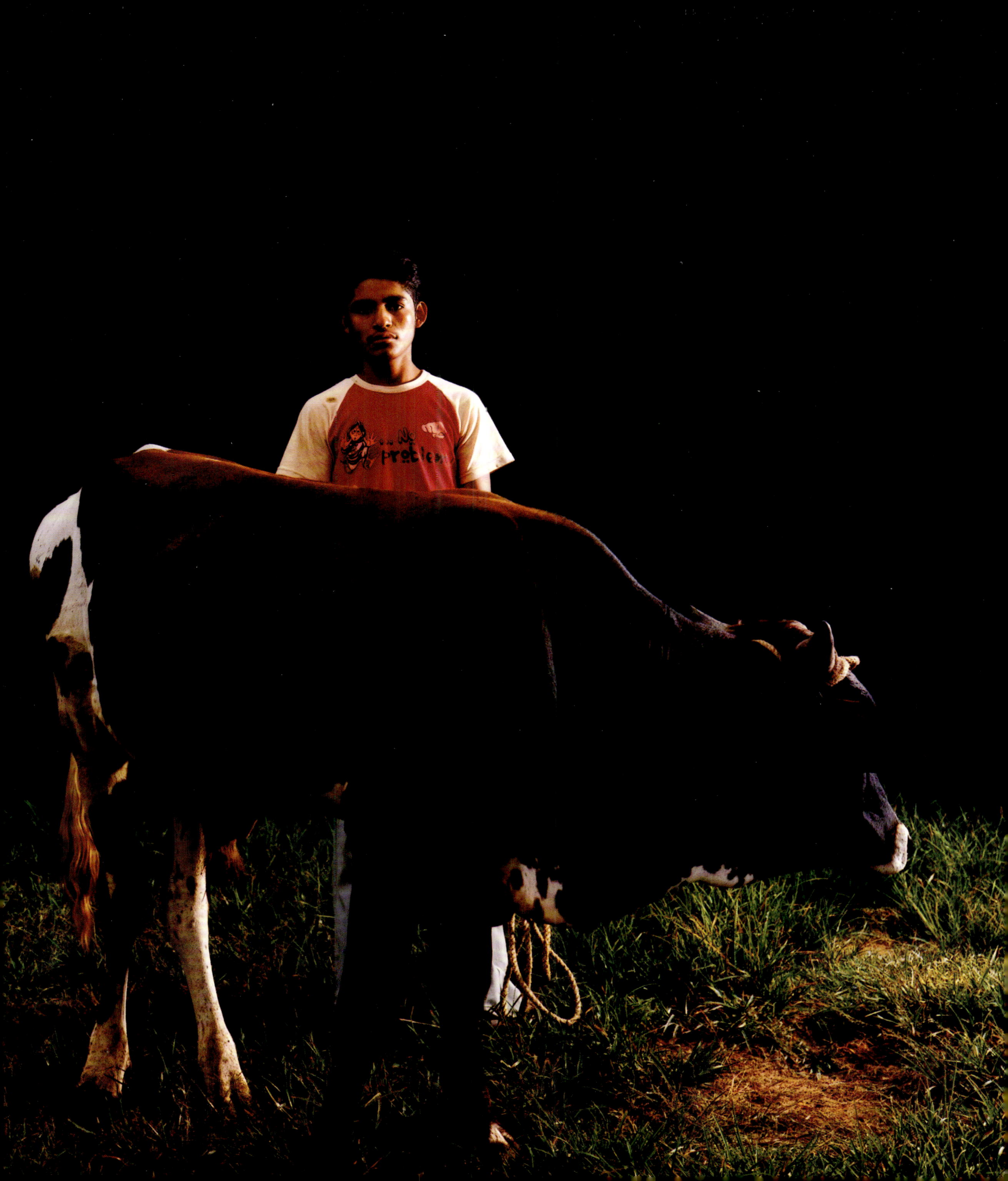

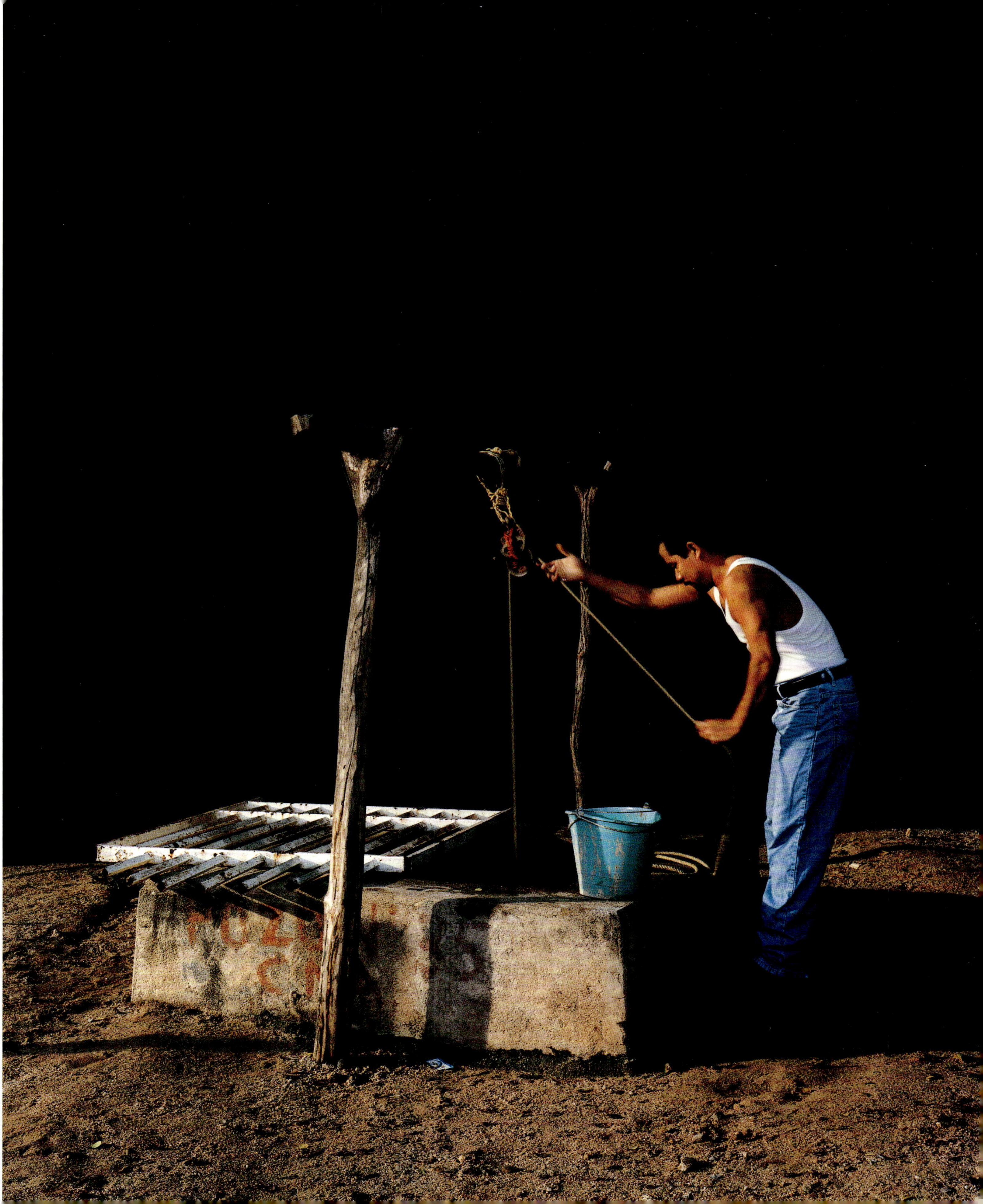

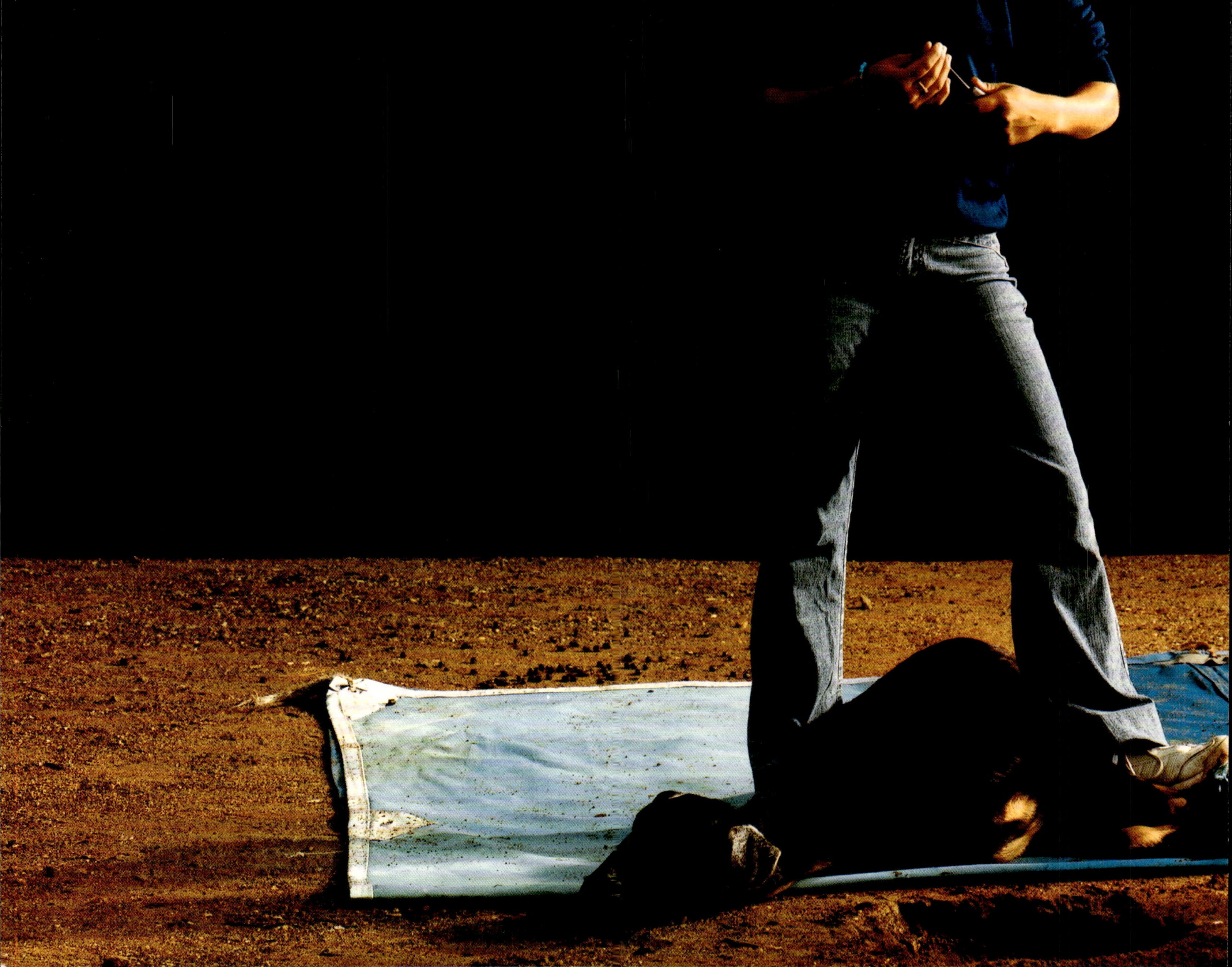

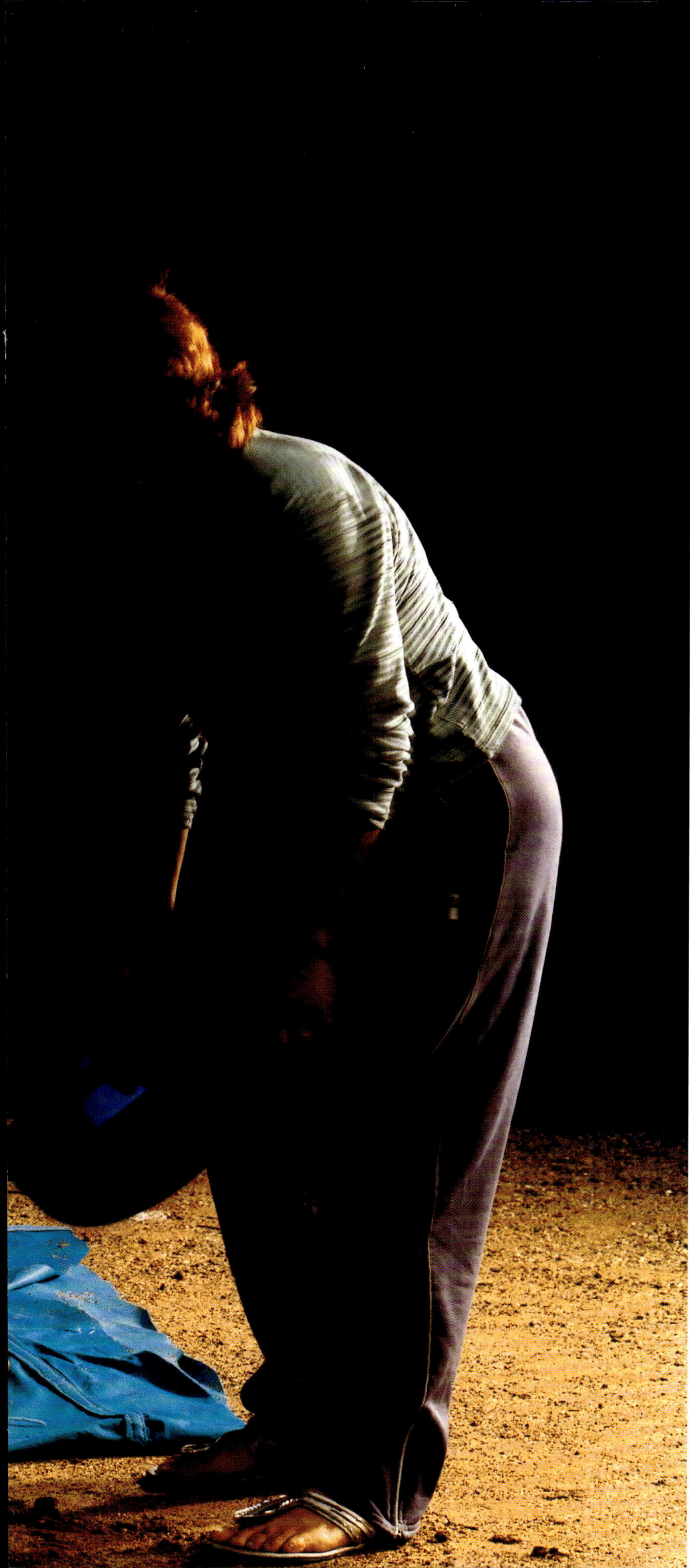

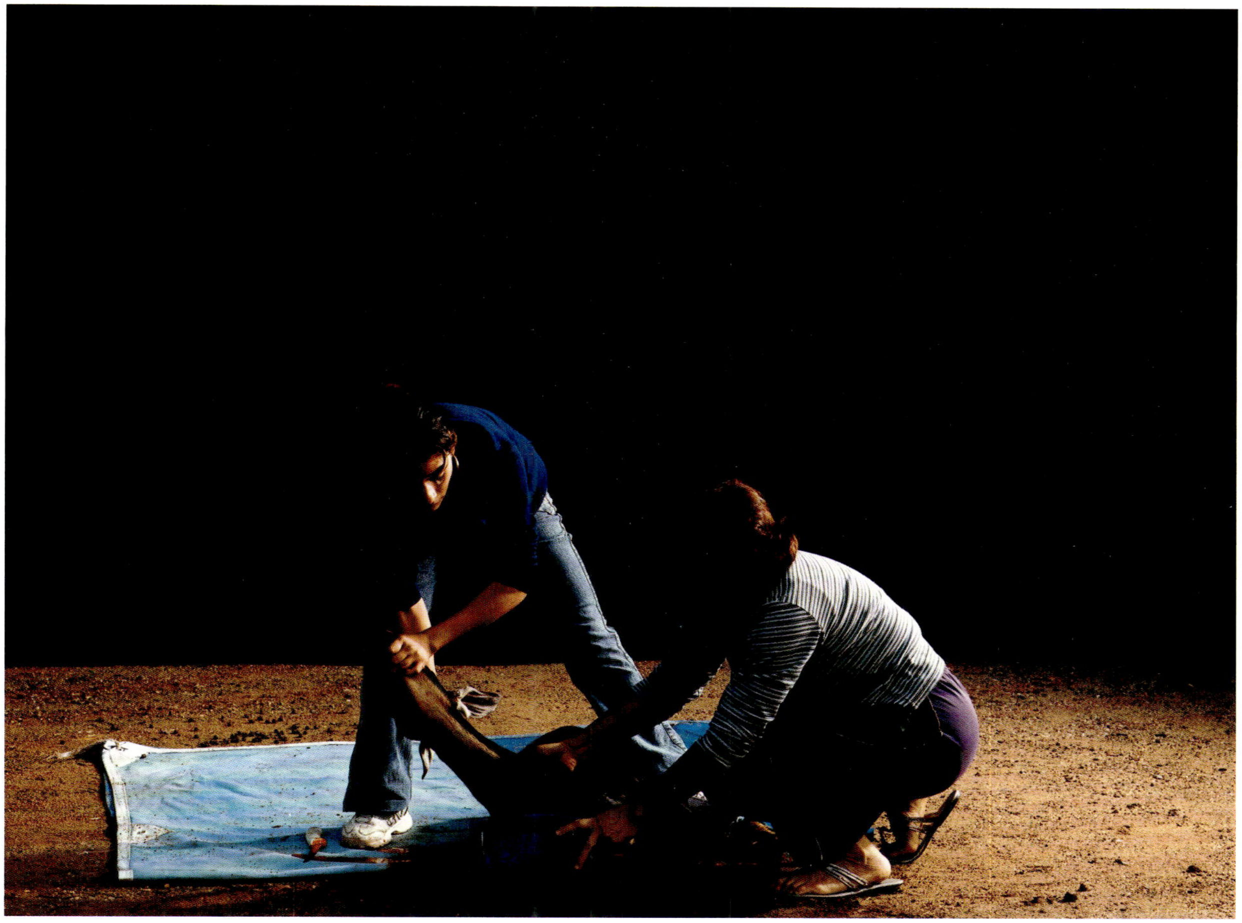

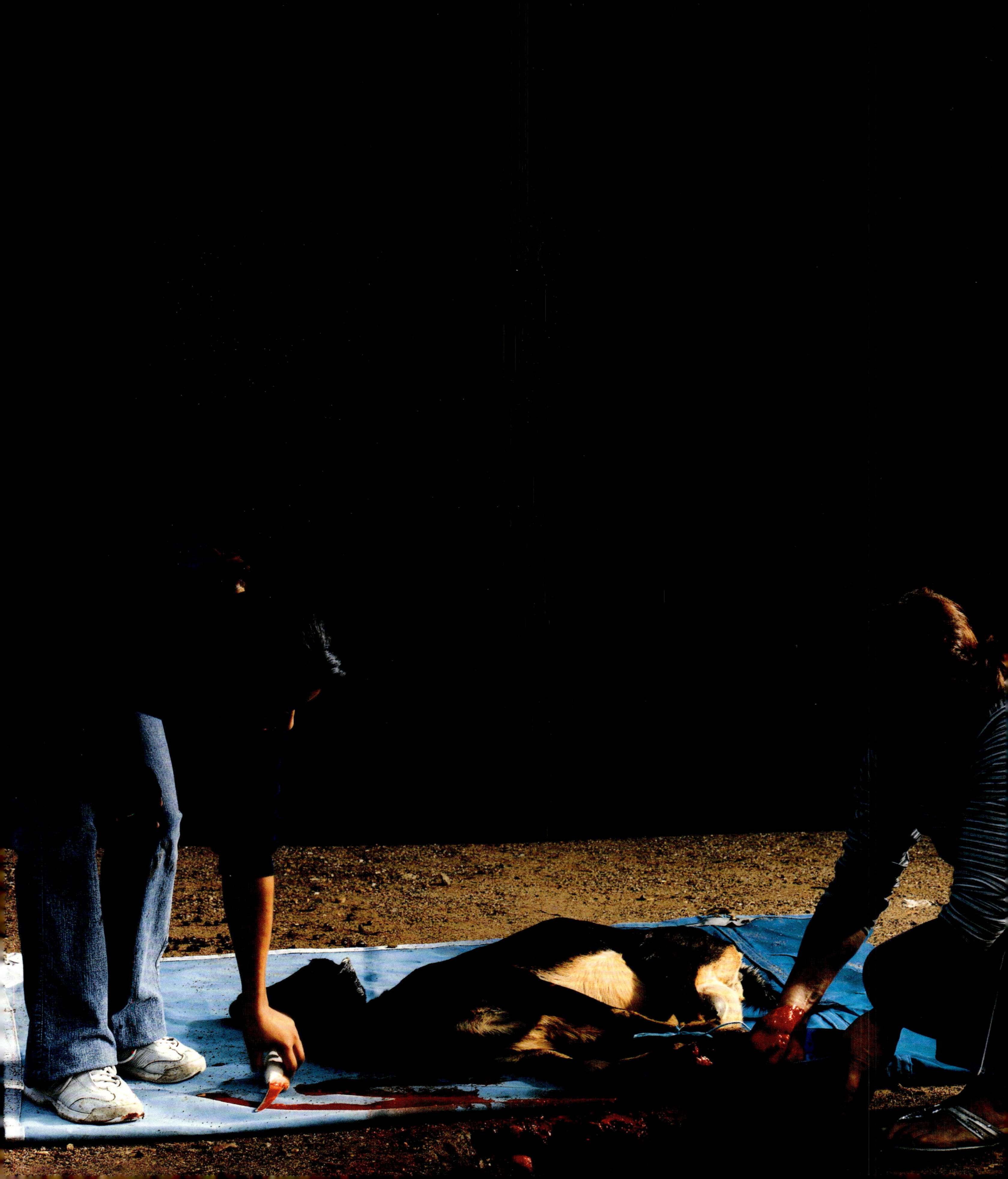

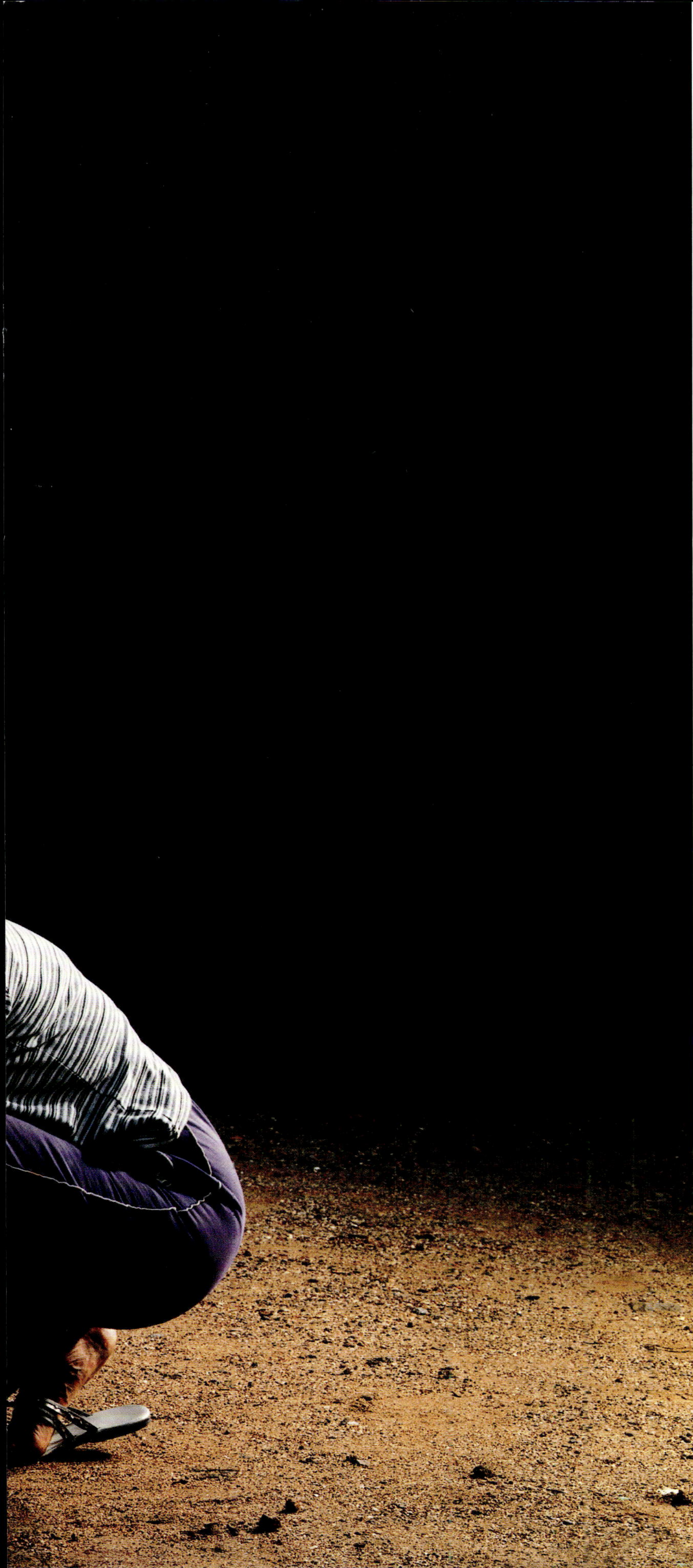

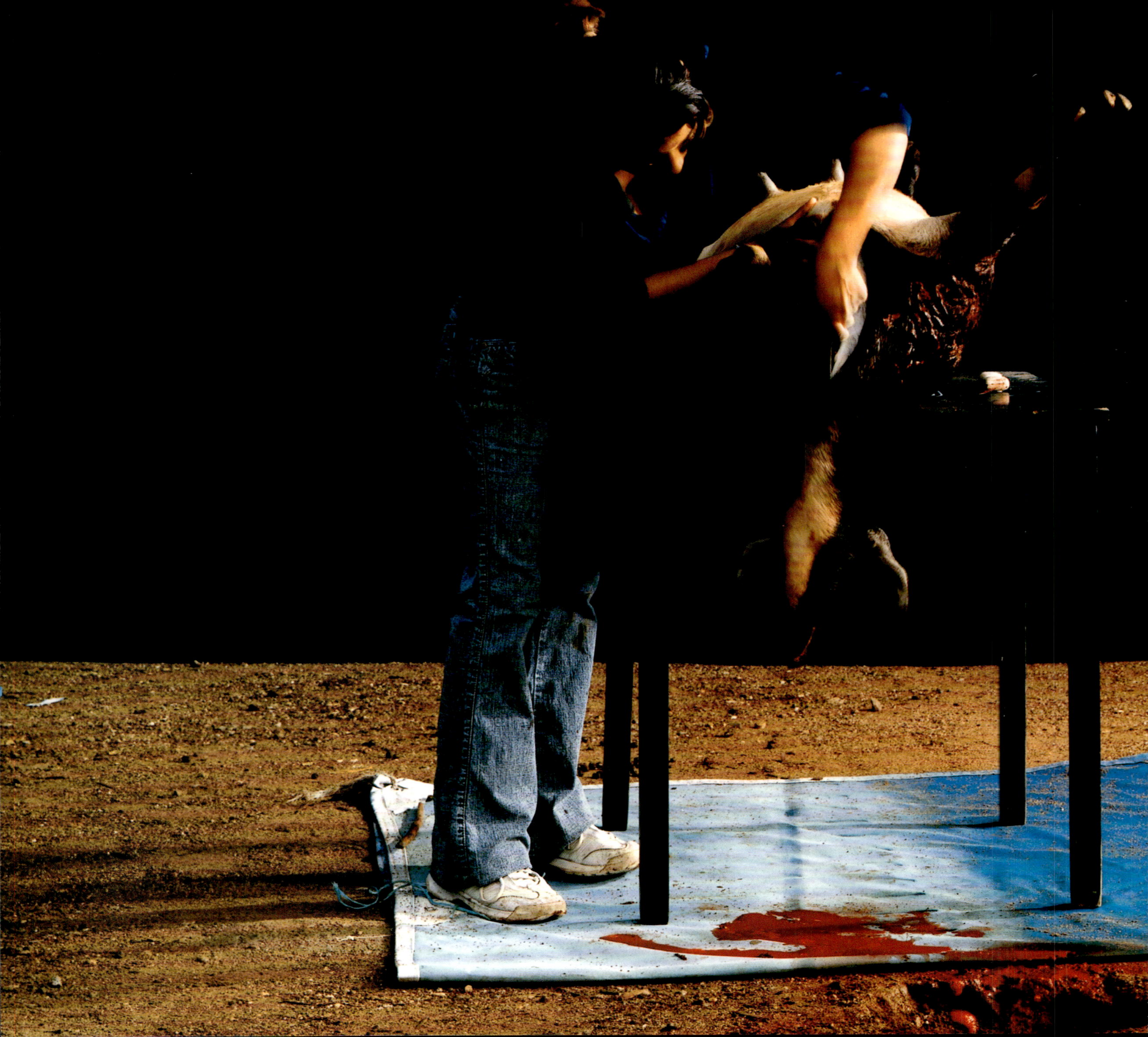

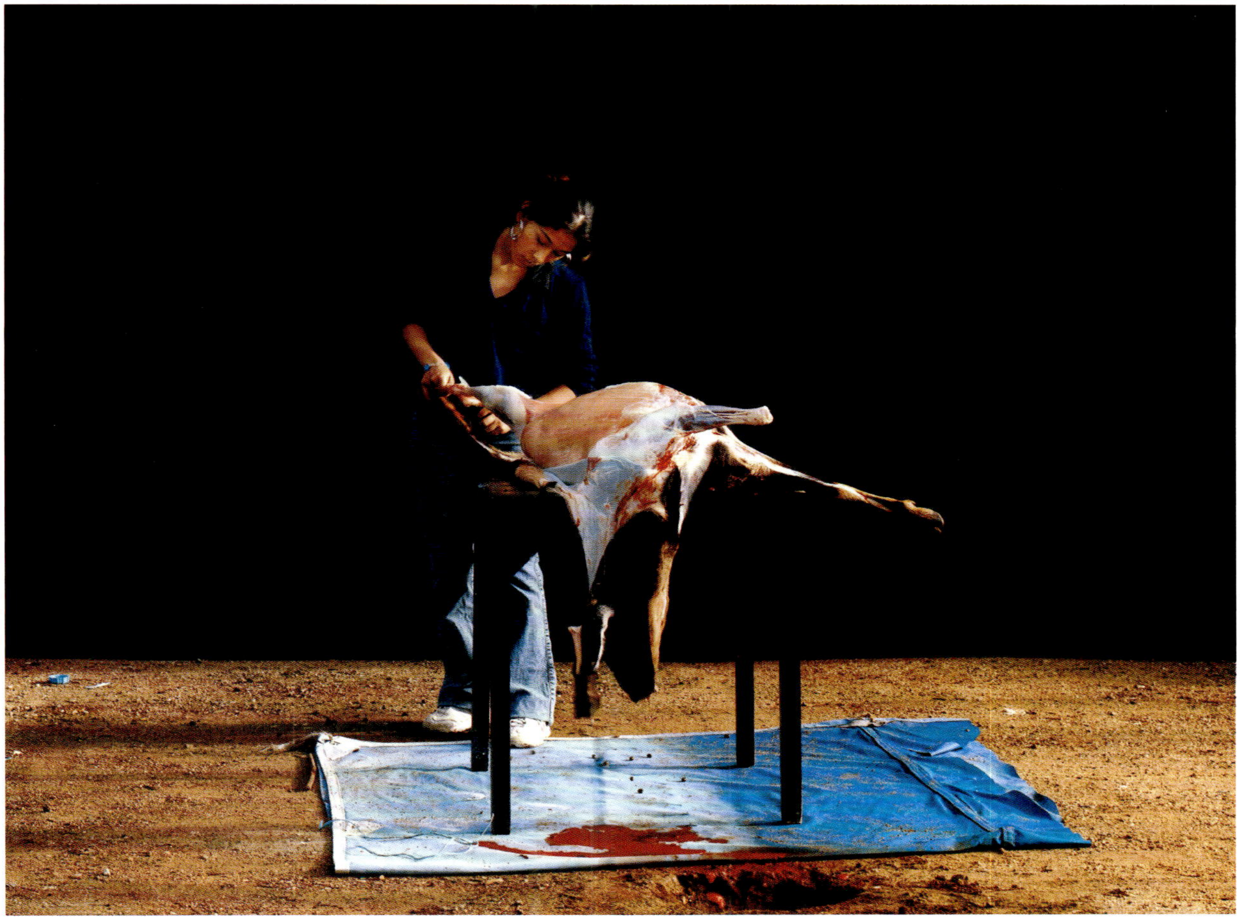

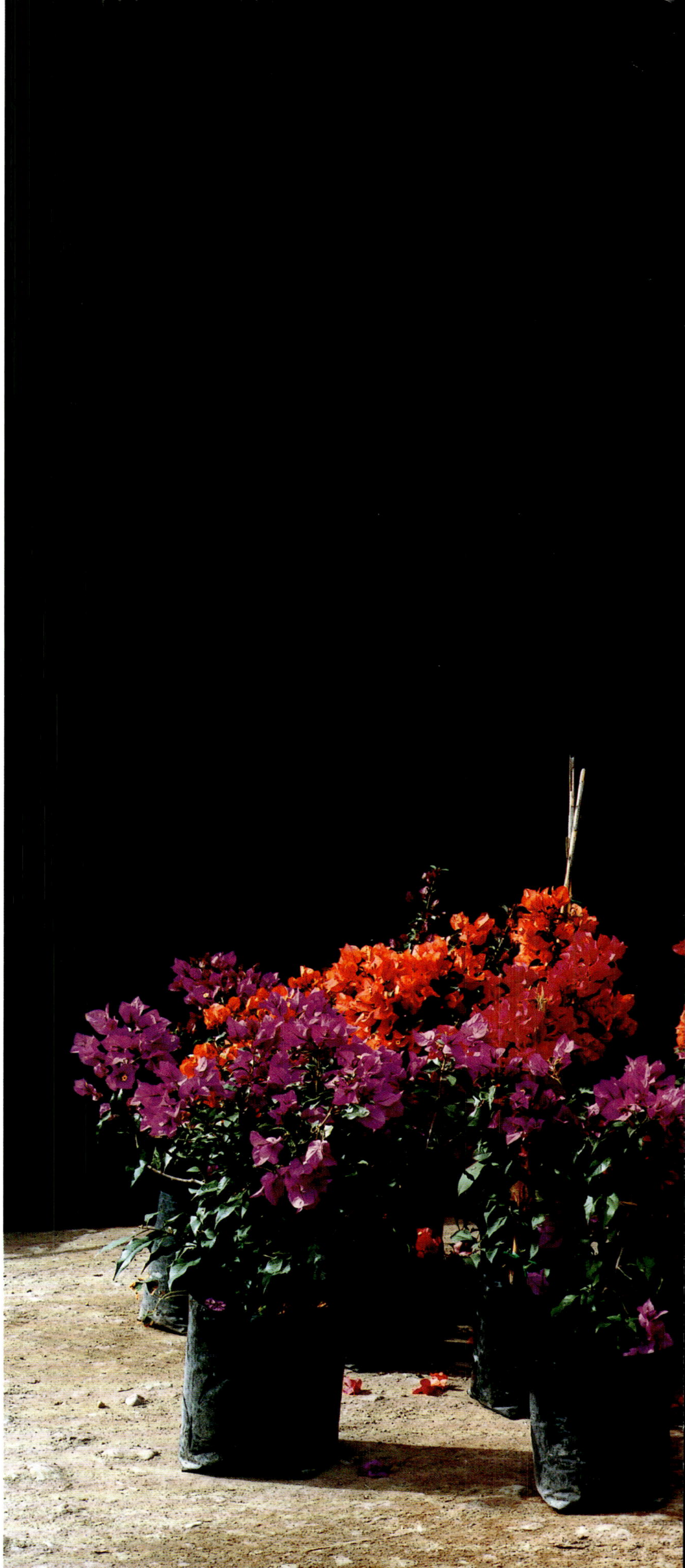

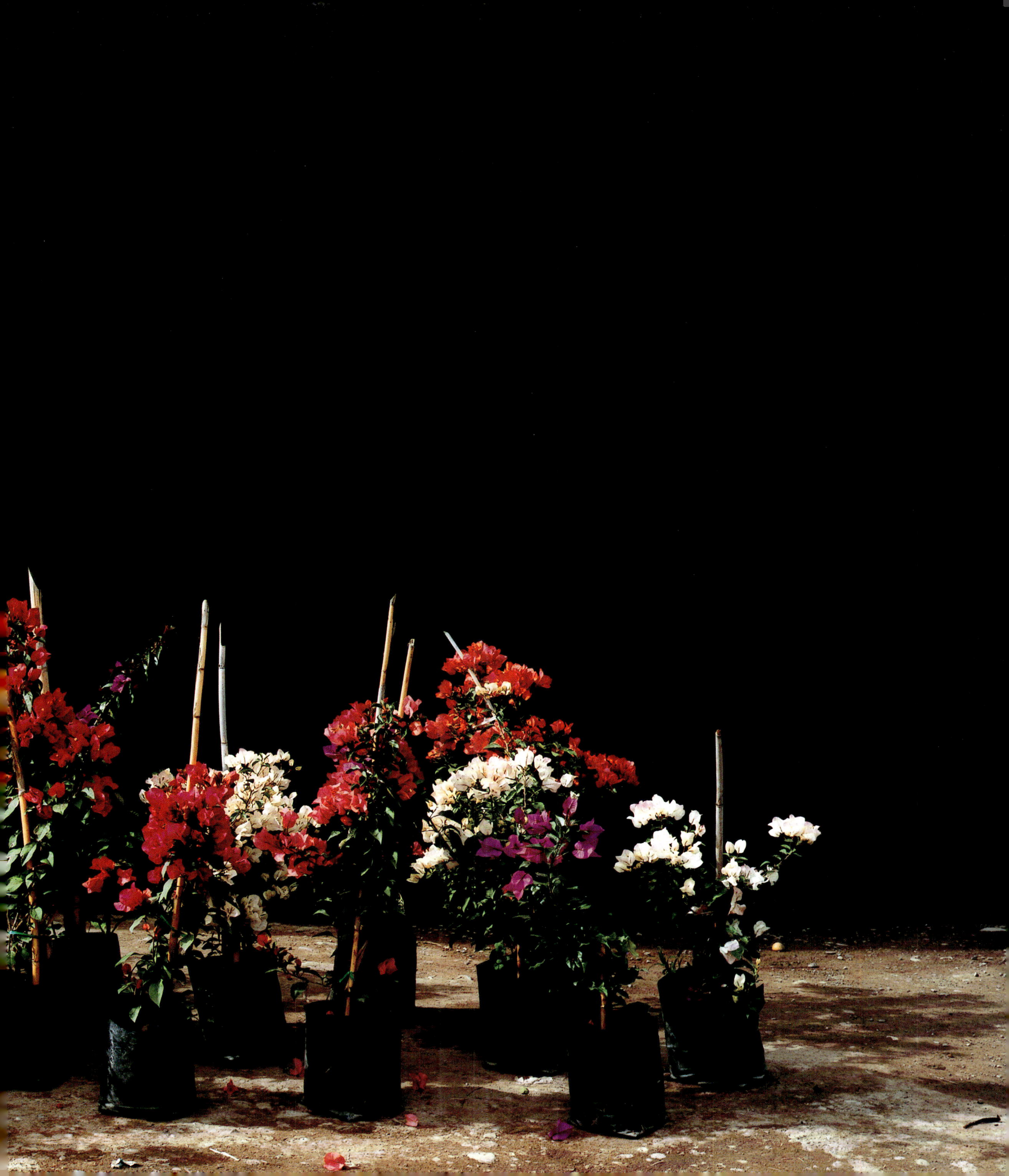

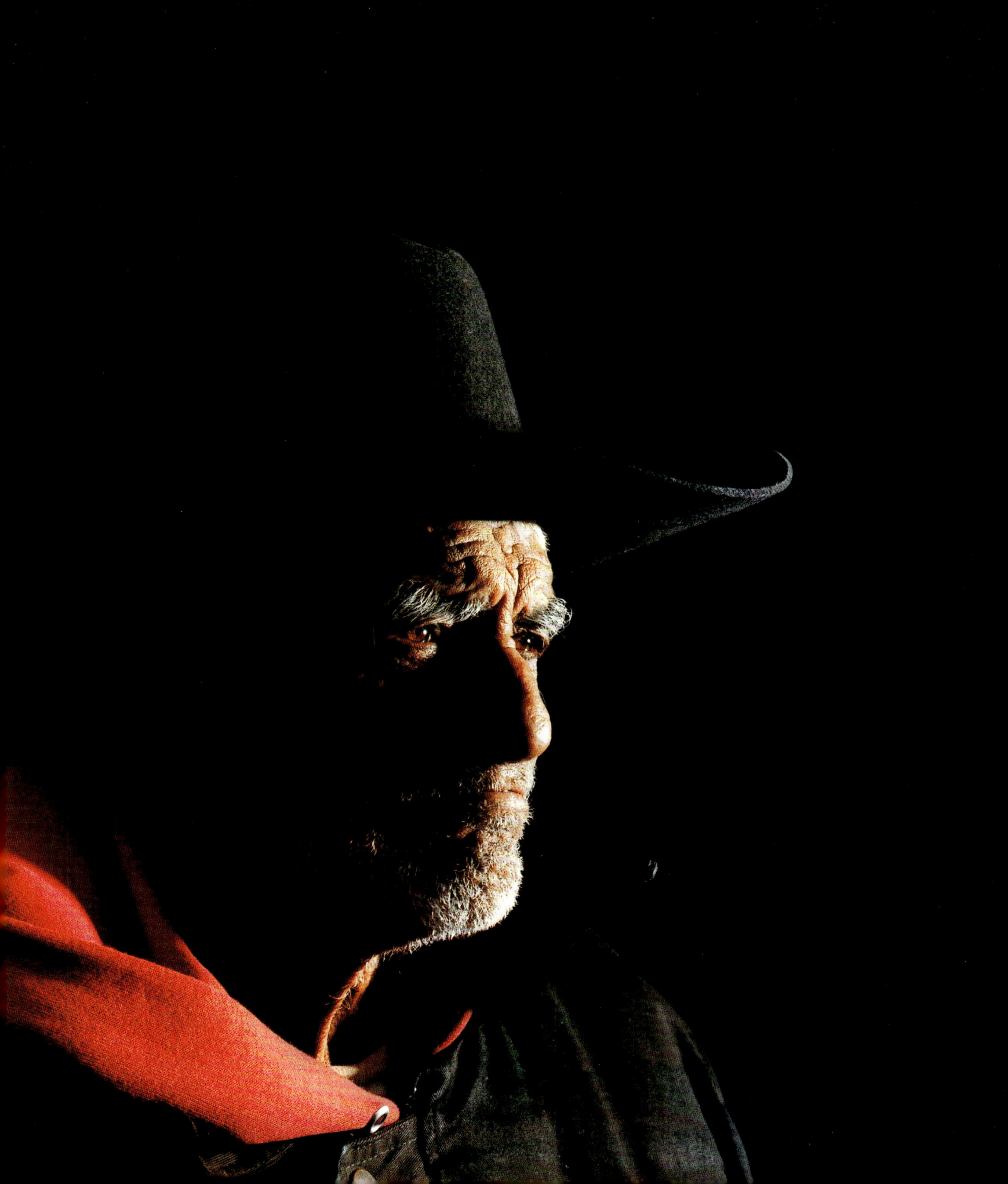

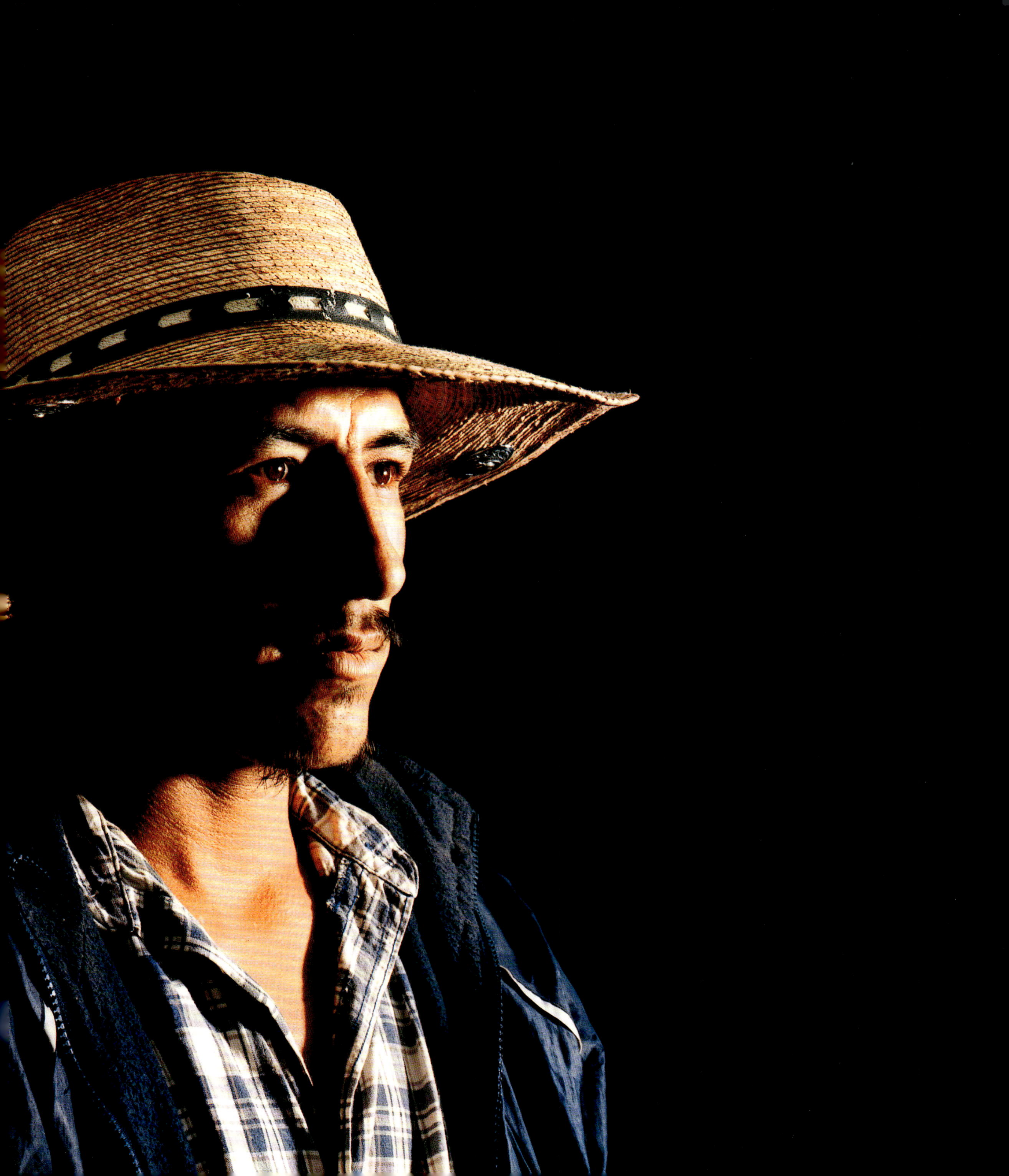

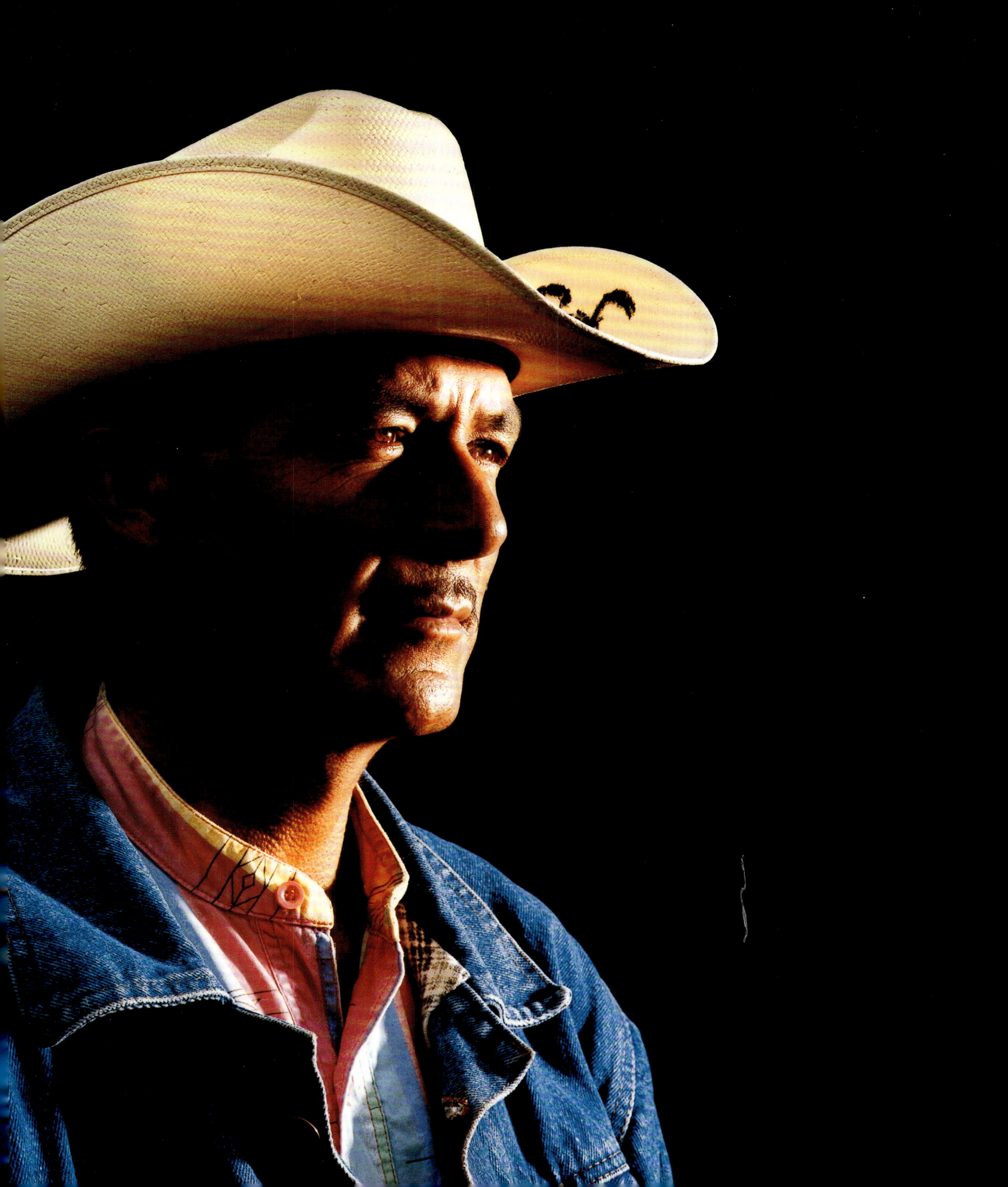

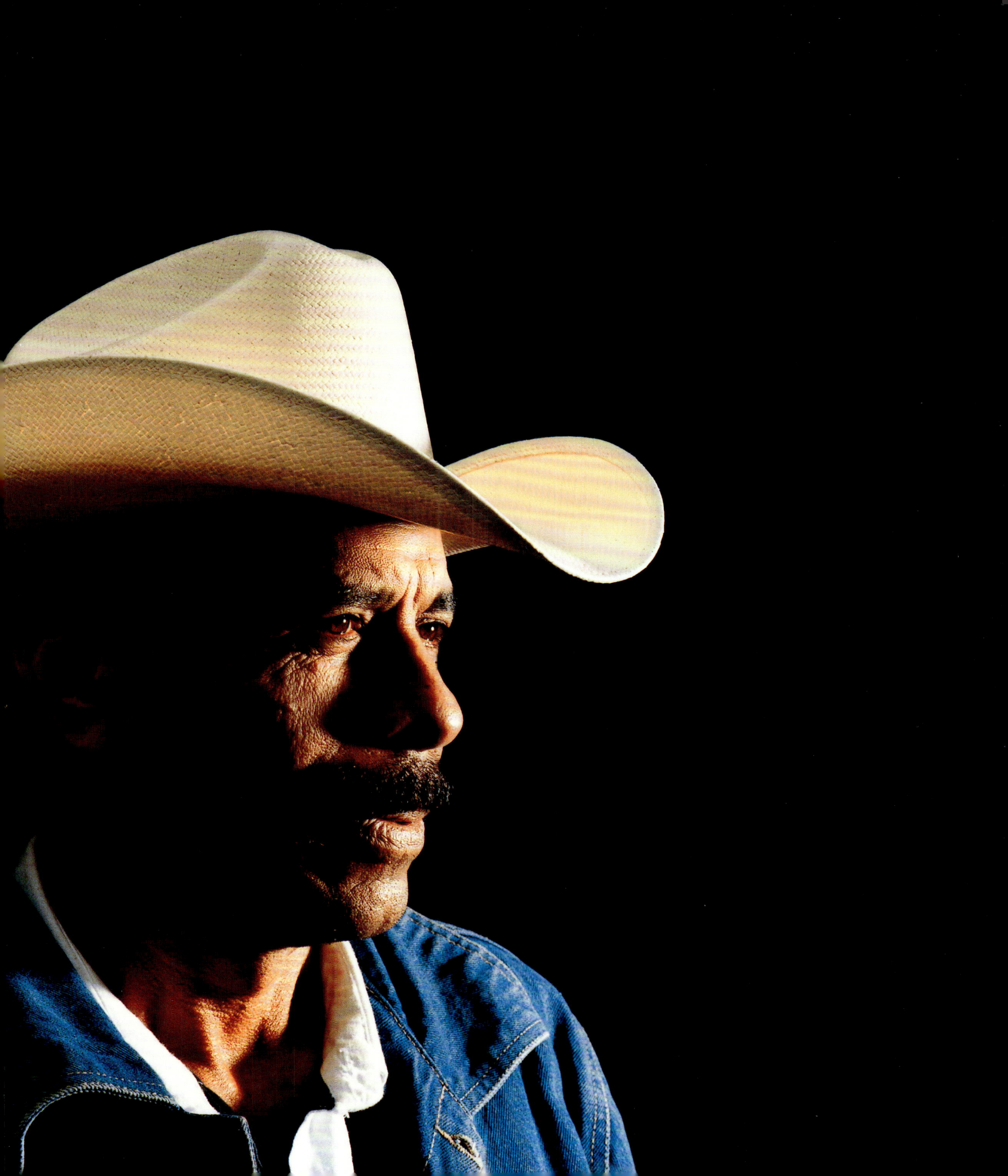

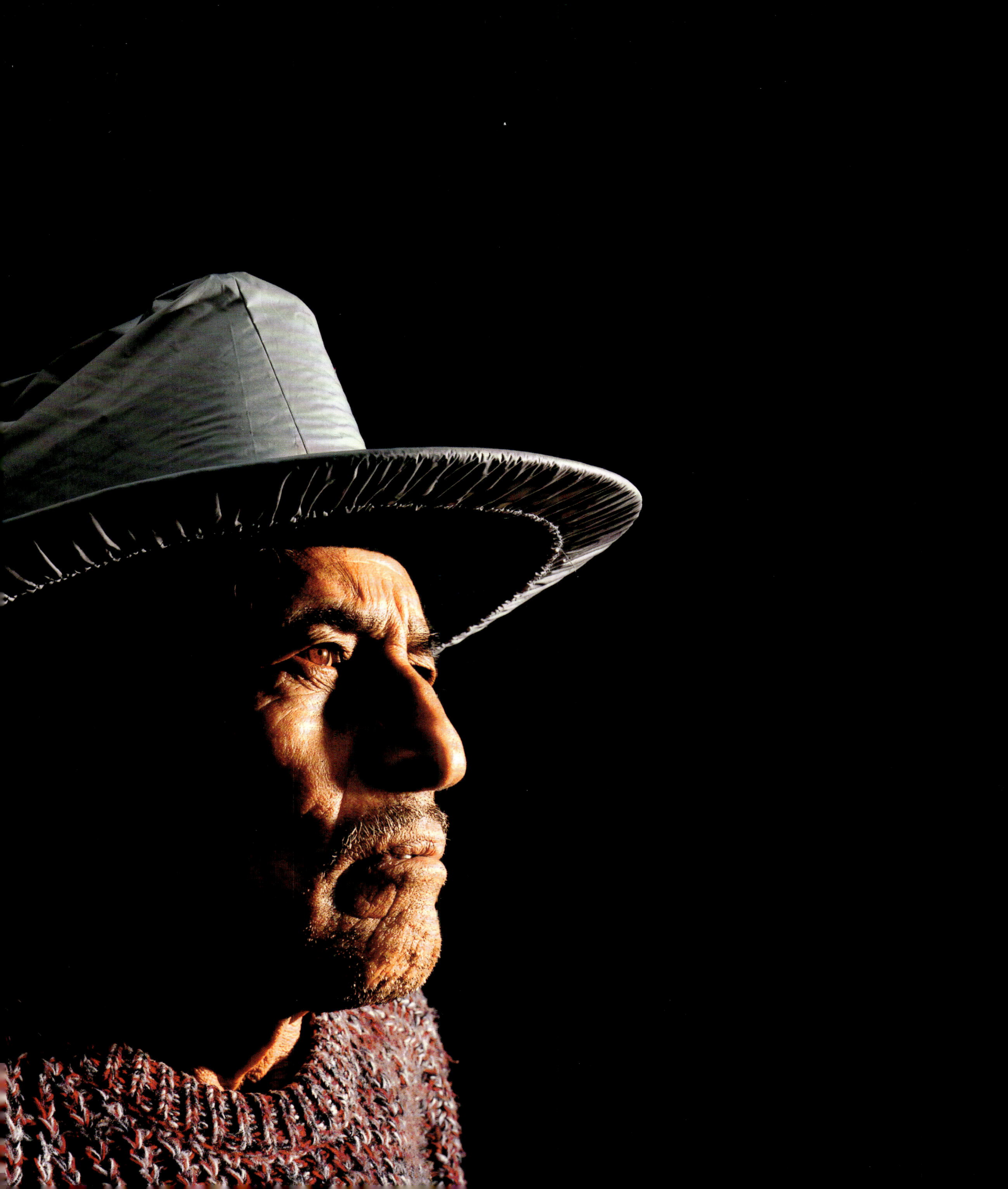

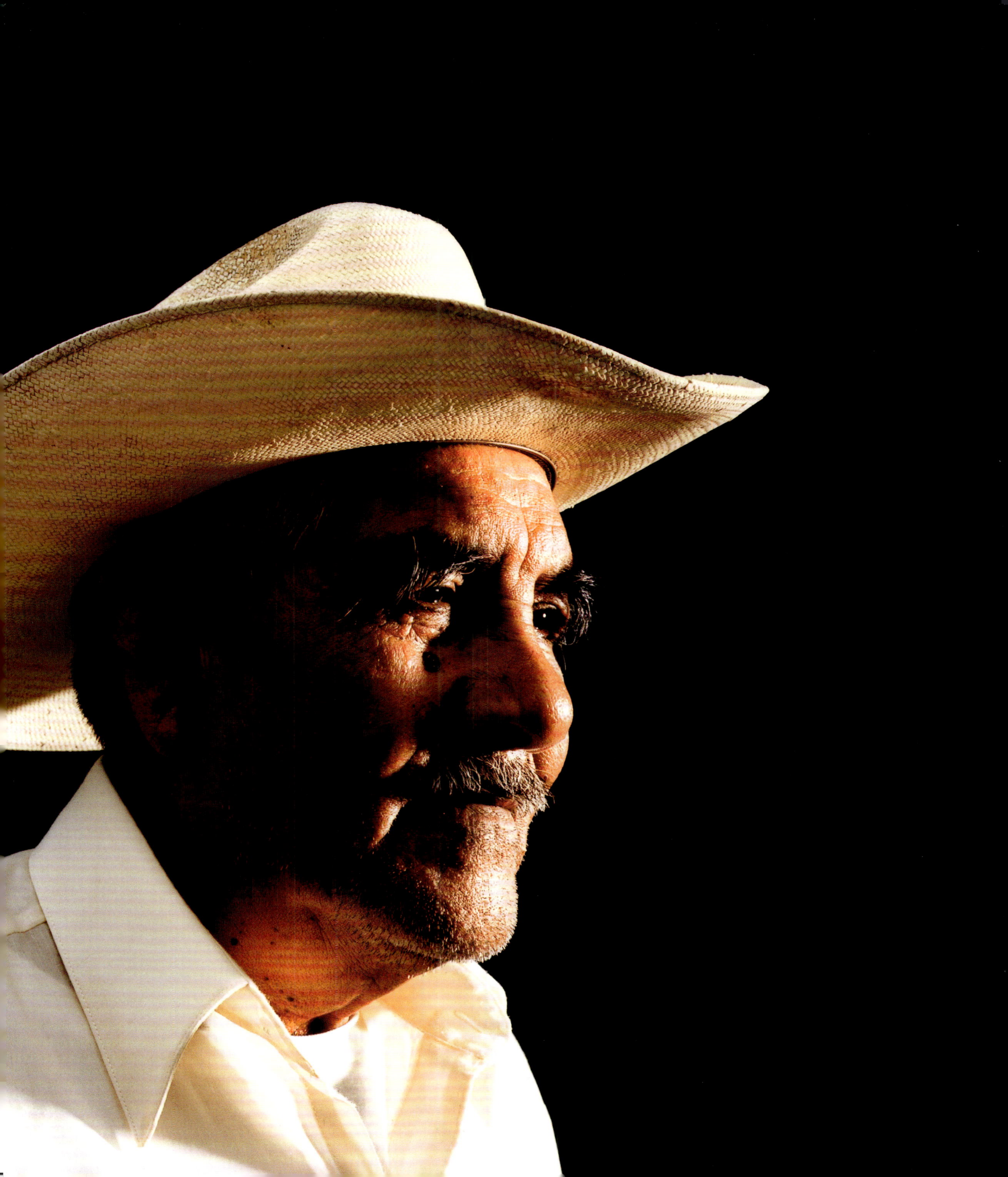

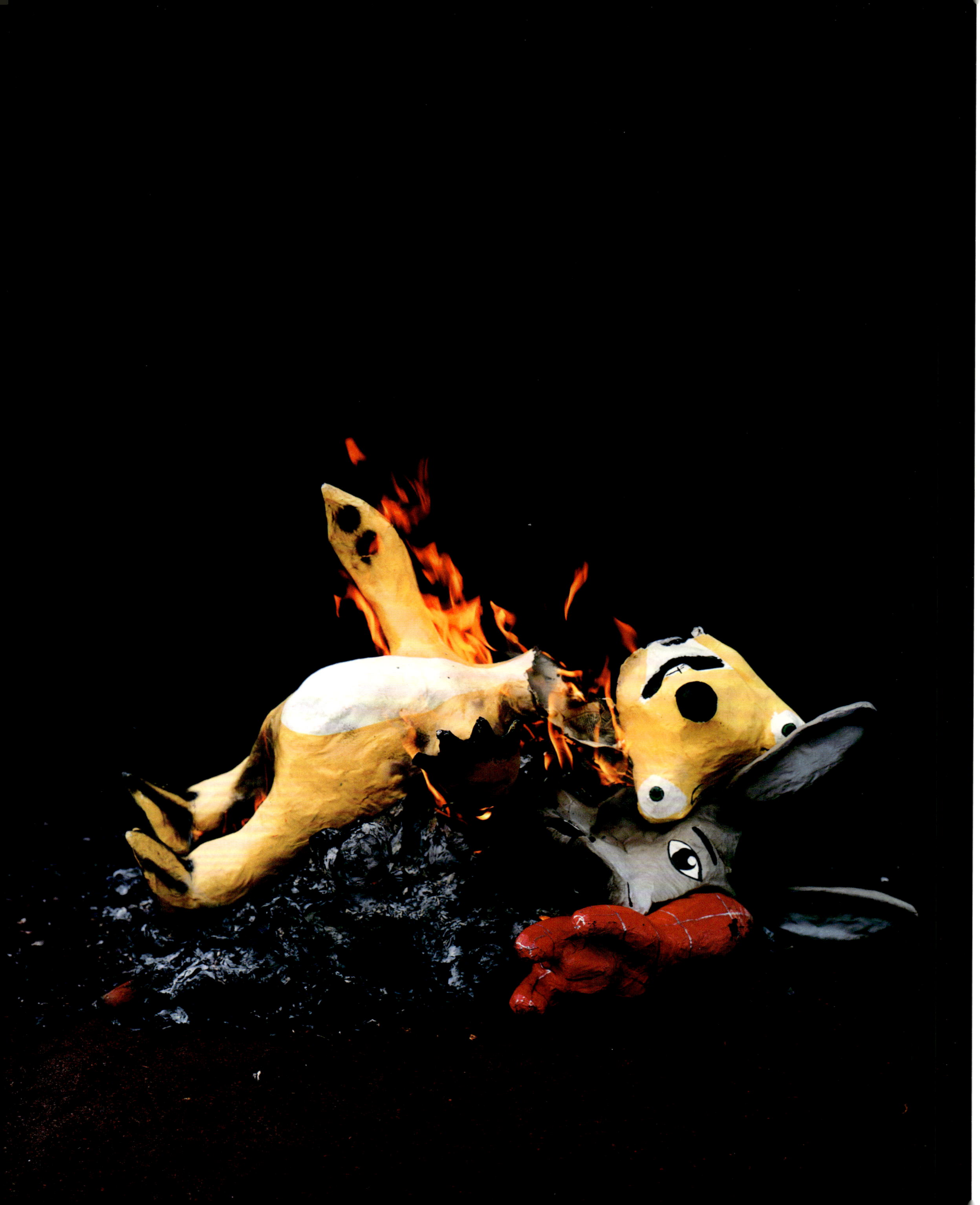

LIST OF WORKS

LOS LOSS

I-XXII

I Central de Abasto / Merced, Mexico City

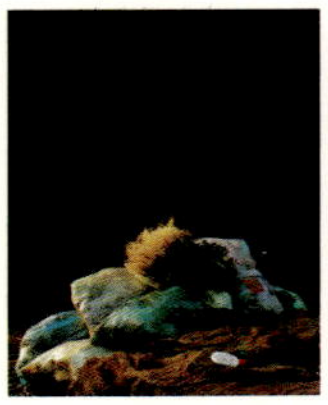
Untitled

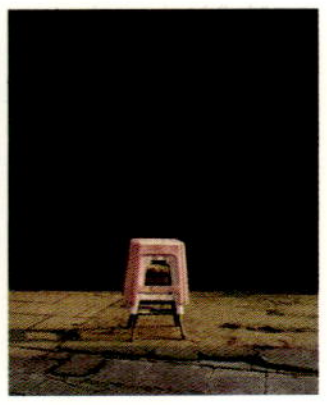
Stacked

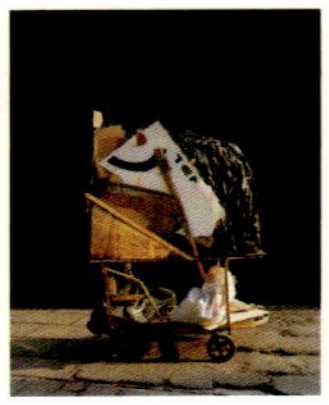
Hot Cart

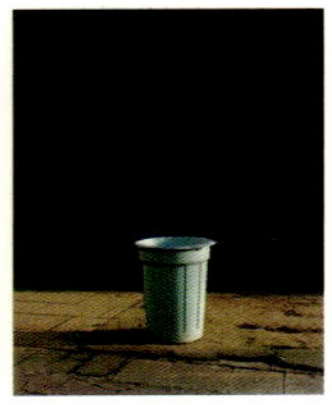
Green Bin

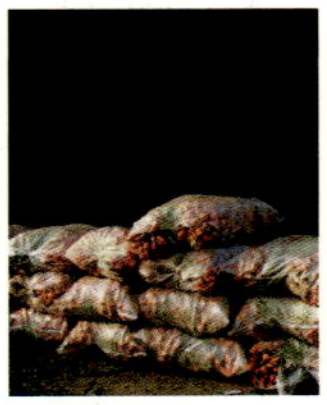
Hundreds of Radishes

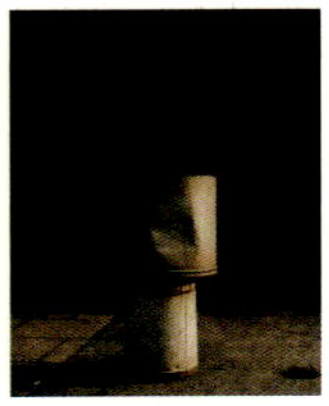
Two Bins

II Boxers

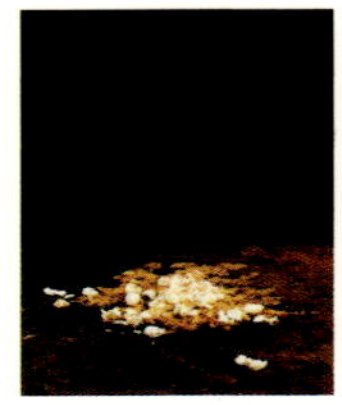
Crack

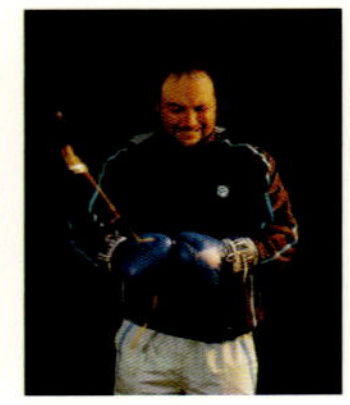
Jose Guadalupe Mendez

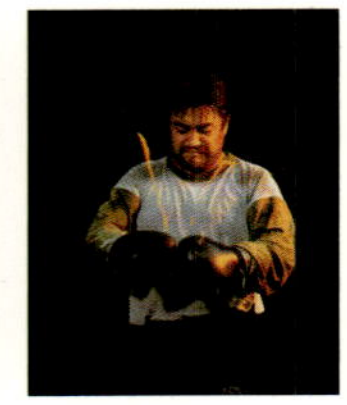
Andres Martinez Vargas

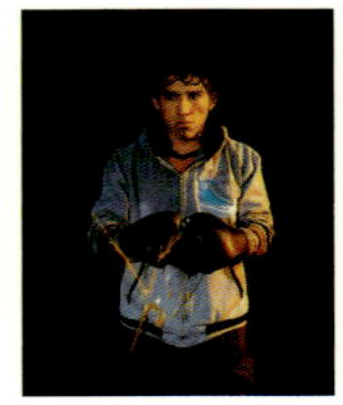
Luis Ernesto Soto Parader

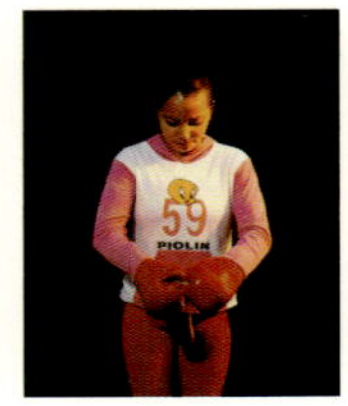
Reyna Floresa

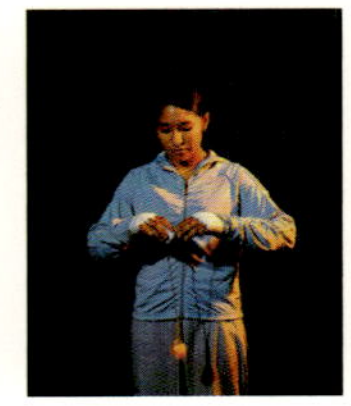
Maria Del Carmen Tlaxcano

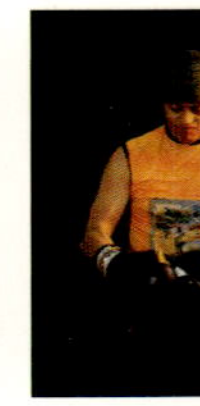
Arturo Del Martinez

VII Rancho la Esperanza, Concepcion

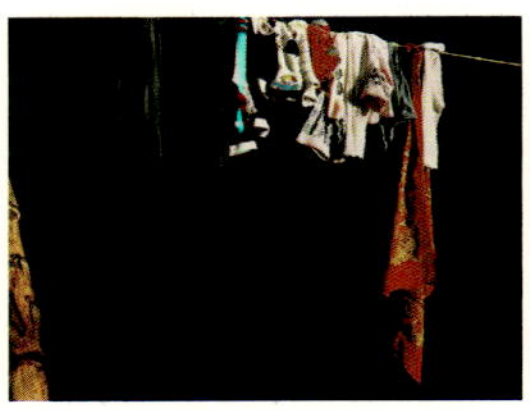
Strung Out 2

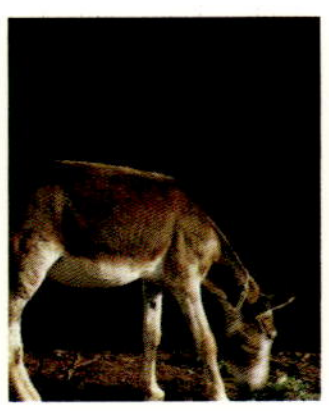
Untitled

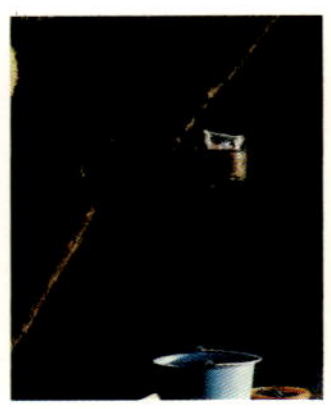
Bucket / Pot

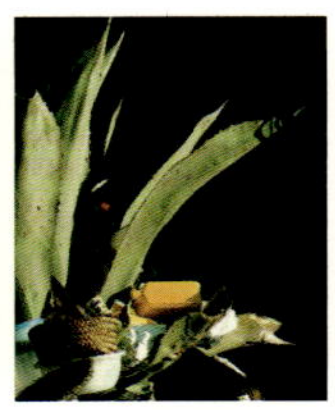
Broken Arms

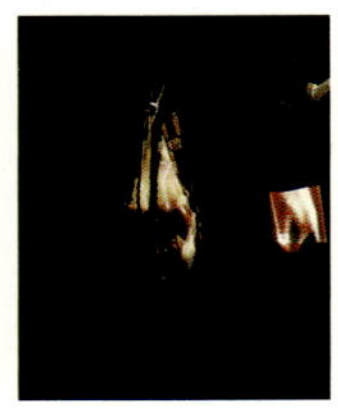
A Bag of Tomatoes

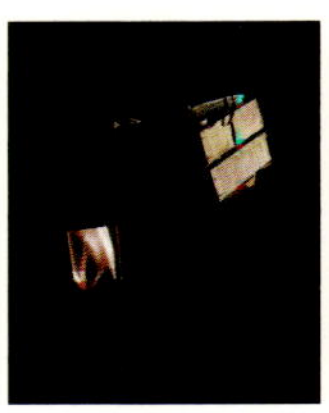
Red / Bag

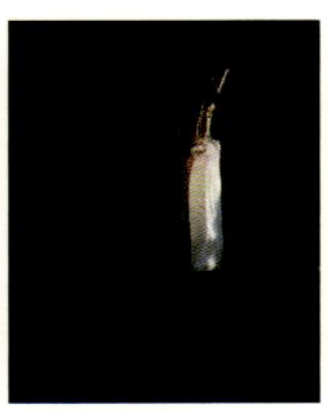
Light

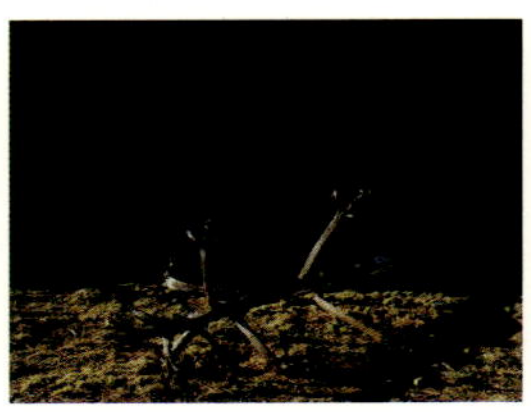
Lung

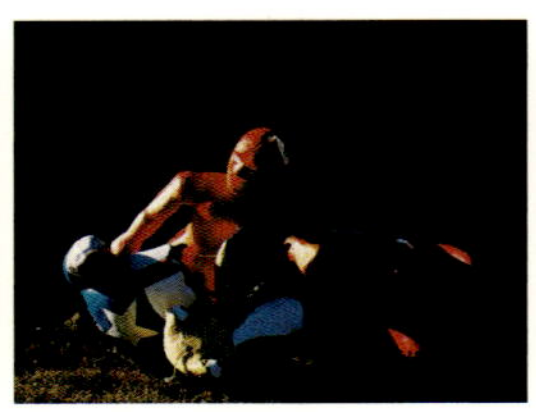
Untitled

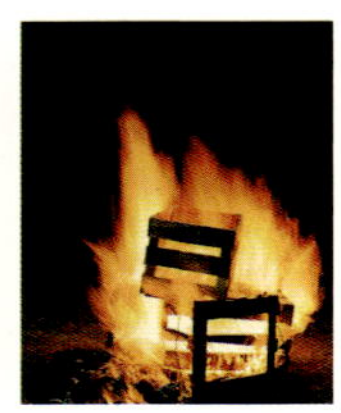
Boxes / Torched

VIII Girls, Oaxaca Zoca

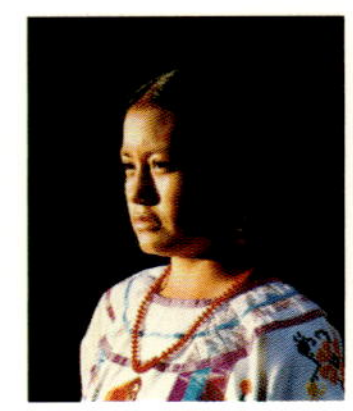
Ilse Karina Diaz Santos

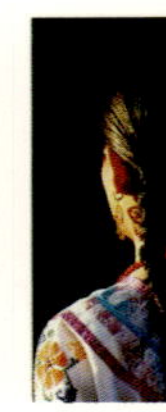
Ilse Ka Diaz Sa

XV Beach, Barra de la Cruz

Green / Grass

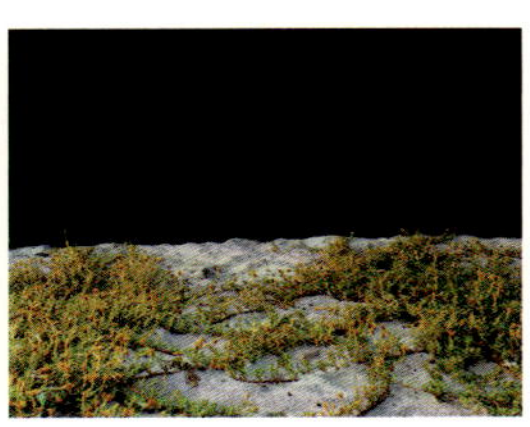
Yellow / Plant

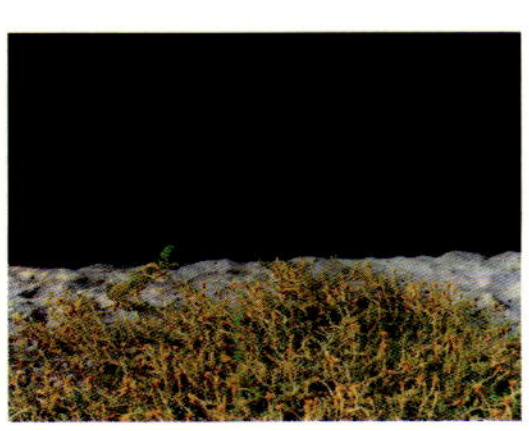
Fire / Plant

XVI Cemetery, Barra de la Cruz

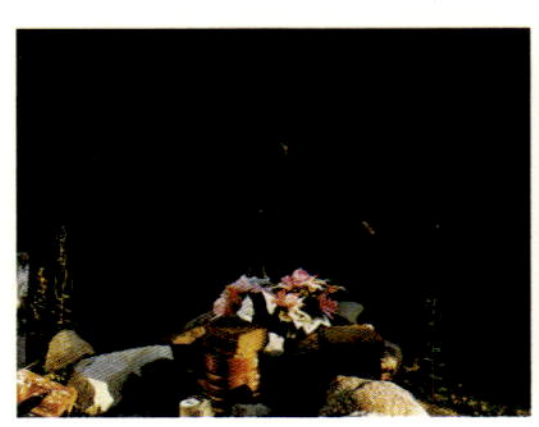
Gold / Can

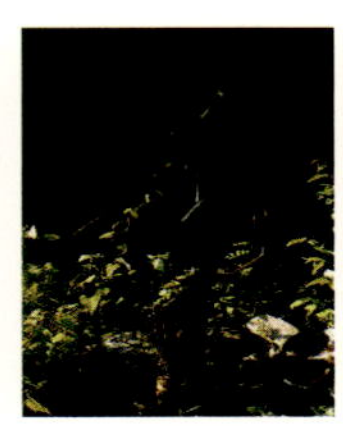
Black / Cross

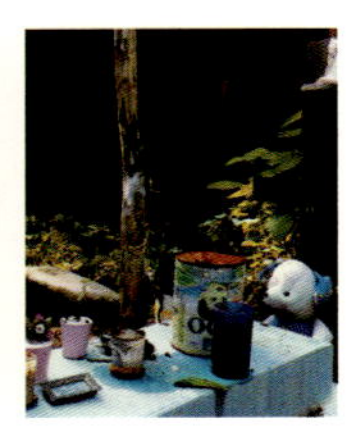
Baby Blue

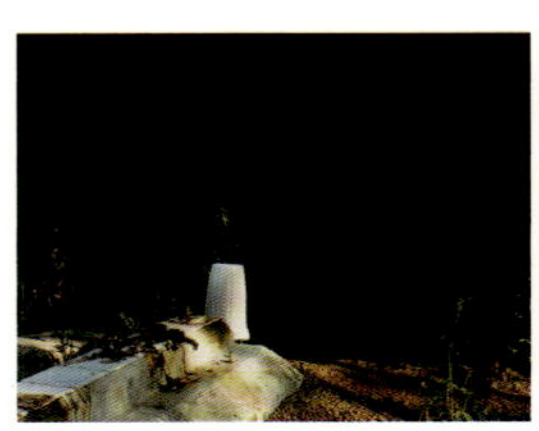
White / Vase

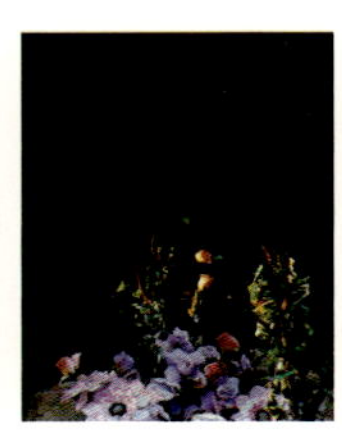
Pink / Flower

Blue / Grass

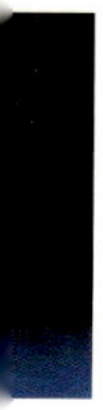

VI Ring Girls, Arena de Mexico

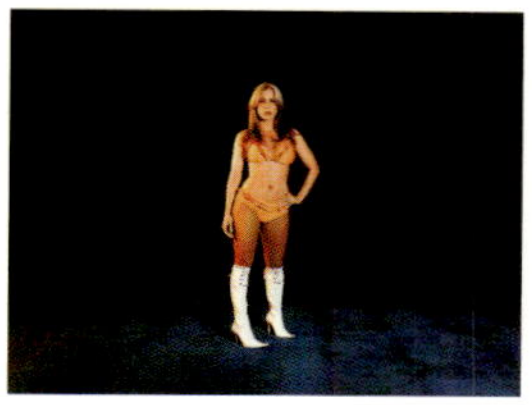
Linarys

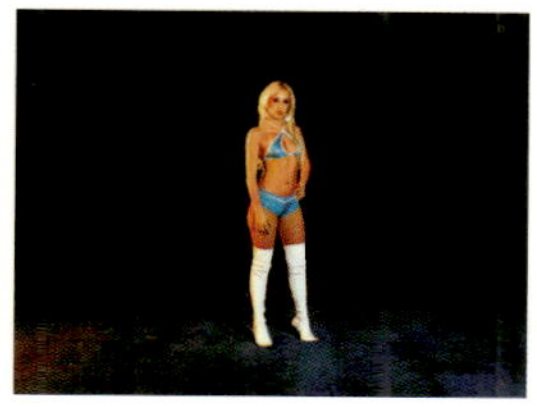
Ariana

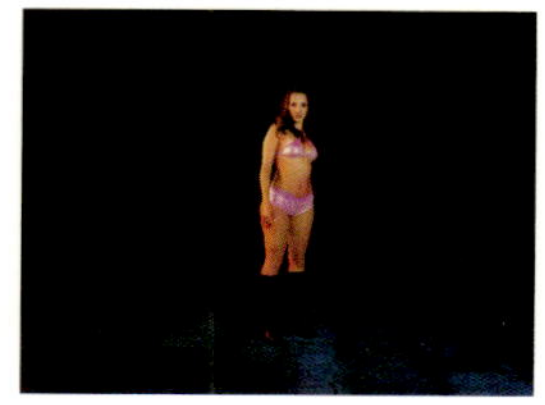
Scarlet

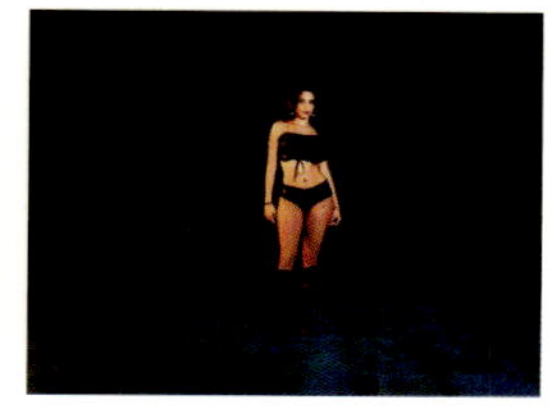
Analen

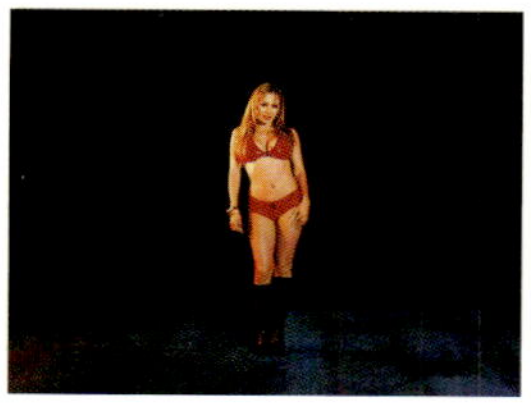
Areli

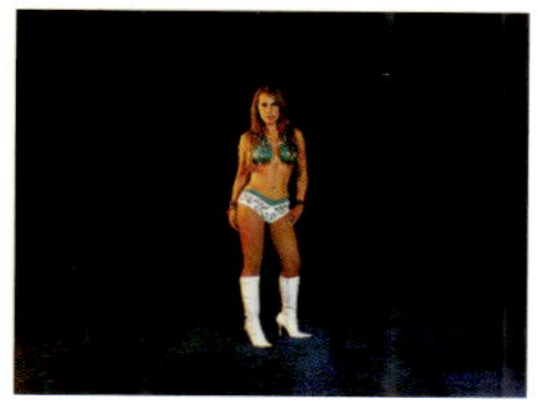
Gretel

atio, Copalita

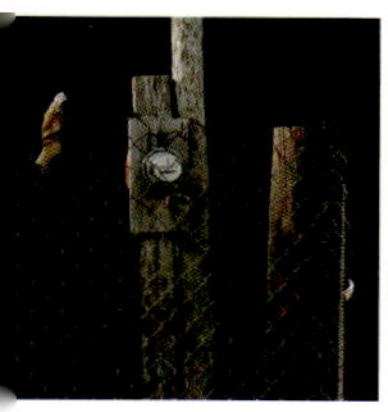

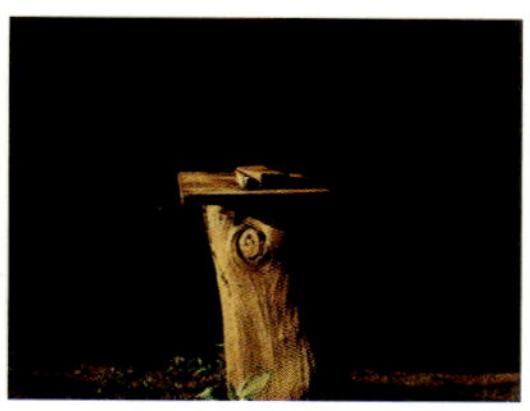
Eye

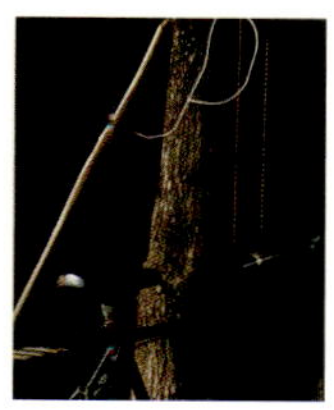
Chain

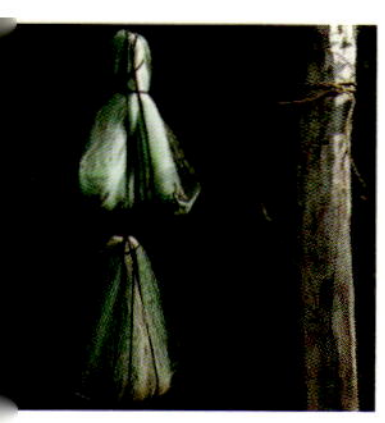

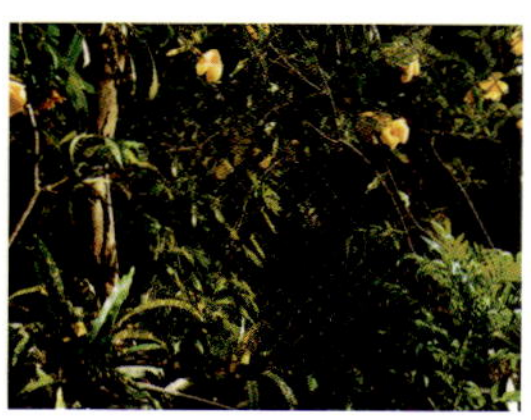
Hole

XIV Palm Field, Barra de la Cruz

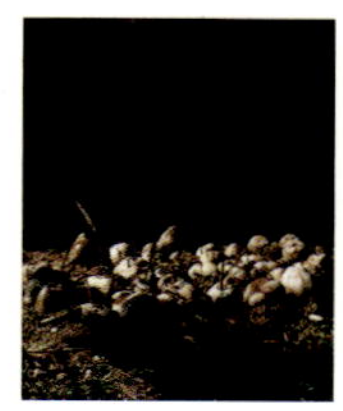
Skull

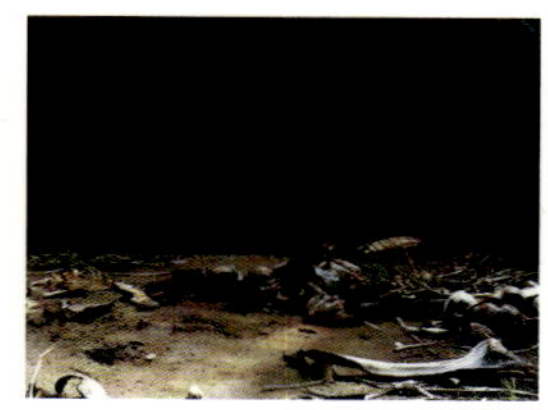
Fallen in the Morning

Stars

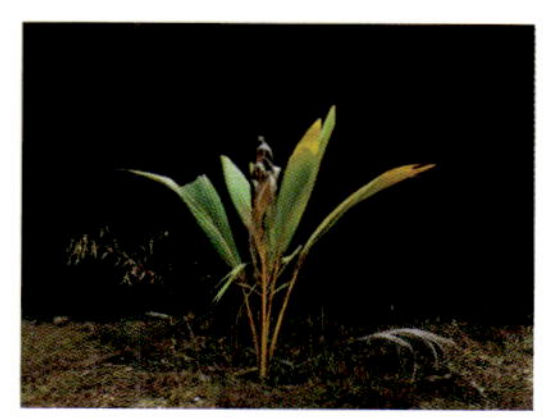
Dry

ezuma

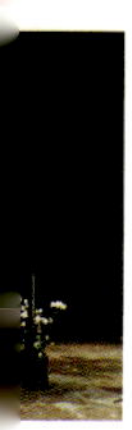

XXII Hats, Charcas Zocalo

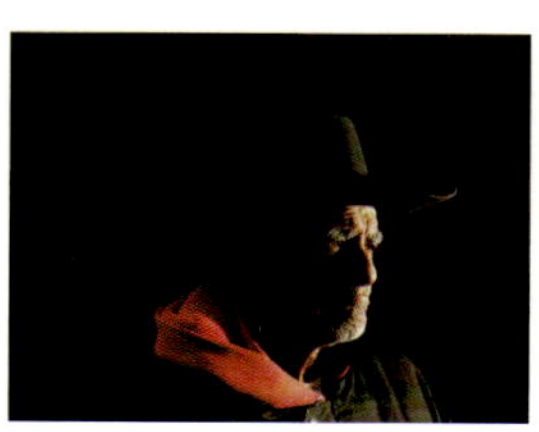
Eugenio Puente Arredondo

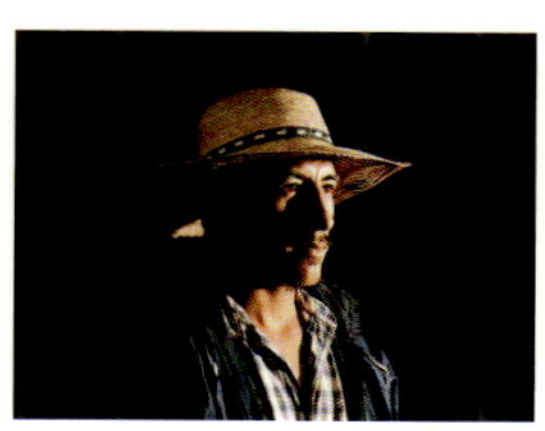
Mario Alonzo

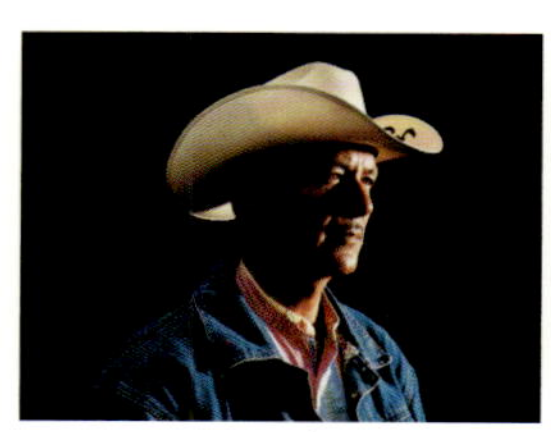
Cecilio Armando Flores

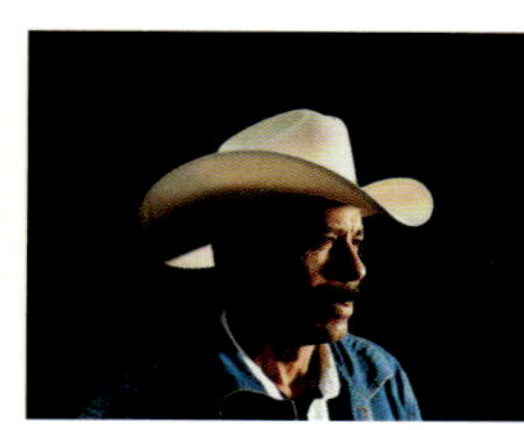
Marcelino Aleman Pena

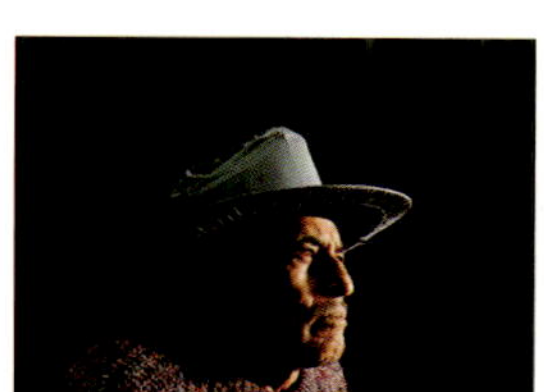
Raymundo Alcantar Gonzalez

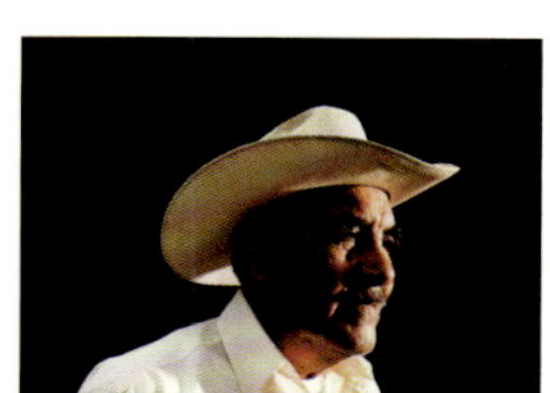
Genaro Luna

THANK YOU

Shoba Mistry

Edward Booth-Clibborn
Guy Briggs
Hazel Dexter
Michael Dodson
Stuart and Margaret Evans
Paul Gavin
Alison Green
Miguel Guttierrez
Paul Hedge
Thomas Hull
Paul Maslin
Sean Murphy
Guy and Marion Naggar
Corina Neuenschwander
Patricia Ortiz Monasterio
Cydney Payton
Jaime Riestra
Richard Slater
Ella Whitmarsh
Dushka Zapata

Arena de Mexico, Lee Piper at Rapid Eye,
Casa Xachiquetzal, Arturo Delgado Martinez,
Rancho La Esperanza,
Familia Garnica Ciriaco, Familia Ricardez Alberto,
Roman Pinacho Martinez,
Guadalupe Monserat Altamarino Lopez,

and all the others
who helped to make this project possible.

Designed by Value and Service

First published in 2008
by Booth-Clibborn Editions
in the United Kingdom
www.booth-clibborn.com

A Cataloguing-in-Publication record
for this book is available from the Publisher.

ISBN 978-1-86154-306-6

Printed and bound in Hong Kong

Born in South Africa,
Trevor Appleson is a self-taught photographer
who lives and works in London.
He has exhibited widely, and his works are
included in numerous public and
private collections.

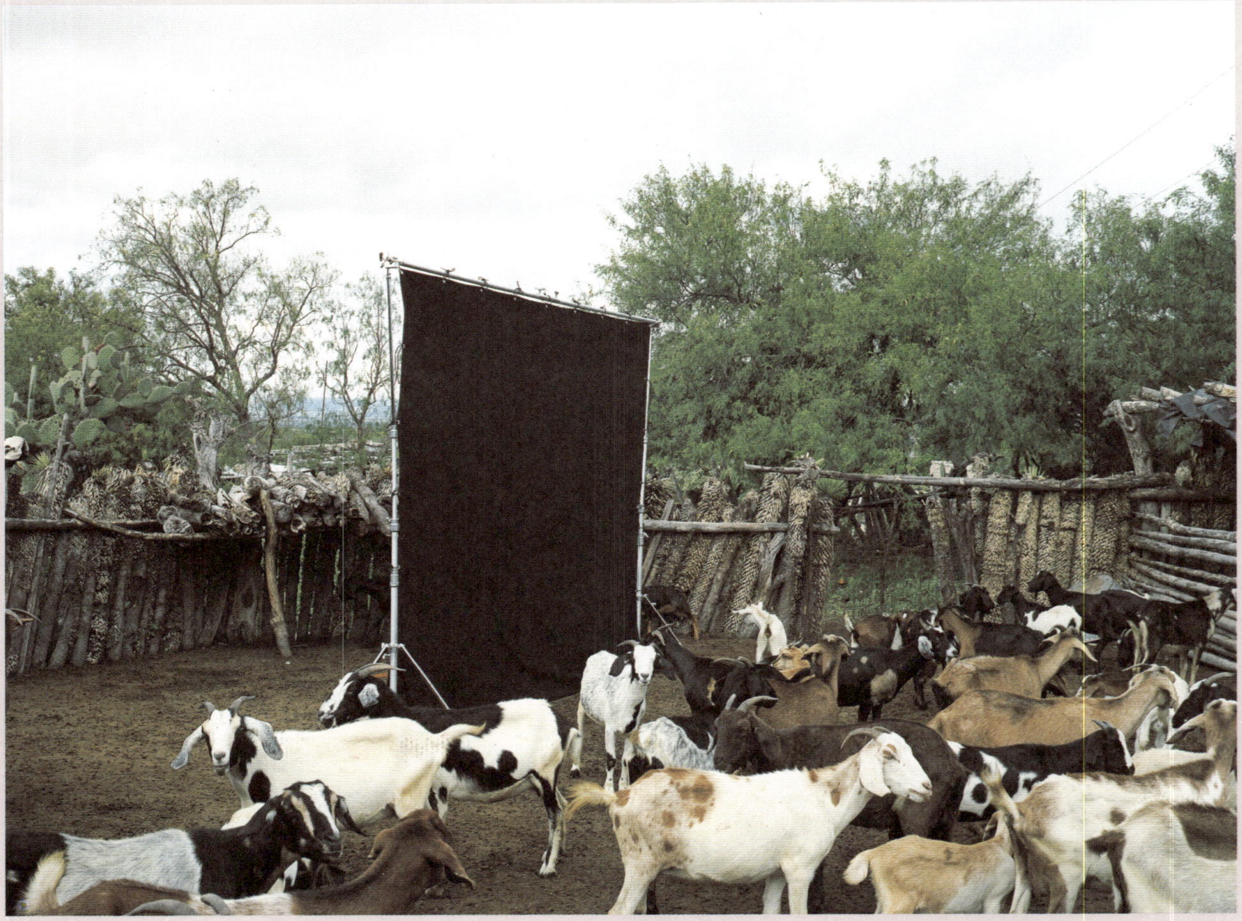